The Unknown
Max Weber

The Unknown Max Weber

Paul Honigsheim

**Edited and with an introduction by
Alan Sica**

Transaction Publishers
New Brunswick (U.S.A.) and London (U.K.)

Library of Congress Catalog Number: 00-034405
ISBN: 0-7658-0015-2
Printed in the United States of America

Library of Congress Cataloging-in-Publication Data

Honigsheim, Paul, 1885-1963
    The unknown Max Weber / Paul Honigsheim ; edited and with an
introduction by Alan Sica.
        p. cm.
    Includes bibliographical references and index.
        ISBN 0-7658-0015-2 (alk. paper)
    1. Weber Max, 1864-1920—Contributions in social sciences   I. Sica,
Alan, 1949- II. Title.

H59. W4 H65 2000
300—dc21   00-034405

Contents

Acknowledgements

Philip Schwadel scanned the four original articles and the printed book so they could be republished in this new form; his labors were heroic and indispensable given the limitations of scanning technology, which leave much to be desired when converting old texts into contemporary fonts. Thanks also to my Penn State colleagues, who allowed Phil to work as my research assistant for this and other projects.

Anne Sica, as always, was there to help in as many ways as needed, including retyping complex notes which "would not scan" for conversion to word processing, and also with the tiresome tasks of proofreading and indexing. She has been at this task now for over twenty-five years. How can one thank such a woman sufficiently?

Thanks also go to the original publishers of Honigsheim's work:

"Max Weber as Rural Sociologist," *Rural Sociology*, 11:3 (September, 1946), 207-218.

"Max Weber as Applied Anthropologist," *Applied Anthropology: Problems of Social Organization*, 7:4 (Fall, 1948), 270-35. (Journal was renamed *Human Organization*.)

"Max Weber as Historian of Agriculture and Rural Life," *Agricultural History*, 23:3 (July, 1949), 179-213.

"Max Weber: His Religious and Ethical Background" first appeared in *Church History*, 19 (1950), 219-239.

On Max Weber, translated by Joan Huber Rytina (New York: Free Press, Collier-Macmillan Limited, London/East Lansing, MI: Social Science Research Bureau, 1968).

Introduction

Paul Honigsheim and
Max Weber's Lost Decade

Alan Sica

Paul Honigsheim's voice is unique among those who knew Max Weber personally and decided to write about him, and in its own way remains as useful to understanding Weber and his times as are the celebrated remarks of Karl Jaspers. In 1960 Howard P. Becker, famous for his brutal honesty, reflected on "Paul Honigsheim's linguistic facility, amazing industry, tremendous range, and incredibly accurate memory."[1] And with the posthumous publication in 1968 of *On Max Weber*,[2] scholars who, during the preceding forty-seven years, had not noticed Honigsheim's published essays about his famous friend, were thereby treated to a style of memoir and substantive commentary which bore the mark of the genuine article. He was one of the select few who regularly participated in the Weber-*Kreis* in Heidelberg during the second decade of the century, whose "excellent" dissertation (on Jansenism) Weber approvingly cited in his most famous work, *The Protestant Ethic and the Spirit of Capitalism*,[3] and who outlived his herculean friend by over four decades.

The young man's frequent visits to the mansion on the Neckar are faithfully recorded in Marianne Weber's monumental biography of her husband.[4] Because Marianne's book remains the undisputed foundation of whatever intimate knowledge we have of Weber—even allowing for the selective portrait she produced, and while we await a complete edition of his correspondence to appear (in either German or English)—it is worth quoting her at length regarding Honigsheim's enviable proximity to the century's preeminent social analyst (circa 1908):

> Weber very seldom let himself be lured out of the house, but he always enjoyed the company of stimulating visitors [from Marianne's diary]: Almost every day someone is here; of the scholars, it is particularly Troeltsch, Jellinek....The friends usually come in the afternoon, now and then also in the evening. Max retires at nine o'clock, but first he does an enormous amount of talking.

> With the older intellectuals there were important scholarly discussions each time....The young people stood in awe of Weber and always stayed at a respectful distance...[Marianne here names the Jaspers and Simmel couples, Roberto Michels, Sombart, Emil Lask, and many other regular guests.] P. Honigsheim and K. Löwenstein frequently were among the younger men, future scholars who sought stimulation from Weber.[5]

> Our life is full to the brim; every day there is a visitor, at least one searching soul (December, 1910)...[Marianne quotes Weber's own words]: "Yesterday the menu was as follows: Slept well till 8:00 [visits of Gottl, Lina Radbruch, Gundolf, Salz]. Thus four of us until 5:15. Then exit Lina R., thus I, Gundolf, and Salz until six, then + Gothein, somewhat later also exeunt Gundolf and Salz, then Honigsheim and I until 7:30, then + Lask...until eight, then exit Lask. Supper with Honigsheim who remained until ten o'clock. Then Berta sent him away: 'Frau Professor would really be angry.' Then I turned on the electric light in my room to read the newspaper. Berta brought a lamp and turned off the electric light: 'Herr Professor would only forget. 'Then slept tolerably well with a lot of bromide. Talked about the whole world + three villages."[6]

Though idyllically responsive in these passages, especially for young intellectuals and artists in search of a leader, the company of Max Weber was not always so pleasantly Socratic. Other eyewitnesses recall a furious temper and granite stubbornness that left no room for the easy style of give and take which Honigsheim and his peers had obviously come to expect at the Weber "salon." Among many examples, consider Felix Somary (1881-1956), banker and diplomat, who witnessed an exchange in Vienna between Weber and Joseph Schumpeter in 1918:

Max Weber had asked me to be present at the discussion he was to have with Schumpeter about the succession to his chair at the University of Vienna. Weber wanted to return to Germany and he was thinking of Schumpeter as his successor, but the two men knew each other only superficially although Schumpeter had written an outstanding history of ideas to accompany Weber's handbook on social sciences. I was worried about the meeting, because a greater contrast between two personalities was hard to imagine.

Max Weber was a restless, nervous type, full of "drive,"a Huguenot with deeply-held convictions, for which he strove with every atom of his energy. He battled on without letting up, even when only minor issues were at stake. He was explosive in temperament, verging on intolerance; those who did not know him well could easily have been put off or even frightened at first meeting him. Hugo von Hofmannstahl tried to explain him by saying: "He has the gifts of a Caesar who is unable to find a field large enough for his energies. "There was much truth in that observation: Weber was never in his life able to give his tremendous intellectual and spiritual powers full expression. He took nothing lightly.

Schumpeter, on the other hand took nothing hard. He had been educated at the Vienna Theresianum, where the pupils were taught to stick to subjects and not to get personally involved. The rules of the game in every part and ideology were to be learned thoroughly, but nobody should join a party or subscribe to a dogma....

We met in the Café Landmann opposite the University. Ludo Hartmann, a historian of the Classical world and son-in-law of Mommsen, accompanied Weber, and I came with Schumpeter. I took no notes of our conversation, but can recall the elements of it that impressed me most strongly. The talk turned to the Russian Revolution [whereupon they disagreed about the likely outcome]. Weber said with some heat that communism at the Russian state of development was a crime—he knew the language and followed Russian affairs closely. He added that developments in Russia would lead to unheard-of human misery and end in a terrible catastrophe. [Schumpeter countered that it was "a good laboratory to test our theories."] "A laboratory heaped with human corpses!" Weber replied.

"Every anatomy classroom is the same thing," Schumpeter shot back...Weber become more vehement and raised his voice, as Schumpeter for his part became more sarcastic and lowered his. All around us the café customers stopped their card games and listened eagerly, until the point when Weber sprang to his feet and rushed out into the Ringstrasse, crying "This is intolerable!" Hartmann followed

> with Weber's hat, and vainly tried to calm him down. Schumpeter, who
> had remained behind with me, only smiled and said, "How can some-
> one carry on like that in a coffee house!"

> I felt unhappy about the incident. Here were two individuals of rare
> gifts, who were not far apart in their fundamental views on the economy,
> and in their deep intellectual seriousness. But it was the curse of the
> German and Austrian haute bourgeoisie that its all too few original per-
> sonalities, if they ever met at all, immediately became deadly enemies.
> They all had too much temperament to compromise on issues.[7]

Expressive explosions of this kind, based as much on strongly
held intellectual positions as on quirks of personality, were often
reported whenever Weber spoke in a public or semi-public forum.
Only in his private home, among students and friends of the sort
that Honigsheim was, did Weber "lighten up"and take on the inter-
personal style more common to ordinary people. He was known
even to joke.

Considering all this, Honigsheim's special place within Weber's
world compels us to grant his reminiscences, as well as the Weberian
scholarship his privileged position made possible,[8] a degree of cred-
ibility and informativeness which can be matched by very few others whose works are in English, for example, Karl Jaspers and Karl
Löwenstein.[9] On the basis of the intimate knowledge thus gained
about Weber, his colleagues, his personal style and intellectual concerns, Honigsheim wrote over the years a series of masterful essays,
the first of which appeared almost immediately after Weber's death
in 1920, the last left in manuscript in 1963, just prior to the author's
own death.[10] But since many of them have remained either
untranslated or in journals seldom consulted by today's students of
Weber, Honigsheim's portrait of his colleague as man and sociologist has suffered unwarranted neglect, when compared to those of
Parsons, Gerth and Mills, Bendix, and others.[11]

This omission is not only unfortunate on the simple grounds that
Honigsheim alone, of all these chroniclers (except Jaspers and
Löwenstein), knew Weber and was esteemed by the master of
Heidelberg. More importantly, there are certain of his essays which
open up portions of Weber's work to English-language scholars that
are otherwise obscured for lack of translations.[12] To be precise,
Honigsheim published in the late 1940s a set of four essays which

address what might be called Weber's "lost decade." Between 1889 and 1898 (and the onset of his emotional ailment), Weber published an enormous amount of sociological, political-economic, and historical writing. His dissertation on late medieval trading companies in the Mediterranean[13] is reasonably well known by name, but has not yet substantively penetrated Anglophone scholarship, since most students rely upon capsulizations for their knowledge of this important work.[14] Very quickly he composed an habilitation on the history of agrarian practices in Rome which so impressed Theodor Mommsen, so goes the oft-told tale, that the elder publicly "anointed" young Weber as his successor in ancient historiography.[15] With hardly a breath, he directed what for that time was a gigantic research project on behalf of a social policy organization, in order to ascertain the state of agrarian economy and social structure east of the Elbe (at the time a "hot" political issue), analyzing all the data himself. This was published as a volume in the proceedings of the organization, and came to 891 pages, all of which Weber either wrote, compiled, or edited for publication.[16] His next major publications included a study of the stock and commodity exchange, published in segments between 1894 and 1896, totalling 390 pages, only sixty-five pages of which found their way into the collected essays.[17]

In addition to these, Weber managed to publish numerous position papers, book reviews, contributions to symposia, and so on. But only taking into account the major writings from 1889 to 1896, one confronts 1,700 pages of Weber's work, less than 10 percent of which were included in the *Gesammelte Aufsätze*, and little of which has been translated into English. In fact, from the entire decade in question, only four essays have entered English-language scholarship,[18] literally leaving 95 percent of Weber's hectic first period of creativity untouched. This, then, is truly a segment of a promethean career lost to our knowledge, the same period during which Weber established his reputation in Germany as the most versatile and brilliant of the younger social scientists. It was, in fact, these very studies which drew young men like Honigsheim, Georg Lukács, and Karl Löwenstein to Weber after his partial recovery in 1903. Today "Weberian" sociologists usually strive to imitate the substance or method of the mature work, material written for the most part after 1911. For the earlier writings, and especially for those involving ancient history, it proves enlightening to turn once again to

Honigsheim's solid essays on the subject, little gems which have virtually escaped notice since their publication fifty years ago. The first of the group "Max Weber as Rural Sociologist,"[19] concisely treats Weber's essays on Russia, Poland, and other works in economic history, attempting to demonstrate Weber's proper claim to the label "rural sociologist." The article is still important since with rare exception,[20] little of the material Honigsheim deals with has been translated or commented upon in subsequent secondary studies. It might be argued that Honigsheim overplayed his hand somewhat in order to "place" the essay within a particular journal—a strategy not unknown among practitioners today. But this in no way diminishes the importance, for instance, of Honigsheim's treatment of the "feoffment in trust" (*Fideikommis*) and the importance of this feudal anachronism in late nineteenth-century Europe, or his comments upon Weber's interpretation of the Serbian *Zadruga* and the Russian *mir*. Though less ambitious than the other three essays, Honigsheim's initial statement about Weber in an American journal still offers a point of departure for students wishing to probe Weber's celebrated and misconstrued distaste for traditional Slavic social structure. (He was at the same time, however, a champion of revolutionary movements, particularly the events of 1905.)[21] Additionally, the only scholar in more recent years who has assayed Weber's rural sociology based most of his conclusions upon Honigsheim's "spadework," as evidenced by numerous references to the latter's essay.[22]

Two years later Honigsheim turned his attention toward "applied anthropology," in hopes of proving that his old friend could be counted among scholars in this field as well.[23] Here again the contemporary reader finds an examination of Weber's interest in subjects which have too often been ignored, in favor of the warhorses: bureaucracy, stratification, charisma, routinization, the market, and so on. For instance, Honigsheim aggressively makes a case for Weber's intellectual commitment to the study of race, ethnicity, and nationalism as mediated by ethnic attachments, social policy formation, handicraft economies, comparative social structures, and also what he calls "Ethno-Politics" or "Ethnic Social Politics" (p. 28). With slight repetition from the preceding article, Honigsheim swiftly guides the reader through a set of essays which have mostly eluded translators, especially those in which Weber combines the results of empirical research with prognostications about the likely political fates of given countries and areas. His essays on Poland, Prussia, Russia, Bavaria, Bismarck's foreign policy, the nation-state, the role of the national president, the condition of agricultural laborers, and various racialist theories (of which Weber held a low opinion), are among these.

The earlier two essays to appear in English apparently served as Honigsheim's working papers for the third, "Max Weber as Historian of Agriculture and Rural Life."[24] This article must certainly be judged a minor masterpiece of exegesis and comparative inquiry. It is comparative in the sense that Honigsheim takes upon himself the enormous task not only of stating concisely Weber's achievements in the field, but also to show, point by point, whose ideas Weber used, whether and how he modified them in his own research, and which later scholars made use of Weber's major notions, and to what degree. This immense labor of love requires nearly twenty-four thousand words and four mighty tables, on which the author directly relates Weber's work to that of dozens of writers from all the major European countries, and through scores of research monographs.[25] It is an exercise in the sociology of knowledge which is rivaled by few within its genre. In addition to the prodigious tabular layout, Honigsheim also composed notes to the article which are quintessentially German, and must be read to be believed. In the first, page-long footnote, for example, he writes, "The following authors seemingly deal with the same matters in some of their books as Weber, but actually they do not mention him, even in their footnotes and bibliographies, and accordingly they can be omitted [from Honigsheim's consideration]:...,"whereupon sixty-two scholars from the U.S., England, France, Germany, China, Russia, and elsewhere are listed alphabetically (p.180n).

The essay begins by enumerating the "eleven fundamentals" of Weber's epistemology (p. 180), certainly the most parsimonious report of this material one is likely to find. Thereafter Honigsheim immediately begins his long journey, during which he elucidates Weber's work on pre-state society, oriental and pre-occidental state cultures, classical antiquity, and the Christian world. To do this he must range over Weber's entire output, but, as before, he concentrates on the half-dozen historical and empirical studies which Weber wrote before his debilitation in 1898. What is most useful for today's student, whether regarding Weber or historical sociology in general, is the extraordinary parsimony with which Honigsheim presents a deluge of factual and theoretical information. This is especially vivid in the tables, where one column of each is given over to the stating of propositional theories, noting whether they were accepted by Weber after initial enunciation by his predecessors. By using this format, Honigsheim makes it easy for the reader to follow important notions from one historian to another, and from this country to that (for instance, about changing family structure through history). Herbert Spencer's unequalled but forgotten *Descriptive Sociology*, in 12 volumes, comes to mind when reading Honigsheim's tabular representation of Weber's research. Also notable are the subdivisions within each of the four major areas of historical interest, for example, animal husbandry, nomadism, land communism, seignorial property, the matrilinear family, and so on, all under the first topic, "Pre-State Society" (pp. 182ff). To this writer's knowledge, this article is in a class alone, for no other (in English) has attempted to juxtapose systematically Weber's historical and theoretical analyses of premodern society with those of his contemporaries and immediate followers to the extent and with the completeness that Honigsheim achieves in this selection. But not only can one quickly "locate" Weber in the intellectual current of his time, it is also simple to learn what he himself discovered about a range of historical phenomena which have not often been associated with his name (e.g., the Etruscans, or the powerlessness of handicraftsmen in ancient Greece). Had Honigsheim written nothing else on his mentor, his reputation as a Weber scholar would have been assured through wide dissemination of this one article, which unfortunately did not occur.

The last of the four articles might best be thought of as a minor corrective and addendum to Marianne's biography (cited above). In "Max Weber: His Religious and Ethical Background and Development,"[26] we learn things about Weber which in Marianne's circumspect, sometimes recondite book, lay beneath the surface—for instance, that Weber's pessimism about "man's perceptive capacity" and "inborn goodness" resonate with Kant's *Religion Within the Limits of Reason Alone* (p. 235), but that the major difference between the two stemmed not from arid epistemology, but from dissimilar emotional reponses to Pietism and the conception of "the tragic."

Honigsheim cites as his basic references for the article remarks in Weber's letters and his last two speeches, information provided by Marianne, and the author's own memories. Though many of Weber's letters have been available for some time,[27] Honigsheim remains one of the few commentators to have consulted them to any extent. Perhaps the greatest service this article performs is in sorting out, definitively one might think, the thorny questions about Weber's intellectual and emotional attachment to his Pietist heritage in conflict with his neo-Kantian epistemology. A careful reading of this last essay helps tremendously in disclosing the "tension" in Weber's life and work which resulted from the perpetual collision of "fire and ice": the "irrational" demands of his religious heritage and familial dilemmas smashing relentlessly against the steely edifice of his professional method and goals. Honigsheim fearlessly related Weber's passion for Dostoevsky and Schopenhauer to his larger *Weltanschaung*, and by taking these sorts of interpretive risks, softens the lines of Weber's famously humorless visage.

With interest in the work and person of Max Weber growing with each year,[28] it would seem only prudent to look again at the work of a man whose intellectual youth was spent in the extraordinary company of the twentieth century's greatest social scientist. From him we may learn not only the bold outlines of a theory or two, but more importantly, the finer shades and contours of thought which are revealed by one person to another only during private exchange. Through these essays we luckily become party to those private moments.

Notes

1. Howard P. Becker, "Forteen Years After, "in Howard Becker and Harry Elmer Barnes, Social Thought from Lore to Science, 3rd edition (New York: Dover Publications, 1960), Vol. 1, p. xvii.
2. Translated by Joan Rytina (New York: Free Press; and East Lansing, MI: Social Science Research Bureau), a posthumous collection of four essays and the first book-length item on Weber published over Honigsheim's name.
3. *The Protestant Ethic and the Spirit of Capitalism*, trans. by Talcott Parsons (New York: Charles Scribner's Sons, 1958, pb ed.), pp. 212, 222, 226, 229. Weber writes, "On the attitude of Port Royal and the Jansenists to the calling, see now the excellent study of Dr. Paul Honigsheim, *Die Staats- und Soziallehren der französischen Jansenisten im 17ten Jahrhundert*

(Heidelberg Historical Dissertations, 1914...)", p. 212. He later called it "an acute analysis," p. 229.

4. *Max Weber: A Biography*, trans. by Harry Zohn (New York: Wiley-Interscience, 1975), pp. 370, 454, 455. (Reissued in 1988, with a new introduction by Guenther Roth, by Transaction Publishers.)

5. Marianne Weber, *Max Weber*, trans. by Harry Zohn, intro. by Guenther Roth (New Brunswick, NJ: Transaction Publishers, 1988), 368-370.

6. Ibid., pp. 454-455.

7. Felix Somary, *The Raven of Zürich: The Memoirs of Felix Somary*, trans. by A. J. Sherman, with a foreword by Otto von Habsburg (London: C. Hurst and Company/New York: St. Martin's Press, 1986 [1960]), pp. 120-121.

8. After immigrating to the U.S., Honigsheim prepared detailed course syllabi for use at Michigan State College which give some indication of the Weberian scope of his interests, and serve to remind today's teachers how distant we are, pedagogically, from those of Honigsheim's era. The syllabi include "An outline for the study of the war and conflicting social philosophies" (1942, 54 leaves), "An outline for the study of primitive peoples in North, Central, and South America" (1942, 19 leaves), "An outline for the study of races and nationalities, revised" (1945, 37 numbered leaves), "Europe: Its peoples and cultures; an area course. The Romantic western, southwestern, and southern Europen countries and peoples; syllabus" (East Lansing, MI: Institute of Foreign Studies, 1945, 44 leaves), and "The Mohammedan World: an area course; a syllabus" (Institute of Foreign Studies, 1946, 52 leaves). Finally, in 1970, K. Peter Etzkorn made available "Sociology of Music; bibliography of titles selected by Paul Honigsheim" (St. Louis: University of Missouri Press, 1970, 196 leaves), which later made its way into a book which Etzkorn edited, *Music and Society: The Later Writings of Paul Honigsheim* (New York: John Wiley and Sons, 1973), reissued with new material as *Sociologists and Music: An Introduction to the Study of Music and Society*, 2nd ed. (New Brunswick, NJ: Transaction Publishers, 1989).

9. Karl Jaspers, "Max Weber: A Commemorative Address" [1920] in *On Max Weber*, tr. by Robert Whelan, ed. and intro. by John Dreijmanis (New York: Paragon House, 1989), 1-27, *passim*; Karl Loewenstein, "Personal Recollections of Max Weber," in *Max Weber's Political Ideas in the Perspective of Our Time*, tr. by Richard and Clara Winston (Amherst: University of Massachusetts Press, 1966), pp. 91-104.

10. "Max Weber als Soziologe," *Kölner Vierteljahrshefte für Sozialwissenschaften*, Vol. 1, No. 1 (1921), pp. 32-41, and "Erinnerungen an Max Weber," *Kölner Zeitschrift für Soziologie und Sozialpsychologie*, 15 (1963), pp. 161-271, both translated for the first time in *On Max Weber*, pp. 125-33 and 1-122 respectively.

11. Talcott Parsons, *The Structure of Social Action* (New York: McGraw-Hill, 1937), pp. 500-694, plus dozens of later works; H.H. Gerth and C.

Wright Mills, trans. and eds., *From Max Weber* (New York: Oxford University Press, 1946), pp. 3-74; Reinhard Bendix. *Max Weber: An Intellectual Portrait* (New York: Anchor Books, 1962; reprinted by the University of California Press, 1977, with a new introduction by Guenther Roth). Others include Karl Loewenstein, *Max Weber's Political Ideas in the Perspective of Our Time* (Amherst: University of Massachusetts Press, 1966), pp. 91-104; Arthur Mitzman, *The Iron Cage: An Historical Interpretation of Max Weber* (New York: Grosset & Dunlap, 1971; reprinted with a new introduction by the author, Transaction Publishers, 1985); and Dirk Käsler, *Max Weber: An Introduction to his Life and Work* (Oxford: Polity/Chicago: University of Chicago Press, 1988).

12. An interesting exception is Fred Rosenberg's dissertation, *Society and Civilization in Max Weber's Earlier Work, 1890-1907* (New School, 1983), especially pp. 209-275. Rosenberg used Benjamin's Nelson's "civilizational analysis" as an entry into this *terra incognita*, yet he relies for the most part on translations into English rather than the German originals. Nevertheless, his study is informative and unusual given the enormous amount of Weber literature which exists and has managed somehow to avoid these earlier years entirely, particularly 1890 through 1897. For bibliographical details, see Alan Sica, *Max Weber and the New Century* (Oxford: Blackwell Publishers, forthcoming), which includes a 3,000+ item bibliography of Weberiana in English.

13. *Zur Geschichte der Handelgesellschaften im Mittelalter* (Stuttgart: F. Enke, 1889), reprinted in Weber's *Gesammelte Aufsätze zur Sozial- und Wirtschaftsgeschichte* (Tübingen: Mohr, 1924), pp. 312-443.

14. The best known are Bendix's *Max Weber*, pp. 1-2, and Guenther Roth, "Introduction," pp. xxxiv-xxxvi, in *Max Weber, Economy & Society*, trans. and ed. by Guenther Roth and Claus Wittich (New York: Bedminster, 1868). These, of course, are very slight sketches of a technically demanding work, for the preparation of which Weber forced himself to master medieval dialects both of Spanish and Italian; see Marianne Weber, *Max Weber*, p. 113.

15. *Das Römische Agrargeschichte in ihrer Bedeutung für das Staats- und Privatrecht* (Stuttgart: F. Enke, 1891), 286 pp. This work was not incorporated in Weber's collected essays. For details of Mommsen's famous acclamation, see Marianne Weber, *Max Weber*, p. 114.

16. *Schriften des Vereins für Sozialpolitik:* "Die verhältnisse der Landarbeiter im ostelbischen Deutschland," Vol. 55 (Leipzig: Duncker & Humblot, 1892). This work was not included in the collected works that appeared in the early 1920s, was finally reprinted in 1984 as volume 3 of the *Gesamtausgabe* project, yet none of it has been translated. A useful portrait of the *Verein* is in Anthony Oberschall, *Empirical Social Research in Germany, 1848-1914* (New York: Basic Books, 1965), pp. 21-27, *passim*. Oberschall says a few words about Weber's role in the *Verein* study of 1892, but goes into much more detail concerning a later field study of factory workers which Weber conducted in

1908 ("The Psychophysics of Industrial Work;" *GAzSuS*, pp. 61-109). Again, the writings of the "lost decade" are slighted in favor of later research. Other useful analyses include Keith Tribe, "Prussian Agriculture and German Politics: Max Weber 1892-1897" in Tribe (ed.), *Reading Max Weber* (London: Routledge, 1989), 85-130, and Martin Riesebrodt, "From Patriarchalism to Capitalism: The Theoretical Context of Max Weber's Agrarian Studies (1892-3)," in Tribe, ibid., 131-157. See also, for comments on the *Verein* study, Bendix, *Max Weber*, pp. 14-23, 30-41.

17. "Die Börse," reprinted in *Gesammelte Aufsätze zur Soziologie und Sozialpolitik*, pp. 256-88; "Die Ergebnisse der deutschen Börsenenquete," *Zeitschrift für Gesammte Handelsrecht*, 43 (1895): 83-219, 457-514; 44 (1896): 29-74; 45 (1896): 69-156; and "Die Börse," also reprinted in *GAzSuS*, pp. 289-322. See also Bendix, *Max Weber*, pp. 23-29

18. The translated articles include: "The Social Causes of the Decay of Ancient Civilization," *The Journal of General Education*, 5 (1950), 75-88; translated from the reprint in Weber's *Gesammelte Aufsätze zur Sozial- und Wirtschaftsgeschichte*, pp. 289-311. Weber delivered this address in 1896 in Freiburg. The English translation has been reprinted in J.E.T. Eldridge, ed., *Max Weber: The Interpretation of Social Reality* (New York: Charles Scribner's Sons, 1971), pp. 254-75; "Developmental Tendencies in the Situation of East Elbian Rural Labourers," *Economy and Society*, 8:2 (May, 1979), 177-205, reprinted in Keith Tribe (ed), *Reading Weber*, 158-187; "The National State and Economic Policy (Freiburg Address)," *Economy and Society*, 9:4 (November, 1980), 428-449, reprinted in *Reading Weber*, 188-209; "'Roman' and 'Germanic' Law," *International Journal of the Sociology of Law*, 13:3 (August, 1985), 237-246. For a brief review of this period, see Käsler, *Max Weber*, 51-66.

19. *Rural Sociology* 11:3 (Sept. 1946): 207-17, lead article.

21. One of Weber's essays on Russia was translated for the first time not long ago: "The Prospects of Liberal Democracy in Tsarist Russia," in *Weber: Selections in Translation*, ed. by W.G. Runciman, trans. by Eric Matthews (Cambridge: Cambridge University Press, 1978), pp. 269-84. More recently made available is Max Weber, *The Russian Revolutions*, tr. and ed. by Gordon C. Wells and Peter Baehr (Oxford: Polity Press, 1995), which includes his prescient essays of 1905-1906 and also of 1917. Victoria Bonnell, a leading U.S. sociologist of Russian politics, was astonished at Weber's acute ability to foretell Soviet history long before its lineaments became obvious to other analysts; see her review in *Contemporary Sociology*, 25:6 (November, 1996), 821-823.

Weber typically used his thorough knowledge of agrarian economics to comment upon the political futures of Poland, Russian and Prussia, thus giving his analyses remarkable depth. A more recent stylistic equivalent is perhaps Barrington Moore, in his *Social Origins of Dictatorship and Democracy* (Boston: Beacon Press, 1966), and his legion imitators.

21. Of the few appreciable statements about Weber's political sociology of Russia (as opposed to his agrarian sociology), the most recent and detailed is David Beetham, *Max Weber and The Theory of Modern Politics* (London: Allen & Unwin, 1974), chapter 7, pp. 183-214. This supplements Richard Pipes, "Max Weber on Russia," *World Politics*, 7:3 (April 1955): 371-401.

22. Q.J. Munters, "Max Weber as Rural Sociologist," *Sociologia Ruralis*, 12:2 (1972), 129-146. This essay does include a useful bibliography of everything Weber wrote which touches upon rural sociology, plus a demonstration of the fact that American text writers on the subject have failed to notice Weber. There are nine explicit references to Honigsheim in Munters' short essay.

23. "Max Weber as Applied Anthropologist," *Applied Anthropology: Problems of Human Organization* (long since known as *Human Organization*), 7:4 (Fall 1948), 27-35.

24. *Agricultural History* 2:33 (July 1949): 179-213.

25. Honigsheim is especially keen in showing the interrelation of Weber and Oppenheimer. At around the same time, he enlarged upon the importance of the latter, a neglected figure, in the peerless text assembled by H.E. Barnes, *An Introduction to the History of Sociology* (Chicago: University of Chicago Press, 1948), pp. 332-52: "The Sociological Doctrines of Franz Oppenheimer: An Agrarian Philosophy of History and Social Reform."

26. *Church History* 19 (1950):219-239.

27. *Jungendbriefe, 1879-1893* (Tübingen: Mohr, 1936) and *Max Weber: Werk und Person*, ed. by Eduard Baumgarten (Tübingen: Mohr, 1964). It is also known that Baumgarten is in possession of many letters concerning Weber's private life, which he has not yet published. Interest in these documents was stimulated by Mitzman's book (mentioned above) and by Martin Green's *The von Richthofen Sisters* (New York: Basic Books, 1974). Thus far volumes 5 and 6 of the *Gesamtausgabe* have provided letters from the Weber collection that originate in the years 1906-1908 (vol. 5) and 1909—1910 (vol. 6), published in 1990 and 1994 respectively. Their availability has not yet made much impact on Anglophone Weber scholarship.

28. The most detailed general bibliography of secondary literature on Weber lists 2,400 items in a half-dozen languages; see Constans Seyfarth and Gerd Schmidt, comps., *Max Weber Bibliographie: Eine Dokumentation der Sekundärliteratur* (Stuttgart: Enke, 1977). My own compilation of English-language works numbers more than 3,000 items; see *Max Weber and the New Century* (Oxford: Blackwell Publishers, forthcoming).

Foreword to *On Max Weber* (1962)

Paul Honigsheim came to Michigan State University by way of France and Panama in 1938 as a political refugee from Germany. As incongruous a figure in a provincial midwestern university as a cowboy in Heidelberg, Honigsheim nonetheless provided a model of scholarship for students and colleagues alike. To be with Dr. Honigsheim (never Paul) was to be in a perpetual seminar with the theme ever the same—the role of history in social structure and process, yesterday, today, and tomorrow. He stood firmly in the classic tradition of sociology, and insisted that history, biography, and social issues make up the guts of sociology. And he was ready to prove to anyone that American sociology was too non-historical, too oblivious to world problems, and too dependent upon statistics.

Honigsheim was a person of enormous intellectual and physical vigor. A three-hour lecture was merely a warm-up, a prelude to a discussion that could last for days. A self-labeled fanatic and monk, Honigsheim devoted himself completely to scholarship. There was little else to life. His three-room apartment was filled with books, clippings, records, and notes. Even the kitchen cupboards were crammed with books and papers. He planned prodigious and grandiose writing and research efforts, among which were definitive volumes on Max Weber's sociology, the sociology of music, the Mohammedan world, and the history of social and political thought. Yet he completed none of these. Unconsciously, he kept putting off these tasks to respond to virtually any request to write an article, an encyclopedia piece, or a radio talk on almost any socio-historical subject.

Reluctantly, as a response to the constant nagging of his students and colleagues, he began work on his books in the last years of his life. Yet they remained subsidiary tasks to be turned to in earnest "once this damned article that . . . is plaguing me for is done."

xxiii

Almost as if he had a premonition that turning to the Weber book would hasten his death, Honigsheim was uncompromisingly busy on the Weber memoirs during his last days. He had completed a rough draft of his reminiscences of Weber just before he died. The draft was hand-written in German, and the style showed that he was anxious to get down his main ideas. The Weber book was not to be a mere assemblage of the articles already printed. He had planned to revise his articles, to fill in certain gaps, and to incorporate his personal memories of Weber. But death (or rather, Mephistopheles, as Honigsheim would have preferred) intervened.

Honigsheim's reminiscences of Weber were originally solicited by Dr. Johannes Winckelmann of the Max Weber Archives, University of Munich. As a part of the Max Weber Centennial celebration, they were published almost unedited by Rene König in the *Kölner Zeitschrift für Soziologie und Sozial/psychologie* in 1963.

Paul Honigsheim was born in Düsseldorf on March 28, 1885. He pursued his higher education at the Universities of Bonn, Berlin, and Heidelberg. His Ph.D., granted in 1914 at Heidelberg, was in history, and his dissertation was entitled, "Die Staats- und Sozial-Lehren der französischen Jansenisten im 17. Jahrhundert." It was during the Heidelberg period that he became a member of Weber's inner circle. Although Honigsheim was never a student of Weber's in the formal sense, their intellectual interchange was extensive. He was often a guest in the Weber household and remained in contact with Marianne Weber until her death.

World War I was a personal tragedy for Paul Honigsheim. He called himself "half a Frenchman" (his mother was French), and the war struck him as a horrible fratricide. After induction into the German army, he served as an interpreter for captured French soldiers in the prisoner of war camp near Paderborn. It was during this time that he became an ardent pacifist.

After the War he became assistant and librarian, Institute for Social Research, University of Cologne, and held these positions from 1919 to 1921. He then became instructor and associate, University of Cologne and, simultaneously, director of the People's University, an adult education program of the University of Cologne. He held these positions until 1933. He left Germany soon after the Nazis seized power and became director of the Paris branch of the Institute for Social Research. He held this post until 1936 when he went to the University of Panama as professor of philosophy, history, and anthropology. Two years later he came to Michigan State College in the Department of Sociology and Anthropology. His retirement from Michigan State in 1950 was a formality, for he continued his frantic pace of teaching and writing.

He was guest professor at Lewis and Clark (1950-53) and at Washington State College (1956-57). Returning to East Lansing, he resumed classes and his round of informal seminars at Michigan State University. He also lectured at numerous other American universities, made several lecture trips to Germany, and regularly attended meetings of the American and International Sociological Associations.

Paul Honigsheim ordered his life in accord with the demands of scholarship. He read prodigiously and possessed an encyclopedic memory. His hand-written notes and extracts, carefully classified and filed, would fill an ordinary office. To say that "Max Weber wolfed down eight little cakes," as Honigsheim does in the reminiscences, cannot be dismissed as false precision. We are sure that a note taken about 1913 specifies this fact.

Honigsheim's scholarship ranged over numerous disciplines and his bibliography contains well over 300 citations in German, English, French, and Spanish. Although the majority of his writings focused on the history of ideas, many of his works dealt with such diverse areas as the sociology of the arts, pacifism, ethnology, and adult education. Among his unfinished works is a book-length manuscript on the sociology of music.

Honigsheim was never happier than when surrounded by students, either in the classroom or around a table. His impact upon students was shattering: either they became mesmerized devotees or fled in search of a less enriched academic fare. It is difficult to know whether Honigsheim the scholar, or Honigsheim the human being, was the more appealing to his students, colleagues, and friends.

This small volume offers a sample of Paul Honigsheim's wide-ranging scholarship bearing exclusively on Max Weber. Even this sample would not have been possible without the collaboration of a number of people. Joan Rytina, research associate in the Department of Sociology, brought imagination and great energy to the difficult task of rendering an unrevised German text into English.

Liese von Oettingen, librarian, Grand Haven Public Library, assisted Mrs. Rytina in checking and verifying certain references and idioms.

We wish to recognize the assistance of others who have contributed in a number of different ways. Dr. Rolfe Schulze, Department of Sociology, Northwestern University, served as an assistant to Dr. Honigsheim and spurred him to prepare the reminiscences. Miss Brigitte Utikal, Honigsheim's student helper, and Mrs. Helene Urban, his typist and friend, did yeoman service in preparing the handwritten text of the reminiscences for publication in German. Miss Utikal and Mrs. Elke Kochweser Ammassari provided translations of many articles to give us a basis for deciding what to include in the present volume. Dr. Peter Etzkorn, Department of Sociology, University of Nevada, consulted with Mrs. Rytina on resistent portions of the manuscript. Dorothy Tervo, Nancy Moore, and Sharon L. Graham typed the manuscript, and William D. Emery helped with the editing of the footnotes.

We gratefully acknowledge permission from *Kölner Zeitschrift für Soziologie und Sozialpsychologie,* Duncker & Humblot, Westdeutscher Verlag, and *Handwörterbuch der Sozialwissenschaften* to translate and publish the papers found in this book.

Finally, we wish to express our gratitude to Dr. Louis L. McQuitty, Dean of the College of Social Science, for his enthusiastic support. Not only did he make available the facilities of the Social Science Research Bureau, but he encouraged the enterprise in many other ways.

Readers of this volume should be aware that, as a first draft, Honigsheim's "Memories of Max Weber" is incomplete in many ways. This translation is incomplete, in similar ways, but, unlike Honigsheim's work, ours is a matter of design, not circumstance. Those of us involved in this enterprise have tried to present what Honigsheim actually wrote as he wrote it. To do more, to improve on what we can only imagine were Honigsheim's intentions, was not our wish.

J. Allan Beegle
William H. Form

Part 1

The Unknown Max Weber

1

Max Weber as Rural Sociologist: In Commemoration of the Twenty-Fifth Anniversary of His Death

The United States will be obliged to participate in a decisive way in the rehabilitation of chaotic Europe in general, and of its rural life in particular. This task is inextricably connected with the political problems related to the penetration of the Soviets and their collective farms into central and southeastern Europe. In this connection at least three types of rural organizations came into consideration: (1) Feudalism was and still is in existence in Germany, east of the Elbe, in Poland and in the Rumanian lowland, and was found in its extremist form until recently, as feoffment in trust (*Fideikommis*). This latter term denotes a relatively large estate, being the property of a privileged family and, therefore, not able to be brought up for sale, even if the owning family is indebted. (2) The rural collectivity existed in the past as *zadruga* in Serbia and as *mir* in Russia and at the present time as *artel* in the Soviet Republics. (3) The independent peasant's farm existed and exists to a greater or less extent in same parts of Eastern Europe, including Germany.

In the United States neither feudalism nor collective farms existed except in the South and in a few remote sectarian groups. Accordingly it may be difficult for Americans to appraise these European phenomena. Under such circumstances it may be of importance to know the viewpoint of Max Weber in regard to these problems, for he was one of the most outstanding among the German soci-

Rural Sociology 11:3 (Sept., 1946), 207-218.

ologists, economists, and politicians of the era before, during, and after World War I. Max Weber was very familiar with the United States, its economic and sociological viewpoint, through his studies and travels, and was, therefore, able to compare the Old and New Worlds. Both his friends and enemies agree in considering him a man of vast knowledge, keen methodological perception, incorruptible objectivity, and genuine sense of justice. While he was known in Europe as much for his rural sociological interests as for his researches in historical and theoretical fields, in the USA he is known almost exclusively, not as a rural sociologist, but as a methodologist and pioneer in the field of the sociology of religion. He will be considered in this paper primarily as a rural sociologist. A few preliminary words on his personality and background may be in order at this point. [1]

Max Weber was successively a lawyer, a teacher of Roman and commercial law, and a professor of economics in Freiburg and Heidelberg. Because he was overworked and ill during fifteen years while in Heidelberg, he neither taught nor appeared publicly. Later he re-entered politics during World War I and after the peace treaties for a short time before his death he was professor of sociology in Munich. The basic element of his spiritual life was a religiously founded ethical categorical imperative, which drove him to two duties: (1) to investigate scientific topics objectively, that is, by eliminating personal bias and judgments of value within the historico-economico-sociological sphere,[2] and (2) to make individual decisions and remain loyal to his convictions in the spheres of religion, ethics, and politics.[3]

As a politician Max Weber shifted from moderate liberalism to a more radical democratic conviction which was not of a laissez-faire character, but which, on the contrary, led him to work within the influential "verein für Sozialpolitik" for state-supported social policies. Oriented by his studies in the comparative history of rural life and institutions[4] he debated four rural political problems, three of which involved eastern Germany: (1) the social situation of seigniors and dependents; (2) feoffment in trust; (3) Polish minorities; and (4) the structure of rural Russia before and after the collapse of Czarism. The discussion on the following pages is developed around these four topics.

I. *The social position of seigniors and dependents* is to Max Weber a special case of the sociological phenomenon known as "feudalism." This is a pattern of social life, closely connected with one of Weber's three types of leadership, that is, the traditional one. Here the leader is obeyed, neither because he is supposed to be a unique individual, nor because there exists a written law in an institutionalized society, making him a bureaucrat, but rather because of tradition.[5] Max Weber investigates and describes the sociological phenomena arising out of this traditionalistic feudalism, such as the special concept of honor and luxury, the denial of the calculating and capitalistic mentality, and the refusal to be involved in trade.[6] But independent of this general sociologico-classificatory interest, he had the special and practical interest in and aversion to the power of the Prussian "Junkers." This situation he describes and judges as follows.

The feudal owners of large rural estates were the regular political leaders in the majority of rural societies in the past. In England[7] they have continued to the present time and in eastern Germany until recently.[8] Here actually the leading social class was scattered over the entire land; their castles and estates were centers of power and they themselves were political autocrats, economically self-satisfied, with little knowledge in economics and without much interest in business. Their subordinates [9] were not only domestic servants and valets in the manors of the seigniors, but were either permanent or transient rural workers, the latter being hired from surrounding villages. The former were not unmarried, but had families, and were obliged, if their families had too few workers, to hire themselves a substitute called *Scharwerker*; all these were largely paid in kind, which made them believe that they had the same economic interests as their employers. They accepted this traditional situation without any opposition owing to the indoctrination they had received for many generations.

Changes have occurred during recent decades[10] due to the higher standard of living of the bourgeois class in the cities. Especially now it was necessary for the Junkers to maintain their social supremacy and to attempt to raise their own standard; but the manor, thus managed was not capable of maintaining the living standard of a noble family. The sons had to become officers in the army or members of very exclusive, and expensive student associations, and the daughters, in order to be married according to their rank, were supposed to have a big dowry. Thus the Junkers were obliged to became entrepreneurs with an increasingly "bourgeois" mentality and accordingly changed their attitude toward their subordinates.[11] The importance of perquisites decreased, while cash payments and the number of persons receiving them increased. The dependents also began to prefer this method although it was less secure but offered greater independence. They also began to develop antagonism toward the proprietor, even an inclination to class struggle and some of them emigrated to the cities to become factory workers. Last, but not least, the nobles felt themselves compelled to change the interrelationship between political power and economic status. Formerly they had based their political power on their unshaken and undisputed economic status; now they found it necessary to maintain their seriously threatened economic status through political power. The result was that they became an economic group which turned into a pressure group using political resources for economic class purposes. This was done by enacting new state laws favoring the maintenance of the economic productivity of their estates especially by requiring laws protecting the feoffment in trust.

II. *The feoffment in trust,* according to Weber, although it had already been known in ancient Indies, was re-originated in Byzantium, where land, to avoid its confiscation by the Emperor, was transferred to the Church under the agreement that nine-tenths of the land rent be paid to the family. From the Greek-Roman Empire this institution shifted to the Mohammedans, with them to Christian Spain and from there to England and other Christian countries, including Prussia.[12] Here, under the pressure of the Junkers, the government published in 1903 the draft of a new bill concerning feoffment. Immediately after its publication Max Weber, who had already shown an interest in the problem[13] and continued later to maintain his interest in this field,[14] collected material and published his criticism, protest, and his own program. He describes the situation as having existed hitherto as follows:[15]

Land which has relatively high and riskless rent, has a tendency to be incorporated into feoffments. This arose in considerable part because those capitalists who had all the money they wanted but desired security, desired to invest money in such land, in that way obtaining nobility from the monarch, and gaining the opportunity of living on the standard of a highly esteemed "rentier." This possibility would even increase if through tariffs protecting the grain production, the land-rent of grain-producing land could be maintained and even increased.[16]

The draft of the new bill provided[17] for the possibility of the establishment of new feoffments with the king's permission and pretended to protect and strengthen by such measures the interest in family and home. In opposition to this, Weber asserts[18] that it is the intention of the government to combine protectionism with feoffments, thus to maintain, and to create artificially big estates, giving to the capitalistic bourgeoisie class the opportunity of becoming nobles, thus making them conservatives dependent upon the supporters of the monarchy, and allies of the declining eastern nobility. He opposes the new bill for this reason and believes—as he will also repeat later[19]—that the effects of existing feoffment are the following[20]: capital which Germany should use in trade, is removed out of the world's trade and industry; peasants are driven from good to bad land; rural workers settle down definitively on or near to the feoffment's land, become again bound to the soil, and in reality dependent upon the landlord, as happened in the feudal era; rural workers not willing to accept such a situation, are induced to emigrate, and the owners themselves to hire foreign seasonal workers.

Under such circumstances, Weber had always opposed[21] every measure calculated to hinder rural workers from moving to the city or to return them back to their former rural districts, or to have them settle as small part-time farmers on or near the large estates. He concedes[22] feoffments for only a small percentage of soil used mostly for forestry but insists that all the other feoffments, which already exist, or the establishment of which may be asked for, should be eliminated. As a transitory measure he requires[23] expropriation with compensation of the untenable large estates by the state, the conversion of this land in demesnes, the assignment on leave of the latter to crown-land-lessees, and the protection of the workers hired by and dependent upon these tenants with a contract which should be signed by both the state and the lessees.

The government became enraged at this sharp opposition and criticism by the Heidelberg professor but felt itself impelled to withdraw the draft of the bill. Thus actually Weber was successful, but only to some extent, for neither his claim for abolition of feoffment nor the positive part of his program became realized, and the Polish minority problem in rural eastern Germany also remained, the other aspect of the feoffment question.

III. *The Polish minority in rural Eastern Germany* originated thus: By the partition of Poland at the end of the eighteenth century, some of the Poles had become subjects and later citizens of Prussia and Germany respectively. Previously, feudalism in Poland had been even stronger than in Prussia and the latter had to some extent protected the Polish lower rural classes from the nobility which caused the Polish masses for some decades of the nineteenth century to acquiesce to Prussian domination. With an increasing tendency toward Prussification and with a simultaneous development toward Russificiation, Polish Catholic propaganda arose against Prussian Protestantism and against Russian Greek-Orthodoxy, thus making the antagonism between the nations more acute. This manifested itself, among other things, in the Prussian laws, which restricted sharply the use of the Polish language in the Eastern provinces.

Max Weber had always strictly opposed anti-Polish language laws,[24] acknowledging at the same time the loyalty of the Poles in Upper Silesia,[25] but from the very beginning of his public appearance he likewise opposed the increasing Polonization of the East. Because of this and other reasons, he blamed the Junkers and the conservative party. His accusation ran somewhat as follows: they give themselves an air of nationalism but actually sacrifice national good for their own socioeconomic interests. These Junkers use hired Polish seasonal workers coming front Russian-Polish districts because of the cheapness of the labor and the absence of any obligation to furnish welfare assistance in time of need. Last, but not least, the feoffment in trust as they are, and most of all as they would be, if the bill mentioned in the previous section became law, would increase, for reasons mentioned above, the amount of seasonal workers, especially those of Polish descent. Only Poles[27] would be willing to settle on or near the large estates of the manor holders in the completely dependent form described above. Therefore Weber's twofold challenge:[28] forbid the entrance of Polish seasonal workers, coming from Polish-Russia into Eastern-Germany and abolish the feoffments, especially for advancing Polish immigration. Apparently the national point of view plays a role in Weber's thinking but it is not the most important. This emphasis upon the national viewpoint comes to light here because he considered it his duty to labor where God or destiny had put him; and one of these values according to him is the nation. This national point of view was not the only one which led Weber to the anti-feoffment campaign, but rather it was his religiously founded deep sympathy for the lower classes.

This feeling may help us to explain Weber's interest in the changes of Russian rural structure before and after the collapse of Czarism, which is regarded as his latest rural sociological interest.

IV. *The rural structure of Russia* had always attracted Max Weber's attention. Even more than that, he had always been affected by the collectivity feeling of the Russian peasant, by the Greek-Orthodox Saint and the passive sufferer in the fictions of Dostoevsky, and by Tolstoy's attempt to teach and to live a life conforming to the precepts of the Sermon on the Mount. Weber did not believe in the possibility of regulating state and politics according to those principles. On the contrary, he had emphasized more than anyone else the essentially tragic role of the politician because the latter was responsible for the future of his group or country. Thus, he could not act exclusively according to his own individual ethical conscience without taking the future into consideration; rather he had to act in regard to his responsibility and take upon himself the burden of becoming, ethically speaking, guilty and, religiously speaking, a sinner. Max Weber had been deeply touched by the problem and by Tolstoy's attempt to solve it in a way, different from his own. He had even planned to go beyond the occasional remarks and to write a book on this Russian disciple of the Sermon on the Mount.[29] Under such circumstances, one can hardly wonder that Russian rural life meant so much to him, not only after the great changes occurring during World War I, but even before. He had always been interested in and familiar with the history of agriculture and rural life. With this background he investigated Russian rural social structure in its uniqueness comparing it with that of other countries. His description may be summarized as follows:[30] the landed nobility was always dominant in the local government of the rural provincial districts and yet this same nobility did not have any organization of its own to protect itself from the czarist government and to ameliorate its economic conditions. When the economic situation was insufficient to permit the members of an increasing family to make an adequate living they were, more than in other countries, compelled to cultivate connections and in that way obtain high positions in army and administration. They, therefore, became dependent upon the czar and carried on only in the role of a court nobility. Much more than with this nobility, Weber was concerned with the lower classes and with the rural collectivity, characterizing not exclusively the Russian but also the other Slavic language-speaking peoples. Thus, the Serbian zadruga was also of importance to him.[31] This South Slavic form of rural collectivity had for a long time attracted the attention of historians of agriculture as well as that of politicians.[32] Even romantically minded anarchists had used it as an example to prove the truth of their own theory. Their arguments had been, that the zadruga is a form of life, without any legal compulsion and that, if such a kind of existence were possible in Serbia it could also became a possibility elsewhere. Thus, for these romanticists it would be a proof that any kind of legal compulsion is superfluous. Max Weber opposed such use of the existence of the zadruga to justify anarchistic claims. He showed that where the zadruga exists there also exists legal compulsion, even if not administered by the state, nevertheless carried out by a village community. On the other hand the fact that the zadruga exists is for him important because it gives him an opportunity to demonstrate, in opposition to the state-idolaters, the possibility of a stateless legal coercion. More than by the zadruga, Weber felt himself attracted to the Russian mir. The age of the mir is controversial,[33] and he did not feel himself qualified to ascertain its exact age.[34] The mir centers around a village with houses built along a single street; the fields are divided into big areas and these are sub-divided into long strips. The latter are allotted to the families, which are members of the mir, according to the number of working members in every family. Periodically repartition takes place and there exists the right to reparticipation in such a new partition for former members who having left the community had returned again.[35] The czarist minister, Peter Stolypin, at the beginning of the nineteenth century had instituted rural reform laws in opposition to these traditional mores. These laws made secession from such collectivity possible. Stolypin considered his measures liberal and favorable to the independence of the peasants.[36]

Max Weber, studying, describing, and opposing this measure evaluated it in the following way:[37] the measure splits the peasants into two antagonistic groups with private owners seceding from the community and the others still remaining members of it. The tendency was for the peasants, like the veterinarians and other rural intellectuals increasingly to become adherents of the Social-Revolutionaries. These were the successors of the former Narodniki and like these a revolutionary party with less industrial and more rural inclinations, less internationally and more Russian-minded than the two Marxian groups, the Bolsheviks and the Mensheviks.

The Heidelbergian sociologist had the opportunity to know intimately many Social-Revolutionaries who studied at his university and he considered their movement, socio-psychologically speaking, similar to a religious one. He admired these idealists, who were willing and ready, to make the greatest sacrifice for their convictions.[38] When Stolypin attempted to split the peasants by these measures, there appeared at the same time an attempt to split the adherents of the dangerous Social-Revolutionaries. It was especially for this reason that Weber opposed very passionately the reforms of Stolypin.[39] Nevertheless, the attempt made by the latter was successful although only to same extent, since the Social-Revolutionaries remained one of the most important revolutionary parties, especially immediately after the abdication of the czar. Their more moderate right wing became, in coalition with the right-wing Marxists, the Mensheviks, for a short period the rulers of Russia who had as their immediate problem peace with Germany or continuation of the war.

Since the beginning of World War I, the Heidelbergian sociologist, because of convictions which he continued to hold, had advocated peace without annexations.[40] However, he doubted that the government led by Kerensky who was the leader of the right-wing Social-Revolutionaries, would be willing and able to carry this out, especially because of the new rural problems in Russia. Weber considered[41] the Russian peasants of that period to be almost exclusively interested in the expropriation of the property of the rural proprietor of non-peasant origin. He reasoned as follows: they desire to leave the army, return home and enjoy peace; this is also the desire of the Social-Revolutionaries, who are dependent on these peasants. But all groups, interested in individual rural property, are interested for the same reason in hindering the return of the revolutionary-minded peasants. To keep the peasants from returning, these groups must prefer war to peace, because the latter would bring the peasants back. Within the anti-peasant and anti-social revolutionary groups there are (in addition to the independent peasants already mentioned, who left the mir following Stolypin's reform) numerous "bourgeois," who invested money in rural property for its comparatively high degree of security. Included also in these groups are the bankers, and last but not least, similar groups outside of Russia upon whom the Kerensky government is dependent for financial support. It is for this reason that the right wing Social-Revolutionaries, even though they desire peace are not able to promote it. They also are handicapped because of lack of support by the urban workers.[42]

The old prerevolutionary antagonism between the Marxists of both nuances—Bolsheviks and Mensheviks—and the Social-Revolutionaries of both kinds—right and left wing—reappear. Even Plekhanov, the old theoretician of the Mensheviks, asserts that cheap bread is the first requisite and considers the peasant's claims as romantic and reactionary. The peasants, adherents of the Kerensky government, also do not agree with one another. As an illustration,[43] within one smaller political unit the partition of land may give to every peasant only six hectares while in the neighboring one, fifteen hectares. In such cases the peasants living within the first one of these two units will insist on equal partitions of the land and, of course, want to base the division on the larger political unit, thus forcing those who hoped for fifteen hectares to get less. The peasants, on the other hand, who live within the second area, where the fifteen-hectare unit is hoped for, will insist on the monopolistic attribution of the good land of their own district only to themselves, excluding from the partition all land outside their own small unit and all the other peasants living together in the larger political unit.

Finally,[44] the Kerensky government is still dependent on the Duma, that is, the elected parliament still in existence. In the latter there is a strong majority favoring the maintenance of the specific Russian supremacy over the many non-Russian rural minorities, such as Ukrainians, Latvians, Estonians, and so on. This results in another antagonism within the already weak government led by the social-revolutionary Kerensky.

Max Weber's prophecy that this government would not be inclined to make peace with Germany was true.[45] However, the later events have disproved his prophecy that the Bolshevik regime would not exist long.[46] To be sure, after it had been established, both—the Soviets as well as Weber—had to face the problem of the rural collectivity the Artel, as it now was called, and its transferability to other parts of Europe. Our sociologist under consideration had always been free from any prejudice for or against private agricultural property or collectively owned land.[47] He considered the artel adequate for a population like the Russian, which had always lived in an agrarian communism. The Western European peasant on the contrary sets his heart on hereditary property, fears the socialistic workers, even prefers, when he feels himself endangered by the latter, to cooperate with the noble landlord. Therefore the probability of an imitation of the Russian pattern in Western Europe is, according to Weber, not likely.[48]

This judgment is actually the last one within Max Weber's rural sociologico-political activity. The man, who, although ill and handicapped, nevertheless felt himself religiously and ethically bound to participate in public affairs has been hindered from accomplishing his scientific as well as his political work by an untimely death. This work began with investigations in the field of the history of agriculture and rural life and embraced many fields, as indicated in the beginning of this paper. It was motivated by two viewpoints: (1) objectivity within the scientific field and (2) feeling of equity, justice, and religiously-founded brotherly love for the lowly, guiding his participation in the fields of politics and practical activity.

Both viewpoints—objectivity and brotherly love—were also Max Weber's guiding stars in that part of his activities, which was the least known in the United States, that is, his activity in the field of rural sociology.

Notes

1. After the death of Max Weber almost all of his publications were collected and edited by his widow, Marianne Weber, in part with the help of friends. The volumes and the articles within them, coming into consideration for us, are the following: M. Weber, *Gesammelte Politische Schriften*, München, Drei Masken Verlag, 1921, (especially the following articles: "Der Nationalstaat und die Volkswirtschaftspolitik," cited in the following footnotes "Nationalstaat," "Zwischen zwei Gesetzen," cited "Gesetz," "Bismarcks Aussenpolitik und die Gegenwart," cited "Bismarck," "Deutschland unter den europäischen Weltmächten," cited "Weltmächte" "Deutschlands äussere und Preussens innere Politik," cited "Deutschland," "Russlands Übergang zur Scheindemokratie," cited "Russland," "Wahlrecht und Demokratie in Deutschland," cited "Wahlrecht," "Innere Lage und Aussenpolitik," cited "Innere," "Politik als Beruf," cited "Politik"); idem, *Wirtschaftsgeschichte*, München und Leipzig, Duncker und Humblot, 1923, cited "Wirtschaftsgeschichte," idem, *Gesammelte Aufsätze zur Religionsriss der Sozialökonomik*, Vol. III, Tübingen, Mohr, 1922, cited "Wirtschaft;" idem, *Gesammelte Aufsätze zur Religions-soziologie*, ibid., 1921-1922, cited "Religion;" idem, *Gesammelte Aufsätze zur Wissenschaftslehre.* ibid., 1922. (Especially the following articles: "Die Objektivität sozialwissenschaftlicher und sozialpolitischer Erkenntnis," cited "Objektivität," "Der Sinnder Wertfreiheit der soziologischen und ökonomischen Wissenschaften," cited "Wertfreiheit," "Wissenschaft als Beruf," cited "Wissenschaft"); idem, *Gesammelte Aufsätze zur Soziologie und Sozialpolitik*, ibid., 1934, (Especially the following articles: "Argarstatistische und sozialpolitische Bertrachtugen zur Fideikommisfrage in Prüssen," cited "Fideikommis," "Der Sozialismus"); idem, *Gesammelte Aufsätze zur social und Wirtschaftsgeschichte*, ibid., 1924, (Especially the following articles: "Agrarverhältnisse im Altertum," cited "Agrarverhältnisse," "Die Sozialen Gründe des Unterganges der antiken Kultur," cited "Untergang," "Die ländliche Arbeitsverfassung," cited "Arbeit," "Entwickelungstendenzen in der Lage der Altgermanischen Sozialverfassung," cited "Altgermanisch,"). Publications dealing with Max Weber: Marianne Weber, *Max Weber*, ibid., 1926, cited "Marianne Weber;" the epistemological and methodological background is dealt with in the following publications: T. Abel, *Systematic Sociology in Germany*, New York, Columbia University Press, 1929, pp. 116-159; H. Becker, "Culture Case Study and Ideal-Typical Method; with special reference to Max Weber," *Social Forces*, Vol. 12, New York, 1934, pp. 403f.; H.P. Jordan, "Some Philosophical Implications of Max Weber's Methodology," *Ethics*, Vol. 48, Chicago, The University of Chicago Press, pp. 221-231; A. Liebert, "Max Weber," *Prüssische Jahrbücher*, Vol. 210, Berlin, Stilke, 1927, pp. 304-320; J.P. Mayer, *Max Weber and German Politics*, London, Faber and Faber, Ltd., n.d., p. 30; H. Rickert, "Max Weber

und seine Stellung zur Wissenschaft," *Logos*, Vol. 15, Tübigen,Mohr, 1926, pp. 222-237; R. Wilbrandt, "Max Weber als Erkenntniskritiker der Sozialwissenschaften,"*Zeirschrift für die gesamte Staatswissenschaft,* Vol. 79, Tübingen, Laupp, 1925, pp. 584-674. The whole personality, the religious and ethical background is dealt with in the following publications: C. Diehl, "The Life and Work of Max Weber," *The Quarterly Journal of Economics*, Cambridge, Massachusetts, Harvard University Press, 1924, pp. 87-107; P. Honigsheim, "Max Weber als Soziologe," *Kölner Vierteljahrshefte für Soziologie*, Vol. 1, München und Leipzig, Duncker und Humblot, 1921; idem,"Der Max Weber—Kreis in Heidelberg," ibid., Vol. 5, 1926, pp. 271-187; idem, "Max Webers geistesgeschichtliche Stellung,"*Die Volkswirte,*V. 29, ibid., 1930l; idem, "Max Weber,"*Internationales Handwörterbuch des Gewerkschaftswesens,* Berlin, Werk und Wirtschaft, 1932; E. Hula, "Max Weber Scholar and Politician,"*The Contemporary Review,*Vol. 34, London, 1928; K. Jaspers, *Max Weber*, Oldenburg, Gerhard Stalling, 1932; K. Löwith, "Max Weber und Karl Marx," *Archiv für Sozialwissenschaft*, Vol. 67, Tübingen, Mohr, 1932, pp. 53-99, 175-214; J. P. Mayer,"Sociology of Politics,"*The Dublin Review,*Vol. 207, London, Burns,Oates,and Washburn, 1940. pp. 188-196; A. Mettler, *Max Weber und die philosophische Problemtikunserer Zeit*, Zürich, Elgg, n.d.; T. Parsons,"Capitalism in Recent German Literature."*The Journal of Political Economy,"*Vol. 36, Chicago, University of Chicago Press, 1929, pp. 31-51; idem,"A.M. Robertson on Max Weber and His School,"Ibid.,Vol. 43, 1935, pp. 688-696; A.M. Robertson, *Aspects of the Rise of Economic Individualism, A Criticism of Max Weber and his School,* Cambridge, The University Press, 1933; G.v. Schulze-Gävernitz, "Max Weber als Nationalökonom und Politiker," *Hauptprobleme der Soziologie, Erinnerungsgabe für Max Weber*, Vol. 1, München und Beipzig, Duncker und Humblot, 1923, pp. XIII-XXI. No one of these publications deals especially with Max Weber as Rural Sociologist. The present author will deal with "Max Weber as Historian of Agriculture"in a special article.

2. Objectivität, pp. 175-178; Wertfreiheit, pp. 485-502; Wissenschaft, pp. 542-555.

3. Ibid., p. 543; Politik, pp. 440 f.; Gesetz, pp. 60-63.

4. Agrarverhältnisse, *passim*; Untergang, *passim*; Altgermanisch, *passim*.

5. Wirtschaft, pp. 130-139.

6. Ibid., pp. 635, 732 ff. 750 ff.

7. Wirtschaftsgeschichte, p. 108; Wahlrecht, p. 307.

8. Entwickelung, pp. 471, 464.

9. Ibid., pp. 474, 479.

10. Ibid., p. 472.

11. Ibid., pp. 473, 475ff., 479f., 489, 493; Arbeit, pp. 479ff.

12. Religion, Vol. III, p. 160; Wirtschaftsgeschichte, p. 107, Wirtschaft, p. 743.

13. Marianne Weber, p. 342.

14. Deutschland, pp. 99-106.
15. Fideikommiss, pp. 329, 331f., 369, 372f.
16. Ibid., p. 322ff.
17. Ibid., p. 324-327.
18. Ibid., pp. 338, 379, 381.
19. Deutschland, pp. 100-104.
20. Fideikommiss, pp. 357, 359, 391.
21. Arbeit, pp. 459f., 462f.
22. Fideikommiss, pp. 361, 378.
23. Ibid., pp. 466ff., Entwickelung, p. 507.
24. Bismarck, p. 41f., Weltmacht, p. 89.
25. Wirtschaft, p. 225, 629.
26. Nationalstaat, pp. 15f., Bismarck, p. 41., Deutschland, p. 95., Marianne Weber, pp. 229f., 237, 542.
27. Fidiekommis, p. 360.
28. Arbeit, p. 456ff.
29. Gesetz, p. 62f., Politik, p. 441f., Wertfreiheit, pp. 467, 469, 479.
30. Wirtschaft, p. 720.
31. Ibid., pp. 398f.
32. For example, F. Engels, the socialistic collaborator of Karl Marx, in his book *Der Ursprung der Familie*, Stuttgart, Dietz, 11th edition, No. 11, pp. 48f. and A. Meitzen, Max Weber's teacher in history of agriculture and in statistics, in his book *Siedelunger und Agrarwesen der Westgermanen und Ostgermanen, der Kelten, Roemer, Finnen und Slaven*, Berlin, 1896, Vol. 1, No. VIII, *passim*.
33. See the history of the theories concerning its age in A. Dopsch, *Wirtschaftliche und Soziale Grundlagen der Europäischen Kulturentwickelung*, Vol. 1, Wien, Seidel, pp. 40-44.
34. Wirtschaftsgeschichte, p. 34.
35. Ibid., pp. 32f., Wirtschaft, p. 608.
36. Russland, pp. 107f.
37. Ibid., p. 108.
38. Wirtschaft. pp. 295f., 751. Russland, p. 117.
39. Ibid., p. 108
40. Weltmächte, p. 76f.
41. Ibid., p. 116f.
42. Ibid., p. 119.
43. Ibid., p. 116.
44. Ibid., p. 122.
45. Innere, p. 324.
46. Ibid., p. 323.
47. Russland, p. 123.
48. Sozialismus, p. 516.

2

Max Weber as Applied Anthropologist

At the present time the United States feels it necessary to aid in reorganizing a completely disorganized Europe. At the same time Americans must face gigantic internal problems of their own. Certainly the problems which trouble both the Old and New World today are not everywhere the same. Nevertheless they have much in common since actually the same clashes occur everywhere, namely a planned vs. a nonplanned economy, nomination vs. election of public functionaries, state bureaucracy vs. monopoly-company bureaucracy. In the last instance, all these antagonisms seem to be of economic character. Actually, however, that is not the case. In more than one instance the century-old antagonism between peoples considering themselves different from and even superior to one another, is basic: Asia vs. Europe, Russians vs. Poles, whites vs. Colored, and last, an almost universal hate of the Germans by the neighboring peoples. All of these but especially the last antagonism happens to play an essential role in an epoch in which American sociologists became increasingly interested in and influenced by the thinking of German social scientists. Not the German refugees themselves, but rather American-born sociologists such as Howard Becker, Charles P. Loomis, Talcott Parsons, and others made the ideas of German sociologists accessible in this country. Examples are the translations and discussions of the books of von Wiese, Tönnies[1], Max Weber and others. Moreover, graduate seminars make them the subjects of discussions in the field of sociological theory. But why are they used exclusively in the field of theory?

Applied Antropology: Problems of Human Organization 7:4 (Fall, 1948), 27-35.

Couldn't these men be of help in solving the troubles of the present time? Among these men, Max Weber especially falls into consideration.

Weber's position within the development of anthropological and social sciences is as follows: in this country he is primarily known and esteemed for his care and sagacity in epistemologically substructuring and restricting objectives as well as for his views as to the possibilities of obtaining knowledge within the field of social science. Moreover, he is accepted as one of the founders of the sociology of religion and for having demonstrated the Calvinistic background of American capitalistic mentality. Less known are his activities as politician, rural sociologist, historian of agriculture and as "applied anthropologist." Indeed, the term applied anthropology does not appear in his writings and very seldom in the contemporary German literature, which can fall into consideration. For at that epoch in Germany the term "anthropology" was restricted largely to physical anthropology and the term "ethnology" to preliterate culture. That Max Weber fails to use the term "applied anthropology" is of no importance. He deals intensively with races, nations, Germans, Poles, Jews, whites, and Negroes in America, with their agriculture, handicraft, industry, administration, mentality, interrelationship, antagonism, uniqueness, or transferability. Finally based upon his travels in this country, he compares the United States and its methods of dealing with minorities with that of Germany and its methods and indicates some possibilities of incorporating American institutions and ways of life into the German Republic. The foregoing and related activities during the epoch of Weber in Germany were called "social politics," "ethno-politics," or "ethnic social politics." Regardless of names, German investigations in these fields overlap with the areas covered by "applied anthropology" in the United States. Accordingly a survey on "Max Weber as Applied Anthropologist" is highly pertinent.

Weber's motive in dealing especially with the peoples and problems mentioned above was his religiously based rigorous sense of duty. He felt compelled: (1) to struggle against social situations which he considered unjust; (2) to eliminate personal bias as a judgment of value while investigating casual relations; and (3) to abstain from evaluating phenomena with which he was not completely familiar. For the latter reason, he does not deal with Latin Americans, Canadians, and American Indians, who accordingly can be omitted here.

The sources [2] of our knowledge about Weber's attitude are theoretical works, letters, in part written while he traveled in the United States, and articles concerning political conflicts. Furthermore there are his writings about special ethnic groups as well as his basic concept of the role of the physico-anthropological factor in social life.

General physico-anthropological problems in Germany, while playing an important role in the discussions at the turn of the century, were not of great concern among the scientific specialists. The specialists, rather, were interested in the antagonistic views of cultural diffusion versus independent parallel development. Surprising though it may seem, physico-anthropological problems played a role in the fields of politics. Out of Darwinism originated the concept of the physico-anthropological superiority of some peoples and social classes.

Weber's attitude toward the general physico-anthropological problems is as follows [3]: we may consider difference between groups as being caused by physico-anthropological differences only when there are unmistakable hereditary differences (among other factors) determining specializations and differences in cultural development. We do not know a single phenomenon of sociological character, Weber said, which unquestionably can be traced to inborn and hereditary qualities possessed by one group and not another. Furthermore, he indicated that at least six theories regarding the physico-anthropologico-biological explanation of social phenomena could be demonstrated as incorrect. These theories and Weber's comments about them are: (1) Differences in the essence, structure and performance of music among various peoples are caused by racial differences = the theory of Richard Wagner's followers in Bayreuth. To this theory Max Weber replied that the music of the ancient Greeks was structurally more like that of the Chinese, Japanese, Malays, Hindus, and Arabs than to that of the modern Germans. Although less complex, the music of some African and Pacific peoples is structurally similar to the modern German music. Weber concluded, therefore, that the music of racially different peoples (such as Mongolians and Mediterraneans or Negroes and Oceanians) can be more similar than the music of racially more related groups (such as Greeks and Germans). Factors other than race, Weber felt, determined the structure of music. (2) Aristocracies are able to maintain their superiority because they are racially purer than the dominated peoples.

To this theory the Heidelbergian sociologist answers that the aristocracies in the Old World originate largely from the patriarchs among the animal husbandry nomads. It was precisely this group who obtained wives through capture from anthropologically different groups. Moreover, the patriarchs as well as their successors, the ruling class in the early state society, bequeathed their wealth and often their dominant social positions, to preferred sons or to the sons of the preferred wives. The recipients often are children born to wives of secondary rank, frequently descended from a subjected people or from a completely different racial stock. (3) Classical antiquity collapsed due to an unfavorable biological selection and especially because the eternal wars eliminated the fittest physical stock. Just the opposite is true, says Weber. The wars of the Roman Empire were waged by hired "barbarians" rather than by the elite. (4) Differences in workers' attitudes, to a large extent, are explained by their different racial background—a theory used to justify the low salary paid rural and industrial workers of Polish and other Slavic origin. Indeed, such differences do exist, Weber asserts. But even under the most favorable circumstances, the investigator has only a few generations as material for observation. How then can we state that the special kind of attitude is inherited? Furthermore many variations have proved to have been caused by environmental factors such as traditional economic mentality perpetuated by education, or the willingness to accept a given situation, especially the dominance of the ruling class. (5) Mankind is in danger of deterioration through the application of such Christian principles as charity since the weak and unfit would thereby tend to be preserved. Weber's answer to this theory is that the charity principle was almost completely eliminated in the transition period from the Middle Ages to modern times and the subsequent rise of Calvinism. Thus, there is no probability that in modern occidental civilization Christian charity may endanger the maintenance of a biologically strong population. (6) The social policies of the modern state protect and maintain the weak and accordingly are a social and cultural danger. This argument was often used by Darwinists and laissez-faire ideologists to justify the opposition of the industrialists to state interference in the form of insurance to protect the lower classes. On the contrary, Weber indicates, state-supported social policies give to those who are mentally strong but economically weak the opportunity to rise and to reproduce themselves. Thus every attempt to give emphasis to the predominance of physico-biologico-anthropological factors in human life has failed. Nevertheless, to be completely sure, the German sociologist under consideration suggests systematized physico-anthropological measuring of large populations, classified according to occupation. Since such studies, at least insofar as Germany is concerned, have not yet been made, it is impossible to insist upon biologically caused differences in social attitude. The only statement which can be made according to Weber, is that solidary units or groups are formed due to the subjective belief of the individual members that they are of the same racial origin and that they actually constitute a race. Others therefore regard that group as a racial unit. Based on such convictions, Max Weber approached the special ethnical problems which he had to face.

Ethnic problems in Eastern Europe, in both internal and foreign politics, played an increasingly important role since the growth of national feeling in the latter part of the nineteenth century. The chief countries and their attitudes were as follows: (1) Russia, supported by the national branch of the Greek Orthodox Church, tried to "Russify" her non-Russian minority peoples, including the Lutheran German feudals and intellectuals in the Baltic provinces, the Catholic Poles, and other Slavs. (2) Austria-Hungary, although composed of twelve different nations, nevertheless tried to maintain her unity and even to bring Balkan Slavs under her control by promising some cultural autonomy. (3) All Slavic peoples wanted national autonomy. (4) Germany, after the partition of Poland, contained a minority of Polish feudal gentry and peasants. The latter were protected somewhat by law against the feudal gentry. They hated Russia more than Prussia and for some time were not directly hostile to Prussia, but only later became hostile as a result of Prussian policies. On one hand, the Prussian policy restricted the use of the Polish language among Poles residing in Germany. On the other hand, under the pressure of the landowning nobility, the so-called Junkers, Polish seasonal workers from Russia were imported since they worked cheaply and did not require social protection against illness and accident.

Weber's attitude toward the Eastern European ethnic problems is as follows[4]: he attempts to combine into a higher unit the postulates of patriotism and justice. Among the recommendations which

Weber gave his people were the following: (1) Abolish all laws which aim at Prussianizing the Poles, particularly those which restrict the use of the Polish language. (2) Block the entrance and use of Polish rural workers, who came from the Polish part of Russia. (3) Eliminate, or at least restrict, the so-called feoffments in trust, that is, the nonmortgagable estates belonging to the aristocratic families, where much of the seasonal Polish labor is used. (4) Settle free and independent peasants on the soil of the former feoffment in trust. (5) Reject any attempt to make acquisitions in the East, a suggestion made during World War I. (6) Recognize the right of all of the smaller Eastern nations to have a state of their own. But does this also apply to the Jews, who were considered by other nations in the East to be a nation rather than a religious body? This problem will be treated next.

The Jews in Europe [5] had become emancipated only to a limited extent through the French Revolution and the democratic movement. The Jews were still blocked from desirable and esteemed posts in city and state administration and were restricted to occupations such as that of lawyers, and businessmen, especially livestock dealers and corn merchants in small rural places, professions which carried little social esteem. Out of this situation Jews developed inferiority feelings which the surrounding population resented. They were numerically overrepresented in some professions and were almost the only representatives of the money economy, with whom the rural and small urban middle class came into contact. The effect of these three facts was the rise of political anti-Semitism. This movement originally was espoused by the middle-class peasant, the handicraft worker, and storekeeper, all of whom were opposed to the money economy, banking, and industry and were favorable to a reestablishment of precapitalistic guilds. The Junkers had begun to lose their unrestricted power, wished to conceal their ultimate aims and accordingly tolerated or even protected anti-Semitic parties. The latter did not originally have a positive ideology, but were fortunate to find ready for their use the racial inferiority theory based upon Darwinism. This theory was then enlarged into a philosophico-historico-sociological system by many German intellectuals and applied to practically every phenomenon. Formerly Ranke and Treitschke had explained social and economic phenomena, insofar as they studied them, as results of foreign policy; now phenomena were interpreted as being caused by the Jewish mentality and activity. An example would be Sombart's interpretation of capitalism.

Weber's interest in the problems of the European Jews [6] was based on the reasons mentioned above. Furthermore, he mastered Hebrew sufficiently to study the sources, especially the Old Testament. His arguments are as follows: (1) At least as early as the epoch of the Pharisees, the Jews did missionary work and accordingly are not of a pure racial stock. (2) The history of the ancient Hebrews, indeed, is that of a diminishing importance of the peasants and of an increasing dominance of the urban population. The prophets, he indicated, are largely supported by the city dwellers. But this increasing urbanization does not mean a rise of capitalistic mentality. Such an association is not indicated by the prophets or their adversaries. (3) The piety of the devout Jew is manifested in a life opposed to the rationalistic attitude toward the world, a basic tenet of the occidental capitalistic mentality. (4) In just those districts of the Old World (such as Western Asia, the seashore of Arabia, and Southern Europe) where Jewish peoples had lived uninterruptedly since the epoch of Christ, the economic traits which characterize capitalism have never been developed. (5) Those special economic phenomena which characterize the modern capitalistic attitude (bonds and joint stock companies, for example) did not originate out of any previous Jewish form of economic procedure, but rather out of Hellenistic and medieval German institutions. (6) Many traits thought to be original Jewish traits actually are the effects of the exceptional Jewish minority status; it is accordingly that there still remains a Jewish problem. (7) Insofar as the Jews consider themselves a nation, they are entitled, as every nation, to have a state of their own. On the other hand, the Zionistic state would not be the ideal solution since it would become a semi-tolerated small state among others. It would never satisfy the Jewish desire for justice and would not eliminate the Jewish inferiority feeling. What solution then might be proposed? Here Max Weber's concept regarding the assimilation of minorities in the United States enters the picture.

Weber's opinion about the assimilation of other nations into the Anglo-American culture was as follows: it has been the most complete and rapid acculturation, which has ever occurred in world history. American democracy in official educational institutions as well as in the existence of common clubs and common activities for schoolchildren is actually the main instrument of assimilation. In contrast to that in Europe, assimilation in America occurs readily in spite of, even perhaps because of, the complete tolerance of minority languages. Actually foreign languages are rapidly abandoned voluntarily. What, then, about peoples who only to a small extent claim to have and use a language of their own? This question brings us back to the Jews.

The Jews in the United States have maintained to some extent a culture of their own. The Russian-Polish Jews in New York and other big cities have their newspapers and theaters in the so-called "Yiddish" language. This language is a mixture of older German with Hebrew and Slavic terms. It has been used for centuries by the Jews in Eastern Europe as an everyday language and as a literary idiom. The literature of the Chassidim,[7] an Eastern Jewish religio-mystical movement of the eighteenth century, especially has been produced in this language. On the other hand, the children of those Jewish parents who still speak Yiddish assimilate easily into the new American culture, especially when they no longer are orthodox Jews and accordingly are no longer involved in an especially Jewish culture. These facts form the basis of the findings made by our German sociologist.

Weber's ideas about the future of the Jews in the United States [8] are as follows: the Western and Central European Jews are no longer orthodox Jews and accordingly are no longer involved in an especially Jewish culture. When they remain in Europe, anti-Semitism will always make them feel inferior, as shown above. For other reasons the same will occur if they build their state in Palestine. But when they emigrate to the United States, they can more easily than elsewhere assimilate into the newly developing culture just as members of almost any other ethnic group already has done. The Jews have even less difficulties in assimilating than many other ethnic groups because the latter usually had to forget their own national language. Did all racial groups actually succeed in being merged into the new North American nation? Specifically what about the American Negro?

Weber's observations concerning the Negro in the United States[9] were connected with his travels, his sojourn to the estate of his relatives in North Carolina and his visits to Negro universities. Furthermore, he incorporated the study of the Southern plantation prior to the abolition of slavery into his comparative historical studies by comparing it with the plantations of Carthage and the later Roman Empire. His observations may be summarized as follows:

There are indeed differences. In Carthage and in the main epochs of the Roman Empire the slaves live under a military regime in barracks and usually do not reproduce themselves. In the Southern states, however, the slaves did reproduce themselves, at least to some extent. Nevertheless, the economic situation in both cases is somewhat similar; for plantations with slaves are rentable only if new slaves can always be furnished and if land as well as food for the slaves is cheap. Accordingly, the abolition of slavery in the South occurred not only for humanitarian but also for economic and social reasons. Moreover, abolition was forced upon the South by the North because since the Revolutionary War period the North feared that a new feudalism, based on slavery, might grow up and because there existed a Puritanical feeling against feudalism of any kind. The effect of the abolition, insofar as the South itself is concerned, is a low economic and cultural standard for the Negro. This is a result of the treatment he still suffers at the hands of the white man. The whites are culturally and especially ethically little higher and certainly anything but an aristocracy, a claim which they sometimes like to make. As to the North, there is already some aristocratization connected with the stratification of society and some disdain for work begins to appear. Every aristocracy, of course, needs an antithesis, that is a social group which can be the object of disdain. The Negro represents such an object. This is one of the reasons why a Negro problem continues to exist in the North. Another reason is the fact that the lower-class white disdains the Negro for being strikebreakers. This attitude is not the result of any inborn racial peculiarity but rather the effect of the indoctrination of submissiveness, unpretentiousness, and acceptance of the given situation, all of which represent the effect of white man's pressure. Under such circumstances the only way out for the American Negro is to assimilate into modern, American culture. Even more, Weber says, they must participate productively in American culture, and by so doing, they must impress those strata of the white population which are not involved in the process of aristocratization. The latter is only one among the factors which change the traditional American democracy. Another is bureaucratization.

The interrelationship between democracy and bureaucracy in general, according to Weber, is as follows: they are of seemingly antagonistic character. Actually, however, they have something in common. For both originated out of the same situation, that is, out of an already largely rationalized culture and mind. Accordingly, how modern countries may have established a balance between bureaucracy and democracy must be investigated. This problem led Weber to study some institutions of the United States more explicitly.

Weber's impressions concerning democracy and bureaucracy in the United States[11] were for his time considered new by Europeans. His point of view may be summarized briefly. He felt that bureaucracy in the United States originally was and still is weak. This may be explained as due to the fact that the power of the mores, the need for trained specialists, and the separation of the private from the public sphere were not very great. The latter manifested itself, for example, in the fact that, much less than in Europe, the "bench" and its judge are separated from the "bar" and its lawyer. In the democracy the latter becomes an important man. Even more important are party bosses and party machines. The persons who have been elected to office through the "machine" are normally less dependent upon their chief but at the same time, less competent experts, than those persons who have been appointed by the chief, who holds his position (for example, the president of the United States or the mayor of a city) by popular election. The number of such nonelected but appointed functionaries as in the civil service, for instance, is increasing, because of an increasing complication of life and administration and because of increasing change in the structure of American democracy through the increase of the so-called second immigration of Italians, Poles, Balkan peoples, and other groups, with their completely different cultural background. However, American democracy rests not only on such institutions but also as well on the countless clubs, on American training in "fairness," and on the practice of democracy beginning in earliest childhood and continuing through formal and informal educational institutions. Similar ideas have been expressed by some American educators and sociologists. The main question for Weber was, can the American pattern of education for democracy be applied elsewhere?

Weber held that, in general, the transferability of democratic and bureaucratic institutions from one nation to another is limited. Historically many institutions may be transferable. These include for instance, the balance established in some countries between bureaucracy and democracy and the attitude of majorities towards minorities. In both cases Weber held a transfer could be accomplished insofar as the United States and Germany are concerned.

Weber's criticism of Germany and his recommended changes [12] were based on his religiously founded individualism, in which he considered the independence, responsibility, and dignity of the individual as the final goal. From this background he criticized sharply both Prussian militarism and the lack of character of the bourgeoisie. The latter, he argued, had tolerated the reduction of the parliament and even the State bureaucracy by Bismarck to the role of a will-less instrument of his desires. Moreover, the majority of student associations educated the sons of the bourgeoisie according to the ideals of the feudal gentry and professional army officers. Notoriously it was just these associations which had the power to award dominant positions in the administration of the state and law to their members. Compared with these state functionaries the solicitor, actually one of the relatively few independent men, remained a socially less respected person. The effect in Germany was that a personality type had become predominant which Weber describes in the following way. The characteristic type has, perhaps, a relatively great knowledge of the matter with which he has to deal professionally and he may be economically irreproachable. But on the other hand, he had received an education through his student association by which he was actually no longer a gentleman.[1] He was devoid of character, subservient to his superior, without real contact with the people; he became as arrogant as a Prussian officer toward his subordinates, the lower classes, and the subjected peoples. It was on these scores that he was ridiculed in other countries and was hated by the lowly and subjected. The unwillingness of the Polish, Danish, and Alsatian minorities to assimilate into the German Empire, among others, is caused by the dominance of this unpopular type. Furthermore this representative of German mentality was a bureaucrat rather than a politician and was unable to make a decision of his own. Bismarck, as long as he himself was in power, actually decided everything dictatorially. After Bismarck had been eliminated, the Germans accustomed to obey, followed a crowned dilettante, William II. Even during the government of Wilhelm II our

German sociologist, Weber, thought that the only way of preventing the downfall of Germany was to eliminate all the laws and violent measures directed against national, linguistic, and political minorities. Rather, Weber said, give the people a political education, develop in them a political responsibility, and give politically gifted individuals a chance to make use of their special political abilities. In so doing, Weber held, it would be necessary to restrict the power of the bureaucrats, by increasing the power of the parliamentarians and by giving to the latter a chance to become responsible statesmen.

Later, Weber further reiterated these recommendations at the collapse of the Wilhelminian Empire, which he had predicted. Many suggestions as to the reorganization of Germany were put forward in that chaotic period. Don't represent the people through professional chambers or by proportional representation, Weber warned. Both measures will merely place little specialists and representatives of special interests in the top positions rather than the politicians.

Much remained to be done, according to Weber, and that much depended upon finding an example, among peoples, whom Germany could imitate at least to some extent.

To Max Weber, the United States provided the example. Indeed, the transferability of ways of life of the United States into the German Republic, according to Weber[13] is manifold. At least the following eight ways of life, developed by the people of the United States can and must be incorporated into the life of the German Republic: (1) National and linguistic minorities must enjoy the same rights as others, especially linguistic ones. (2) Bureaucrats, who inevitably will become indispensable everywhere, must be sharply separated and distinguished from the politicians who have to make political decisions. (3) The power of the parliament must be restricted by the power of the head of the executive. (4) The head of the executive must be elected directly by popular election rather than by a parliament. (5) The head of the executive must be entitled to nominate his own coworkers. (6) The profession of the lawyer must cease to be considered as less honorable than others and must be recognized as one of the basic professions from which future politicians should be drawn. (7) The party machine must be accepted as a given and, at least at the present time, an indispensable phenomenon. This is true, at least in the case of Germany, says Weber, since only two possibilities exist, each excluding the other. One of these two possibilities would be democracy without a party machine. This republic would be a democracy without the true politicians at the top but with an incapable parliament composed of "little" representatives of particular interests. This republic would therefore actually be governed by the bureaucracy of the state and of bodies of economic interests. The other alternative for Germany would be a republic with a party machine. But this state would simultaneously be a democracy with plebiscite, which presupposes the existence of party machines. Such a democracy would have the greater probability of bringing true statesmen into leading positions. That is, men who have a feeling of responsibility and the capacity and willingness to make responsible decisions themselves. This is the pattern of the United States and the only way which seems suitable for Germany. (8) From childhood the people must be educated in "fairness" and thereby in democracy, not by coercion and indoctrination but rather by building up a club system embracing all men and women from childhood, a basic element of American democracy.[14]

In conclusion we may summarize as follows: indeed, these are not unimportant institutions and mores which Weber saw realized in the United States and which he considered ought to be incorporated into German life. He died a short time after the collapse of the Wilhelminian Germany. He still had the satisfaction of seeing at least two points of his program realized. Through his influence the new constitution entrusted increased power to the president. Furthermore, it stipulated that the election of the president be through a plebiscite (rather than through the parliament). Both provisions conform to the American pattern and were incorporated into the constitution of the Weimar Republic. The Germans incorporated even more democratic institutions into their constitution, but they failed to learn how to use them. Psychologically they maintained their old patterns of feeling and thinking. Based in part upon premises other than Weber's, some politicians and educators such as Kerschensteiner, Paul Oestreich and the author of this article, tried to alter German mentality basically through a new school structure, youth movement, and adult education. They remained isolated and, accordingly, they failed. Thus Germany collapsed again and more fundamentally than in 1918. Now she needs the help of the United States in her reconstruction. Even if we do not agree with all Weber's suggestions, couldn't it be that his voice may nevertheless be useful in the work of reconstruction? As a German patriot he certainly loved his country, as a highly scholarly sociologist he was completely familiar with all problems of applied anthropology. To a large extent he admired the United States, although at the same time he did not close his eyes to that country's difficulties and defects. Nevertheless, perhaps for just these reasons, he was firmly convinced that the German people should have to incorporate into its life, certainly not all, but at least some of the American ways of life.

Notes

1. F. Toennies, *Fundamental Concepts of Sociology (Gemeinschaft und Gesellschaft)* trans. and supplemented by C.P. Loomis, New York etc., American Book Company (n.d.); L.v. Wiese, *Systematic Sociology*, on the Basis of the Beziehungslehre and Gebidelehre of L.v.W. adapted and amplified by H. Becker, New York, Wiley, 1932.

2. After the death of Max Weber almost all of his publications were collected and edited by his widow Marianne Weber. Those volumes and articles which concern us, which are not translated into English and which in our footnotes will be cited by the abbreviations mentioned behind the titles in parentheses, are the following: *Gesammelte Politische Schriften*, München, Drei Masken Verlag, 1921, esp. the following articles: "Der Nationalstaat und die Volkswirtschaftspolitik," (Nat.), "Bismarcks Aussenpolitik und die Gegenwart," (Bis.), "Deutschland unter den europäischen Weltmächten," (Welt.), "Deutschlands äussere und Preussens innere Politik," (Pol.), "Parlament und Gegierung im neugördneten Deutschland," (Parl.), "Bayern und die Parlamentarisierung im Reich," (Bay.), "Wahlrecht und Demokratie in Deutschland," (Wahl.), "Innere Lage und Aussenpolitik," (Inn.), "Der Reichspräsident," (Reich.), "Politik als Beruf," (Ber.), "Politische Briefe, (Br.). *Gesammelte Aufsätze zur Soziologie und Sozialpolitik*, Tübingen, Mohr, 1924, esp. the following articles: Methodologische Einleitung für fir Erhebung des Vereins für Sozialpolitik über Auslese und Anpassung der Arbeiter der geschlossenen Grossindustrie" (Einl.), "Agrarstatistische und sozialpolitische Betrachtungen zur Fidiekommissfrage in Preussen," (Fid.), "Discussionsrede zu dem Vortrag von A. Ploetz über die Begriffe Rasse und Gesellschaft," (Pl.), "Zum Vortrag von F. Oppenheimer über die rassentheoretische Geschichtsphilosophie," (Opp.); *Gesammelte Aufsätze zur Sozial - und Wirtschaftsgeschichte*, ibid., 1924, esp. the following articles: "Agrarverhältnisse im Altertum," (Ag.); "Entwickelungstendenzen in der Lage der ostelbischen Landarbeiter," (Ent.); *Gesammelte Aufsätze zur Religionssoziologie,* Vol. I-III, ibid., 1920-1921, (Rel.); *Wirtschaft und*

Gesellschaft, Grundrisse der Sozialökonomik, Vol. III ibid., 1922, 2d ed., with unchanged pagination, (WG.). Publications of M.W., which were translated into English and cited here in the English translation are the following: *General Economic History,* trans. by F.H. Knight, New York, Greenberg, 1927, (ec.); *From Max Weber, Essays in Sociology,* trans., ed., and with an introduction by H.H. Gerth and C. Wright Mills, New York, Oxford University, 1946, (Gerth); *The Theory of Social and Economic Organization,* trans. by A.M. Henderson & T. Parsons, ibid., 1947, (Tr.), (A trans. of *Wirtschaft und Gesellschaft,* Part I, mentioned above). Among the many publications dealing with M.W. see the following: Marianne Weber, *Max Weber,* Tübingen, Mohr, 1925, (Mar.) (here also the very significant letters, which M.W. wrote while he travelled in U.S. are included). Idem, *Lebenserinnerungen,* Bremen, Johs. Storm Verlag, 1948, pp. 79-112; see also the review of this book by P. Honigsheim, "Max Weber as Rural Sociologist," Rural Sociology, Vol. XII, Raleigh, 1947; idem, "Max Weber as Historian of Agriculture," Agricultural History, forthcoming. (The two latter articles also contain lists of other publications dealing with M.W.); H. Becker, "Culture Case Study and Ideal Type," Social Forces, Vol. XII, New York, 1934, pp. 403f.

3. Einl., pp. 27-33; Pl., pp. 457ff., Opp., pp. 488ff.; WG., p. 222.
4. Bis. pp. 32, 40-43, 47; Welt., pp. 89ff,; Pol., pp. 95, 102; Inn., p. 383; Fid., pp. 354, 360, 392; Opp., p. 491; Ent., p. 502f.; WG., pp. 4, 225.
5. R. Wagner, *Gesammelte Schriften und Dichtungen,* 3rd ed., Leipzig, Fritzsche, 1898, Vol. V, pp. 66-85, Vol. VII, pp. 30-124, Vol. VIII, pp. 238-260, Vol. X, pp. 33-53; P. de Lagarde, *Ausgewählte Schriften,* München, Lehmann, 1924, pp. 3, 63, 83ff., 174, 191-221; R. Richter, *Essays,* Leipzig, Meissner, 1913, pp. 137-177, 303-331; H. v. Gerlach, *Erinnerungen eines Junkers,* Berlin, Die Welt am Montag, (n.d.) pp. 107-116; F. Naumann, *Demokratie und Kaisertum,* Berlin-Schoeneberg, Hilfie, many ed. p. 106; A. Stillich, *Die Politischen Parteien in Deutschland,* Leipzig, Klinkhardt, 1908, Vol. I, pp. 236f.; W. Sombart, *Der moderne Kapitalismus,* München & Leipsig, Duncker & Humblot, many ed., esp. Vol. I, 2, pp. 896-919; idem, *Die Juden und das Wirtschaftsleben,* ibid., many ed., esp. chap. VIII-XIV, pp. 183-434; idem, *Der Bourgeois,* ibid., pp. 229-302, 337-348; E. Fischoff, "The Protestant Ethic and the Spirit of Capitalism, The History of a Controversy," Social Research, Vol. XI, 1944, pp. 56ff.
6. Ag., pp.84; Rel., Vol. III, pp. 10-44, 76, 120, 245, 293f., 306, 354, 360, 436; WG pp. 269, 350, Ec. p. 358; Th. p. 138; Mar., pp. 477, 485, 566, 604, 660. As to the discussions between M.W. and the Zionists see M. Buber, *Kampf um Israel,* Berlin, Schocken, 1933, p. 427, & P. Honigsheim, "Martin Buber 70 Jahrealt," Die Friedens-Warte, Vol. 48, Zürich, Polygraphischer Verlag, 1948, pp. 241-245.
7. The most important writings of the Chassidim are now published in a modern German Translation and compilation in M. Buber, *Die Chassidischen Bücher,* Berlin, Schocken, 1932; see also Honigsheim, "Martin Buber, etc.," loc cit.

8. WG., p. 356; Mar., pp. 299, 316f.
9. Pl., p. 460f.; Rel., Vol. II, p. 123, footnote 1, Vol. III, p. 307, footnote 1; WG., pp. 227, 628; Ec., pp. 79-83; 298-302; Mar., pp. 299, 308f., 313.
10. WG., p. 752.
11. Parl., pp. 146, 150; Ber., pp. 405ff., 410, 414, 422f., 427, 431, 434; WG., pp. 501, 635ff., 752; Ec., p. 360; Gerth, pp. 86ff., 102ff., 107-110, 114; T. Parsons, "Introduction," Th., p. 74; H.W. Braun, "M.W. and the United States," Southwestern Social Science Quarterly, Vol. XXV, Austin, 1944. As to American educators and sociologists, who emphasize the inter-relationship between the American educational system and the Ameri-can type of democracy see especially: J. Dewey, *Democracy and Education*, NewYork, Macmillan, 1924, pp. 228-241; idem, *Schools of Tomorrow*, NewYork, Dutton, 1915, pp. 41ff., 164-228, 287-316; idem, *The School and Society*, Chicago, University of Chicago Press, 1924, pp. 3, 12f.; idem *Education Today*, NewYork, Putnam's Sons, 1940, pp. 62-73, 250-259; idem *Characters and Events*, NewYork, Holt, Vol. II, 1929, p. 781; A.N. Whitehead, *Essays in Science and Philosophy*, NewYork, Philosophi-cal Library, 1947, pp. 172ff.; H.W. Holmes, "Whitehead's Views on Edu-cation," *The Philosophy of A. N. Whitehead*, ed., P.A. Schilpp, Evanston & Chicago, Northwestern Univ., 1941, p. 637; A.R. Mead, *Learning and Teaching*, Philadelphia, Lippincott, 1923, p. 160; C.H. Cooley, *Social Organization*, NewYork, Charles Scribner's Sons, 1925, pp. 48f., 53.
12. Nat., p. 26; Parl., pp. 144, 152, 182; Bay., pp. 271ff., Wahl., p. 308f.; Ber., p. 431ff.; Br., pp. 470, 473, 480; WG., p. 511; Mar., pp. 75, 82, 408, 433; J.P. Mayer, *M.W. and German Politic*, London, Feber, (n.d.) p. 18; E. Hula, "M.W., Scholar and Politician," *Contemporary Review*, Vol. 134, Lon-don, 1928, pp. 479ff.
13. Parl., pp. 144, 169; Wahl., p. 309; Reich, pp. 390ff.; Ber., p. 438; Br., p. 483; WG., p. 511.
14. As to the discussion among German educators concerning the Ameri-can school system and its transferability to Germany see: J. Tews, *Schulkämpfe der Gegenwarte*, 2d ed., Leipzig, Teubner, 1911, p. 154; G. Kerschensteiner, *Der Begriff der staatsbürgerlichen Erziehung*, 5th ed., ibid., 1923, pp. 20, 130-139; idem, *Das einheitliche deutsche Schulsystem*, 2d ed., ibid., 1922, pp. 141ff.; P. Oestreich, *Unabhängige Kulturpolitik*, Leipzig & Wein, Oldenburg, 1924, p. 50; idem, *Der Einbruch der Technik in die Pädagogik*, Stuttgart, Cotta, 1930, p. 72; idem, "Hat dieser Wettbewerb einen Sinn," Edison sucht einen Nachfolger, Berlin, FrankfurterVerlags Anstalt, 1931, pp. 73-82; P. Honigheim, "Paul Oestreich 70 Jahre alt," Die Friedens-Warte, Vol. 48, Zürich, Polygraphischer Verlag, 1948, pp. 133-141.

3

Max Weber as Historian of Agricultural and Rural Life

The United States is facing the problem of rebuilding a completely chaotic world and a disorganized agriculture. The possibilities of doing so are limited by the antagonism between the United States and the Soviet Union, by the basic differences between the structure of Old World and North American rural life, and by the varieties of forms of rural life in the various European countries. These differences are largely caused by, and dependent upon, the uniqueness of the development of agricultural life in each country under consideration. Thus, this particular historical development increases the difficulties and even limits the possibility of changing the rural social structure in many countries.

Under such circumstances a knowledge of the history of the agriculture of the countries under consideration is not exclusively of theoretical importance. Indeed, it is the an essential part of history and an indispensable tool for, and step toward, the perception of regularities of more universal character appearing in world history. But apart from this fact it is a tool which is indispensable in understanding and thus indirectly in changing the present situation of the Old World.

Under such circumstances it may be of importance to become familiar with the ideas of Max Weber (1864-1920) concerning the historical development of agriculture and rural life. Everywhere, including the United States, he was considered one of the most outstanding German sociologists and economists. He was recognized

Agricultural History 23:3 (July, 1949), 179-213.

even by his greatest adversaries as a man of undeniable scientific objectivity and justice. His work was based on a vast knowledge of history as well as of the socioeconomic structure of his own time. He was not exclusively interested in the perception of universal rules of history; he was also interested in emphasizing the uniqueness of developments in various countries. To perceive exactly Weber's essential contributions to the knowledge of the agricultural history of particular areas and eras, we shall consider the status of the problems concerning them and the answers given by scholars before him, his own ideas, the spread of his ideas to other peoples and cultures, and, insofar as possible, the causes of these facts.

A few preliminary words on Weber's background are indispensable. For a short time he was a lawyer. He then successively taught Roman law in Berlin, economics in Freiburg and Heidelberg, and sociology in Munich for a short time before his death. This academic career was interrupted for fifteen years at Heidelberg by sickness due to overwork. During this time he concentrated on research.

Weber's philosophical convictions and his political activities lie outside the scope of this study. Nevertheless, to understand his self-limitation in the social sciences, it is indispensable at least to enumerate the basic epistemological fundamentals of his scientific work.[1]

These fundamentals are as follows. (1) There is a fundamental difference between statements of facts and judgements of value. (2) Judgements of value are of autonomous and subjective character, independent of authorities, and essential in the spheres of ethics and politics where the responsible decisions must be made by the individual at his own risk. (3) Objective statements of facts can be made in the sphere of special sciences and are the principal content of such sciences. (4) There exists within the sphere of special sciences a fundamental difference between natural and cultural sciences. (5) Natural sciences, to some extent, are able to perceive general rules. (6) Cultural sciences have primarily to deal with the uniqueness of cultural phenomena. (7) History, including socioeconomic history, belongs to the cultural sciences. (8) Within the sphere of historical sciences, general terms such as animal husbandry nomadism can and must be used, but in doing so one must have in mind that they are actually nothing but abbreviations. These are used, according to an agreement made, to denote the sum of all these particular historical subjects, which have the same characteristic traits in common. (9) Within the sphere of historical sciences it is impossible to make statements concerning an automatically necessitated process occurring within the sequence of forms of social life. (10) Within the sphere of socioeconomic history there exists no more than the possibility to make some statements concerning the probability that some forms of social structure may succeed one another in the same sequence more than once; but no more than that. (11) The knowledge that some forms of social structure may succeed one another in the same sequence more than once can be used for practical purposes; it can especially be used for the realization of special goals that are socioeconomic in character. The realization of such a goal is then supposed to represent a good, especially a good supposed to be of a higher value than the nonrealization of the goal under consideration. But these decisions about such values and value differences are not derived from considerations made within the scientific sphere but rather from considerations based on the autonomous religio-ethical conscience of the individual.

These limits and ends, which Weber set for his own scientific work, we must keep in mind. As scientists we likewise should eliminate every personal bias and judgement even as to the value and justifiability of the Weberian statements. With that in mind, we can proceed to look at the various areas and eras which played a role in Weber's treatment of the history of agriculture.

Pre-State Society

The agriculture and rural life of pre-state society did not play as essential a role in the work of Weber as did some of the more complicated cultures.[2] Nevertheless, they deserve brief consideration.

When Weber began his career, the scientific view with regard to pre-state society was as follows. Positivistic evolutionism was almost completely dominant. This term was then used to denote the conviction that there is independent parallel development from less complicated to more complicated implements, beliefs, and forms of life. Moreover, such shifting is more than just a change; it rather must be considered a progression. At the end of the nineteenth century evolutionism existed in two forms: liberal evolutionism, which was represented especially by the Englishmen, Edward Tylor, Herbert Spencer, and Sumner Maine, the Belgian, Emile de Laveleye and the German ethnologist, Adolf Bastian and his school, as well as the economists, who mostly followed them, including the powerful Gustav Schmoller and his dominant school of thought; and socialistic evolutionism, especially represented by Friedrich Engels.[3]

Only a few men at that time opposed such evolutionistic parallelism and especially the sequence: hunting, herding, and crop raising. The most noted of the opponents were Eduard Hahn, whose position was made known in the 1890s, and the cultural historical school of Bernhard Ankermann and Fritz Graebner, and, with another metaphysical background, Father W. Schmidt and his school and its review *Anthropos*. These, in contrast to evolutionistic parallelism, gave emphasis to the migration of peoples and cultures, even in prehistoric times. These diffusionists suddenly became the most discussed anthropologists—not exclusively among Catholics but also among other groups—in Germany, France, and Latin America, but rather less in the United States.[4]

Weber himself had never received any special anthropological training, for there were very few if any anthropological professorships in Germany at that time. Nonetheless, he was familiar with the English and French evolutionistic writers (he considered Bastian unreadable) as well as the anti-evolutionistically minded Hahn. The diffusionistic school was beginning to become known only a short time before Weber's death. For this reason its publications and viewpoints appear in Weber's writings only to a limited extent. The latter teaches that one should be careful and even skeptical when one makes general statements. One should be skeptical even when one does not go farther back than to the period of hoe agriculture. Weber's own interests and statements centered particularly around the following six topics.

Automatic Sequences

Automatically occurring sequences of primitive forms of life had been described since the eighteenth century. The Swiss, Isaac Iselin, and many evolutionists after him had advanced the theory of the three regularly succeeding stages: hunting, shepherding, and crop raising. Hahn was especially opposed to this theory. Weber accepted this opposition without claiming to add anything in particular. Accordingly the later writers dealing with this subject refer to Hahn rather than to Weber.

Animal Husbandry Nomadism

The evolutionists considered animal husbandry nomadism a form of life through which every more complicated culture had passed. It had existed in prehistoric times in Europe; and out of it stationary settlement had originated. In contrast Hahn asserted that pastoral nomads often originated out of later and more complicated forms of life.

Weber accepted this special theory of Hahn's as well as his general opposition to the evolutionistic three-stage sequence and enlarged it in the sense of denying the truth of the three evolutionistic theories stated above. A short time after the issuance of the posthumous edition of Weber's lectures containing these ideas, one of the most widely read publications of Father Schmidt appeared. In this work, his "circle of pastoral nomads" arose out of pygmy culture. Further discussion in Germany, France, and Latin America centered around this theory, and Weber went unnoticed. In the United States Robert H. Lowie especially discussed the problem, but he likewise took Schmidt primarily into consideration or drew upon Hahn. Regardless of whether animal husbandry nomads ever existed or not, some peoples certainly settled down and lived in part by the raising of crops. What then was their attitude toward the land which they occupied?

Land Communism

Land communism was claimed to have been universally the original kind of land possession. This was asserted by many evolutionists, especially Laveleye, Engels, and his popularizer, August Bebel. But opposition increasingly arose from such scholars as the Englishman, Frederic Seebohm, the Frenchman, Fustel de Coulanges, the Austrian Catholic, Alfons Dopsch, and many Germans. Weber was one of them. He did not claim to be original, and accordingly his writings were never referred to. Although it is granted that private property existed early, there remains the special problem of seignorial property.

Seignorial Property

According to the overwhelming majority of Encyclopedists, laissez-faire liberals, and socialists, seignorial property originated in the following ways. Some individuals within a group became more well-to-do than others. They used their economic power and brought other persons under their control. Thus, by economic means, they became politically powerful.

In contrast to this theory other socialists, especially Claude Henri de Saint Simon, Pierre Joseph Proudhon, and later Eugen Duhring, argued the opposite. Some individuals or groups conquered land, brought the inhabitants under their control, and, by doing so, became well-to-do siegnorial proprietors. Thus they used political means to become economically powerful.

This later theory was almost forgotten at the turn of the century, but it was rediscovered and supported by the Austrian, Ludwig Gumplowicz, and his adherent, Franz Oppenheimer. Both theories were antagonistic as far as the interrelationship between political and economic means are concerned. Nevertheless, both are similar as far as they are unilateral, that is, each accepted only one factor as the cause of the origin of seignorial property.

To both these unilateral theories Weber proposed his multilateral synthesis. He stated that Oppenheimer was right in insisting upon the importance of the use of political means, especially conquest. However, he was one-sided. Rather, there were at least six factors to be considered as causing the genesis of seignorial propriety: (1) The inability of some persons to perform military duties which led them to put themselves under the sovereignty of other persons; (2) subjection (as pointed out by Oppenheimer); (3) the greater opportunity of making land arable, which existed for some persons because they owned more animals and had more man-power at their disposal; (4) the belief that one individual had superior magical forces; (5) commerce outside their own group; and (6) control over water resources in dry districts. This enumeration by Weber also seems to have aroused little interest. So far as the discussion continued in Europe, it centered around Oppenheimer's system. But this development of seignorial property, just as the development of animal husbandry life, according to Weber, was not an isolated phenomenon but rather was connected with changes within the structure of the family.

The Matrilinear Family

For centuries the matrilinear family attracted the interest of white men and especially missionaries. But most of all two men with very different basic philosophies became interested in this phenomenon, namely Lewis H. Morgan, the well-known American evolutionist, and Johann Jakob Bachofen, an orthodox, mystical, and conservative Swiss Lutheran. Their theories were based on different kinds of material; Morgan concerned himself primarily with contemporary North American Indians, and Bachofen with Oriental, Egyptian, Etruscan, Greek, and Roman antiquity.

Although somewhat interrelated they actually came to the following conclusion independently. At one time or another matrilinear society existed everywhere. It was more or less connected with securing food through the cultivation of plants rather than by animal breeding. Everywhere it originated automatically and independently out of a previous promiscuity.

The German professors of history and law either denied, ridiculed, or suppressed this concept. In contrast, Engels incorporated it into the Marxist system of economic determinism; Bebel popularized it; and it became a part of the official socialistic creed in every country including the Soviet Union. Moreover, at the end of the nineteenth century, it was rediscovered by some German Neo-Romanticists, such as Alfred Schuler and Ludwig Klages, as well as by the adherents of the cultural cyclical school. The "exogamous matrilineal culture circle of horticulturists" was incorporated as one of the various culture cycles into the system of Father Schmidt. The discussion between the evolutionists and the cultural historical school in Europe no longer dealt with the problem of the existence or nonexistence of this phenomenon, for the latter was accepted without question. The discussion, rather, centered around the polygenetic or monogenetic origin of the phenomenon.

Weber wrote his main publications before the discussion concerning Father Schmidt's theories began. He himself never denied the existence of the phenomenon, but, accepting the objections made especially by Ernst Grosse, he denied two special parts of the theory, namely the origin of the matrilinear family out of earlier promiscuity and the automatic nature of its appearance. By rejecting the latter, Weber, as with animal husbandry nomadism, opposed the viewpoint of the evolutionists and approached somewhat that of the diffusionists. But for the same reason mentioned in connection with pastoral nomadism, his viewpoint remained unnoticed.

TABLE 1

Theories Concerning Rural Life in Pre-State Society

Theories	Accepted by Weber after elaboration by the following	Countries of these men	Elaborated by Weber	Men influenced by Weber
1. Rejection of the evolutionistic three-stage sequence	Eduard Hahn	Germany	-	-
2. Rejection of automatic passage through the stage of animal husbandry nomadism	Eduard Hahn	Germany	-	-
3. Rejection of original land communism	Coulanges Seebohm Dopsch	France Germany	Bagiand	
New viewpoints supposed to refute original land communism	-	-	x	-
4. Importance of conquest and political action in acquiring seignorial property	Gumplowicz Oppenheimer	Austria Germany	-	-

TABLE 1 (cont.)

Theories	Accepted by Weber after elaboration by the following	Countries of these men	Elaborated by Weber	Men influenced by Weber
Multilateral origin of seignorial property			x	-
5. Essence and structure of the matrilineal family	Morgan Bachofen Engels Grosse	United States Switzerland Germany Germany	-	-
Rejection of the origin of the matrilineal family out of earlier promiscuity			-	-
Rejection of automatic passage through the matrilineal stage	Grosse	Germany	-	-
6. Rural dowry system originating out of the desire of wife's kinsmen that she become the main wife of her husband	-	-	x	Oppenheimer in Germany

Monogamy and the Dowry System

The socialistic theory had explained monogamy and the dowry system in the following way. The husband was interested in having legitimate children and in having them exclusively inherit his property. Therefore, he married only one wife and insisted on receiving a dowry as well as her remaining faithful to him.

In contrast, Weber asserted the man's desire for heirs could have come about in numerous ways. As he saw the situation, the woman's clan stipulated that she was to be the head wife and that only her children could become heirs. Therefore, it was the interest of the woman in assuring to her children the property of the man that was decisive. This Weberian theory of the origin of monogamy and dowry was accepted by Oppenheimer and incorporated into his system, but little more than that. It is true that he sometimes cited Weber in connection with particulars concerning pre-state rural life, but on basic problems Oppenheimer accepted Father Schmidt completely.

By way of recapitulation, Weber's participation in the development of the history of agriculture with reference to pre-state society is summarized in table 1.

Many ideas of Weber's system, cited in the preceding paragraphs, were explained by special examples in which he dealt more intensively with particular peoples, such as the Chinese.

Oriental and Pre-Occidental State Cultures

Agriculture and rural life in oriental and pre-occidental state cultures played a much larger part in the scientific thought of Weber than the prehistoric cultures already dealt with in this study. Some peoples, however, deserve a somewhat more exhaustive discussion than others.

The Chinese

The Chinese had aroused the interest of the occidental world since the end of the Middle Ages.[5] Jesuit missionaries described China and debated the advisability of permitting Catholic converts there to maintain some of their old customs. Hence, the interest and admiration of the physiocrats and of Encyclopedists such as Voltaire were aroused. In contrast, the German romanticists considered China prosaic and therefore took little interest in it. Almost every historico-philological science in nineteenth-century Germany originated in and was based on German romanticism. Accordingly, the Chinese were studied only to a slight extent in Germany.

Moreover, the few German investigators, Hans Conon and Hans Georg Conon von der Gabelentz (father and son), Wilhelm Schott, F.W.K. Muller, August Conrady, Otto Franke, Wilhelm Grube, Alfred Forke, Georg Huth, and the Dutchman, Johann Jakob Marie De Groot (who later taught in Germany), just as the Frenchmen, Edouard Chavannes, Henri Maspero, Paul Pelliot, Silvain Levi, Edouard Mestre, and their school had dealt primarily with the history of language, the religion, and the literature of China and her minority peoples, such as the Tibetans, the Mongols, and the Manchus. Little time was spent, however, studying the social and economic life of the Chinese.

When Weber decided to deal with the latter, he found few antecedents in this field of investigation. Consequently, he did not find it necessary to spend much time discussing other theories relating to the Chinese economy. Not being familiar with the language, he had to base his judgments on translated sources. His own conception of the development of China is as follows.

The existence of an animal husbandry nomadism in the early stages of Chinese development cannot be proven. Instead, two facts point to an original soil culture. In the beginning the Chinese did not consume milk, and the symbol of the emperor was the plow. In this classic period the Chinese were peasants. Many were in a situation similar to that of the medieval English copyholder who was a dependent tenant. They often had brought themselves under the sovereignty of a powerful man in order to secure his protection. This procedure has been described earlier in this study as leading to social differentiation both in and outside of China. In addition to some individual peasants, land was bought in common by a group of family fathers and then distributed. Those who left the village were paid off, but they remained under the jurisdiction of the whole collective and could rebuy their shares when they returned. The city dweller on the other band made his living from land rent. With this exception, the city dweller was not essentially different from the rural resident. He did not even enjoy particular rights and privileges. In this way the Chinese cities were different from the occidental and especially the Christian medieval cities. This heterogeneity with regard to the differences which existed between the status of the city dweller and that of the rural population in the Orient and Occident played an essential role in Weber's interpretation of the different development in Asia and Europe.

This Weberian idea about the development of Chinese rural life did not find many adherents or even create much interest. A short time after his death some Sinologists and anthropologists wrote publications dealing largely or exclusively with China, but they did so from another viewpoint. These include: (1) Karl August Wittfogel, who interpreted Chinese agriculture in a Marxist sense; (2) Richard Wilhelm, who made the antagonism between northern Chinese patriarchalism and southern matriarchalism the keystone of Chinese history; (3) Oswald Menghin, Paul Leser, and Robert von Heine Geldern, all of whom incorporated Chinese phenomena into Father Schmidt's system of cultural migration; (4) Marcel Granet, who used positivistic categories; and (5) countless American rural sociologists and economists who have dealt with the practical aspects of contemporary China. None of these except Wittfogel even cited Weber. Wittfogel, however, referred to Weber's work in connection with certain matters, which Weber himself considered of secondary importance. To an even larger extent Weber's work in connection with Japan was neglected.

Japan

Japan occupied an even less important place in German universities and sciences than did China.[6] The Japanese had begin relatively early to assimilate occidental culture. According to the habitual concept of the field of ethnology in prewar Germany, the ethnologist was supposed to deal primarily with nonoccidental cultures and especially those which had produced no written sources of their own. A science corresponding to American applied anthropology scarcely existed in a country which at that time had almost no colonies and colonial natives. The professional historians on the other hand were dealing almost exclusively with occidental peoples and especially with occidental states. Thus, very few, if any, groups were especially interested in Japan, and accordingly literature dealing with Japan was rare.

Therefore, apart from English publications, the writings of only four German scholars come under consideration. Their investigations were largely based on the travel and residence of the authors themselves in Japan. These were Heinrich Friedrich Hackmann, Karl Florenz, Otto Rudorff, and Karl Rathgen. The two former dealt primarily with the history of literature and religion; the third edited Japanese edicts. The last was an economist and later Weber's colleague in Heidelberg. His main interest was Japanese economics.

Weber's own explanation of Japanese economic development is as follows. Originally the patrilinear gens was almost exclusively the dominating group. Then out of that originated a feudal state. The latter gave political positions to members of the nobility for a time and compensated them by giving them the usufruct of fiefs, likewise for a time. All these vassals were, in the last instance, under the supreme control of the shogun, the head of the crown vassals. Handicraftsmen, tradesmen, and peasants remained groups without any legal protection. Again a change occurred however, and out of this kind of administration originated a kind of *rentier*, a life based on land rent. But this kind of life produced only a *rentier* mentality, and it would have never produced out of itself an occidental-like bourgeois mentality. Rather the latter had been imported in the nineteenth century from the outside. It found as a connecting link some elements of individualistic character, which had been developed out of the contractual element that evolved into the investiture of fiefs for time. Since such contractual elements existed in pre-occidental Japan, this country could readily imitate the occidental pattern. This is in contrast with Chinese culture. The latter was based on the honor concept of a class of intellectuals as were the Chinese mandarins.

This Weberian concept is actually a synthesis of the results of the investigations of the men, mentioned above, especially of Rathgen, and of Weber's own sociological categories, developed and often used by himself. But he considered his own concept incomplete, and if he had lived longer, he would have accepted completely and even appreciated the fact that no one among the subsequent writers even mentioned his explanation of Japan. Weber was much more concerned about the Hindus.

The Hindus

The spiritual and socioeconomic life of the Hindus likewise attracted great interest in the occidental world relatively early.[7] Here as in the case of the Chinese the struggle between Jesuits and Dominicans as well as Voltaire's admiration played a part.

But the strongest stimulus to interest in the Hindus came from German romanticism. Mystical contemplation and elimination of man's will through asceticism attracted the interest of Friedrich von Schlegel, Friedrich Wilhelm von Schelling, Georg Wilhelm Friedrich Hegel, and especially of Arthur Schopenhauer. Out of this romantic interest originated a Hindu philology. It dealt with comparative and historical grammar and the literature in Sanskrit, Prakrit, and Pali and with editing, interpretation, and translation of the corresponding Brahmanic, Jainistic, and Buddhistic texts. After the fifties of the last century, through the influence of German Lutheran missionary, Carl Graul, a Dravidian philology was also added. While it was concerned with Tamil and Telugu grammar and literature, it took a much less important place than the true Hindu philology. The latter was the subject matter of many courses in all German universities. It is true, however, that there were relatively few participants in these special classes. Even fewer were interested when teachers such as Gustav Salomon Oppert in Berlin or Eugen Hultzsch in Halle were able and willing to offer courses on Dravidian matters. Only in the public lectures on Buddhism and similar subjects were there many auditors.

Thus, many scholars, because of small teaching loads, had time to do research. Some time was spent investigating the socioeconomic life of the Hindus and especially their caste systems. Among others, such work was done by the Germans, Albrecht Weber, Georg Buhler, Friedrich Christian August Fick, Paul Horn, Heinrich Zimmer, and Hermann Oldenberg; by the Frenchmen, Emile Charles Marie Senart, and C. Bougle; and by the Englishmen, Grant Duff, John Faithfull Fleet, Henri Baines, and the evolutionist, Sumner Maine; and by the American, Edward Washburn Hopkins.

Weber did not master the native languages. His judgment was based on translated sources, the German, French, and English forerunners already mentioned, and the English census reports and the special census studies. He elaborated the following synthesis.

The castes did not develop out of families but rather, as especially Bougle pointed out, from religio-magical causes. The rural order, especially the village, originated by conquest. Every village had a common pasture and garden area. In the latter were settled craftsmen, barbers, laundrymen, and all kinds of laborers, who belonged to the village—the so-called village establishment. They were not specifically paid for their work but were at the service of the community in return for their share in the land or in the harvest.

The villages differed with regard to landownership. The land itself might belong to a king or to a joint body of full freeholders. Moreover, there were variations in the social status of the villagers, depending largely on the method of land partition used. In any case, perhaps five or six rent collectors intervened between the owner and the peasantry through the farming out and refarming of the taxes. Within this group of rent receivers and large farmers, a nominal communism had evolved. Likewise, peasants might carry on a communistic husbandry, but in this case they divided the harvest, not the land. Thus, in contrast to Sumner Maine's theory of original land communism, this case of so-called rural communism was neither land communism nor original.

As to the craftsmen mentioned above, they sometimes tried to build guilds. These would have become similar to those of the Christian medieval epoch, but such attempts were crushed by the landowners. Moreover, religious reform movements, such as those started by Buddha and Jaina, turned from roaming monks to established monasteries where the members derived their living from an economy based on kind. To avoid confiscation by powerful men and imposition of unbearable taxes, some families transferred their landed property to such monasteries. Nevertheless, by so doing, they maintained an unassignable right of rent; this actually was the first kind of feoffment in trusts to appear in world history. This more than once played a role in Weber's sociohistorical theory and political practice.

These three factors—nonexistence of guilds, monasterial economy based on kind, and feoffment in trusts—had the same effect in India, which, in China, the city dweller's livelihood, based on rent coming from outside land, had produced. For this reason, cities in the occidental sense (places which were inhabited by persons of another juridical status than the surrounding country people) did not appear either in India or in China.

While Weber had accepted many ideas about castes and other aspects of Hindu social life from Bougle, Fick, Zimmer, and Oldeberg, he was completely original on at least two points, namely his refutation of Maine's theory about original Hindu rural communism and his conclusion on the problem of why cities in the occidental sense did not arise in India. This part of Weber's work did not become well known. Apparently the explanation is that interest everywhere turned to the actual problems of contemporaneous India. Weber was somewhat more fortunate when he dealt with the pre-Greek world.

The Pre-Greek Western Asiatic and Eastern Mediterranean World

Except for the Jews, the pre-Greek western Asiatic and eastern Mediterranean world has a relatively small place in Weber's work.[8] Weber was not familiar with the ancient Egyptian, Sumerian, Assyto-Babylonian, Hittite, Median, or Persian languages. But he did know the English, French, and German translations of Mesopotamian and Egyptian inscriptions, the older works of Eberhard Schrader, Gaston Maspero, John Gardner Wilkinson, and William Mathew Flinders Petrie as well as more recent ones, especially those of the Pan-Babylonian school of Hugo Winckler and his partisans such as the three Jeremias, Alfred, Friedrich, and Johannes. Winckler emphasized the central role of Mesopotamia and her religious systems in the cultural and religious development of the other Semitic peoples.

Weber's conception of the rural economic development of the Euphrates, Tigris, and Nile countries is as follows. Inundation and the necessity of caring for dikes was the central fact. Out of this basic fact originated a specialized water-bureaucracy and a centralized administration. The cost was great, but the king could pay it because he owned a great amount of land. The land was administrated in the font of socage farms operated by thousands of serfs who lived in barracks. This kind of organization was imitated by the Phoenicians and Carthaginians, who transferred it to the occidental world.

These remarks by Weber are indeed rare as compared with his comments concerning the Hebrews, but rather frequent as compared with his observations about the Hittites, Medians, Persians, Kariens, Lykians, and Lydians.

These groups Weber scarcely dealt with at all. The explanation is to be found in Weber's scientific approach. He wrote his essential publications at a time when very little about these peoples was really known, that is, before the essential excavating, deciphering, translating, and publishing had been accomplished. For example, the work done by Winckler and Friedrich Hrozny on Hittite inscriptions found in Boghazkeui had not yet been completed. The rigorous Neo-Kantian moralist would never have permitted himself to make decisions about matters, whose accessible sources seemed to him to be insufficient. Accordingly, his comments on Egypt and Mesopotamia are restrained.

Historically, the place of Weber's work may be summarized as follows. His insistence upon the importance of innudations and dikes came from the previously mentioned Assyriologists and Egyptologists. The role of the Phoenicians and the Carthaginians as the transfer agents of the socage farm organization came from Theodor Mommsen, a historian primarily concerned with Roman antiquity. The term water-bureaucracy and the theory about its origin and role were original. The latter was accepted by Franz Oppenheimer. Although Weber refrained from dealing with the ancient peoples of Asia Minor, he could not escape the obligation to deal with the ancient Hebrews.

The Ancient Hebrews

Even in Weber's personal life, the ancient Hebrews played an incomparably greater role than the peoples mentioned previously.[9] Three factors were probably responsible.

Weber's mother, compared with the average wife of an intellectual of that generation, was relatively orthodox religiously. At the same time, his uncle and cousin, Adolf Hausrath and Otto Baumgarten, were both liberal professors of Protestant theology who dealt with Biblical criticism. Accordingly, at a relatively young age he was in a situation where he was forced to choose for himself between the antagonistic concepts. Out of this situation, and in connection with his shifting to the Neo-Kantian philosophy and epistemology, originated his religio-ethical conviction, to eliminate his own personal religious bias and to investigate linguistically, philologically, historically, and sociologically the sources of the religious creed in which he had been reared. That meant primarily the Old Testament.

During his whole life, Weber felt religiously and ethically bound to protect minorities and persecuted peoples, among them the Jews. The latter, according to the anti-Semites as well as the economic historian, Werner Sombart, were the typical representatives and even the founders of capitalism or at least of the capitalistic mentality. Thus, Weber felt obliged to examine critically the beginnings of Jewish life, as described in the Pentateuch, the Book of Judges, and so on.

Weber's own studies on Calvinism had led him to perceive similarities between it and Judaism. For these and other reasons, he not only studied literature dealing with Biblical criticism, part of which he appreciated highly (especially the books of Julius Wellhausen and his pupil, Hermann Gunkel), but also the original sources in Hebrew itself, a language which he mastered completely. In his special book dealing with the ancient Hebrews, he described their rural life as follows.

Pre-Christian Palestine was not a geographico-economical unit. There existed three different districts, inhabited by the following groups with their respective economies. In the south and east was a sterile desert inhabited almost exclusively by nomadic bedouins, whose economy centered around the camel. Districts of periodic fertility were inhabited by semi-nomadic peoples, who made their livelihood from sheep and goats by transhumance. The plains in the center and the north were inhabited by peasants, who grew cereals and cattle supported by the city dwellers. But this increasing urbanization did not mean an increasing capitalistic mentality. Such an association was not indicated by the prophets or their adversaries. Accordingly, in contrast to Sombart, the origin and development of capitalism cannot be traced to pre-Christian Judaism. Thus the cause must be found in the occidental world itself.

This original Weberian idea has created considerable discussion and has played a part in the struggle against anti-Semitism. Furthermore, it has a similar place in the theological debate concerning the question of whether the Old Testament is unique or largely reflects forms of life common to many pre-Christian Semitic and other eastern Mediterranean peoples. According to many theories the Etruscans were connected with these peoples. For this and other

TABLE 2

Theories Concerning Rural Life in Oriental and pre-Occidental state cultures

Theories	Accepted by Weber after elaboration by the following	Countries of these men	Elaborated by Weber	Men influenced by Weber
1. Chinese: Social, economic, and cultural development	Franke Forke Grube Wilhelm Pelliot Chavannes	Germany Germany Germany Germany France France	-	-
New viewpoints concerning the undemonstrability of an original animal husbandry nomadism			x	-
New viewpoints supposed to explain why cities in the occidental sense did not arise			x	-
Particulars of rural life			x	Wittfogel in Germany
2. Japanese: economic, cultural, and religious development	Hackmann Florenz Rudorff Rathgen	Germany Germany Germany Germany	-	-
Application of some general categories such as *rentier* mentality. etc.			x	-

TABLE 2 (cont.)

Theories	Accepted by Weber after elaboration by the following	Countries of these men	Elaborated by Weber	Men influenced by Weber
3. Hindus: Social, Economic, and cultural development	Albrecht Weber	Germany	-	-
	Zimmer	Germany		
	Oldenberg	Germany		
	Fick	Germany		
	Horn	Germany		
	Senart	France		
	Bougle	France		
	Duff	England		
	Baines	England		
	English census reports	England and India		
	Authors of special Census reports	England and India		
	Hopkins	United States		
Hindu epigraphs as source material	Hultzsch	Germany	-	-
	Fleet	England		
	Buhler	Germany		
New viewpoints supposed to reject Maine's hypothesis of an original Hindu rural communism			x	-
New viewpoints supposed to explain why cities in the occidental sense did not arise			x	-

TABLE 2 (cont.)

Theories	Accepted by Weber after elaboration by the following	Countries of these men	Elaborated by Weber	Men influenced by Weber
4. *Pre-Greek Western Asiatics*: Importance of inundation and dikes in ancient Egypt and Mesopotaimia	Maspero Wilkinson Petrie	France England England	-	-
Structure of large rural estates in Egypt and Mesopotamia	(same)	(same)	-	-
Development of water-bureaucracy as starting bureaucracy in Egypt and Mesopotamia	Oppenheimer		x	Oppenheimer in Germany
Some viewpoints concerning the spread of culture from Mesopotamia	Schrader Winckler	Germany Germany Germany	-	-
Role of Phoenicians and Carthaginians as transmitters of the Egyptian and Mesopotamian kind of rural estate	Mommsen	Germany	-	-
5. *Ancient Hebrews*: Historicity, authenticity, and age of various books and reports of the Old Testament	Wellhausen Gunkel	Germany Germany	-	-

TABLE 2 (cont.)

Theories	Accepted by Weber after elaboration by the following	Countries of these men	Elaborated by Weber	Men influenced by Weber
Subdivision of Palestine into three rural economic parts	-	-	x	
City dwellers making their living from land rent derived from ownership of land outside cities	-	-	x	Some liberal Protestant theologians
Decreasing importance of peasants due to increasing predominance of the urban population	-	-	x	Some liberal Protestant theologians
prophets supported by the urban population	-	-	x	
Nonexistence of capitalistic mentality among later pre-Christian Jews	-	-	x	Some Liberal Protestant theologians; some adversaries of anti-Semitism
6. Etruscans: Autochtony in Italy; structure of rural life; land partition methods imitated by the Romans	Indo-European group of Etruscologists	Italy and Germany	-	-

reasons Weber could not escape giving at least a tentative answer to the question of the Etruscans.

The Etruscans

The Etruscans were the objective of the least successful of the anthropological, archaeological, and historical investigations made after the epoch of German Romanticism.[10] Even after more than a hundred years of research, only a relatively few decisions in the field have been made. The most well-known views are that the Etruscans were a pre-Indo-European people who came from Western Asia, that they were the last representatives of matrilinear culture, and that they were a historically unimportant people. Most of the Etruscologists hold the first theory. The second was the view of Johann Jakob Bachofen, while the latter was that of Theodor Mommsen. As the latter was an intimate friend of Weber's parents, Weber knew him intimately and held him in high esteem. Nonetheless he disapproved this dislike for Etruscan studies and proceeded to formulate his own views from archaeological findings rather than upon linguistic investigations.

Weber viewed the Etruscans as follows. Nothing speaks in favor of their Western Asiatic origin. They were ruled by priests and by an aristocracy subdivided into gentes, that is, large families consisting of persons related by blood from the male side. Moreover, they are important for inventing the technique of land partition which the Romans then imitated. This Weberian concept is largely that of the Etruscologists who claimed that these people were Indo-European. Weber considered his judgment as nothing more than hypothetical as long as the Etruscan inscriptions remained largely undeciphered.

Actually Weber's views on the Etruscans remained unnoticed. For a short time after his death, two groups of scholars, who pointed in the opposite direction attracted attention and gained almost general approval. Gustav Herbig put forward many particulars which he considered proof that a relationship between the pre-Greek inscriptions found in Lemnos and the Etruscans had existed. The latter had then migrated from the eastern Mediterranean region by sea to northern Italy. Hans Muhlestein wrote many publications which pointed in the same direction. Indeed, the latter was often criticized for exaggerating the role of the Etruscans in world history.

Nevertheless, he contributed (just as did Herbig's much more philologically based theories) to an increasing belief in the eastern Mediterranean origin of the Etruscans with the result that Weber's conflicting view remained unnoticed.

By way of recapitulation, Weber's participation in the development of the history of agriculture in oriental and pro-occidental state cultures is summarized in table 2.

For the peoples considered thus far, except the ancient Hebrews, Weber was compelled to use translations of the sources. This is not true for those of classical antiquity.

Classical Antiquity

The agriculture and rural life of classical antiquity was one of the first subjects to hold Weber's scientific attention, and many influences contributed to the development of this interest. He had received nine years of training in Greek and Latin in a humanistic gymnasium. Since boyhood he had known intimately Theodor Mommsen, at that time the most discussed historian of ancient Rome. Weber studied law when the field included intensive training in Roman law and its history. At the beginning of his academic career, he lectured on Roman law at the University of Berlin, a field which necessitated consideration of Greek and Hellenistic law, the latter being increasingly based on the study of papyri. Accordingly Weber's studies on the agriculture of classic antiquity in contrast with those concerning oriental peoples are based on an exact knowledge of the sources in their original languages. Moreover, Weber had to deal with many theories put forward in a vast body of literature which became increasingly almost impossible to master. On the basis of all this material, Weber characterized ancient Greece as follows.

Ancient Greece

In contrast with the orient, the economy of ancient Greece was based upon the conversion of woodland into arable land.[11] Moreover—in contrast with the Christian Middle Ages—it was not an inland but rather a seashore culture. Kings originally resided in castles on hills and were surrounded by many persons who occupied the king's houses and enjoyed the monopoly of exchange and commerce. Around the king's castle the nobility lived organized in sibs. Out of this sib-society originated city and state. Meanwhile cavalry and chariot combat became increasingly important in warfare. Since equipping a cavalryman was expensive, only well-to-do persons were able to do so. Consequently, the cavalry became increasingly and then exclusively limited to nobles. Others, who were not able to do so, brought themselves under the protection and domination of the nobility, became their clients, and worked on their fields. The latter were located outside the towns. The clients also were to be found here.

In this way the city itself became a place where primarily *equites* lived, economically based upon the agricultural efforts of the rural workers. The *equites* themselves were always ready to go to war, especially in connection with the increasingly expansionistic policies, which aimed at conquest, subjection, and a new possibility for the conquerors to live a life based upon the labor of subjected people. This life was the life of *rentiers* without capitalistic mentality.

Moreover, there were handicraftsmen who lived in the city. They produced necessary economic goods with the help of slaves. The latter lived in the houses of their masters and with them formed small economic units. These craftsmen never succeeded in becoming powerful socially. Accordingly, the Greek city was certainly a place of socioeconomic antagonisms. But in contrast with the modern occidental city, the dominant antagonism within the Greek city was not between the social class which owned capital on the one hand and urban craftsmen and proletarians who did not own capital on the other. The decisive antagonism in Greek antiquity was rather between the aristocracy, who owned land and based its life on land rent, and the masses who did not own land and accordingly were dependent workers.

Where does this Weberian synthesis of the Greek rural-economic structure stand in the development of the knowledge of the history of agriculture?

Two of the viewpoints mentioned above had already been put forward before Weber started. Eduard Meyer, more so than any of the historians of antiquity, had emphasized the structure and importance of the sib in the development of social life. Gaston Maspero, primarily an Egyptologist, had emphasized the importance of the development of cavalry in all antiquity. Weber accepted both ideas, but he added a new viewpoint. He held that the sib was the rudiment out of which city and state originated and that the development of cavalry and chariot combat was one of the essential causes of change in the social structure of the rural population.

Having these two viewpoints in mind, Weber's original contributions in the field may be enumerated as follows: (1) The difference between the oriental water-culture and the Greek culture, which was based upon the conversion of woodland into arable land; (2) the difference between the Greek seashore culture and the medieval inland culture; (3) the sib as the rudiment of city and state; (4) the importance of cavalry in changing the structure of rural life; (5) the policies of expansion, whereby it was possible to base the life on the labor of subjected people; (6) the nonexistence of capitalistic mentality among the landowning nobility; (7) the powerlessness of handicraftsmen; and (8) the class struggle centering around land rent rather than around the interest on capital. Of these concepts number 4 was accepted by Gustav Schmoller, numbers 1-3 by Franz Oppenheimer and numbers 5-8 by Johannes Hazebroek. Among the investigators in the field of ancient history the latter more than any other writer emphasized the importance of the economic factor in the development of Greek culture. Accordingly there is a strong influence exercised by Weber. The same is not true of Hellenism.

Hellenistic Age

Since the end of the nineteenth century, the investigation of the epoch between the partition of the empire of Alexander the Great and its conquest by the Roman Empire has been based on two new kinds of sources, the ostraka, or fragments of earthenware containing inscriptions used in elections, and papyri as mentioned above. Ulrich Wilsken and Ludwig Mitteis became the most outstanding editors and decipherers of these two new kinds of sources. Both M. Rostovtzeff, a Russian who emigrated to the United States, and Weber based their work largely on these sources.[12]

As noted above, earlier Egyptologists had asserted that a long time before Alexander there were few independent peasants in Egypt but rather latifundia often owned by the state. Rostovtzeff insisted that these latifundia and their bureaucratic administration had continued without interruption into the Hellenistic epoch. These three scholars, along with Weber, held each other in mutual esteem, and the special interrelationship is as follows. Weber accepted almost completely the work of the other three scholars; he added only a few particulars, and these in turn were in part accepted by Wilcken and Mitteis. Through Weber Oppenheimer became acquainted with the material used by the three and their findings and incorporated the results into his own system.

Rome

The rural history of Rome is usually divided into the epochs before and after the beginning of the overseas conquests.[13] Weber described the development and changes as follows. Originally there existed patricians who were castle owners and plebeians who were not directly the serfs of the former but rather semi-dependent owners of allotments. Moreover, there existed the ager publicus. This was originally fallow land, property of the state and not of the family clan, later increasingly also conquered land, having belonged originally to the native people who had been subjugated. To some extent, this ager publicus could be occupied privately, and the socioeconomic history of Rome, at least before she became a conquering power overseas, is largely a struggle over this fallow land and the title to its occupation. The plebeians ascended by being hoplites or heavy-armed infantry soldiers. In this way they increasingly became entitled to participate in the partition of the ager publicus and thereby interested in the conquest of non-Roman land in Italy. But changes occurred.

This interest in the acquisition of land led to overseas conquest, that is, to the second era of Rome's rural history. Overseas expansion in general and ownership of slaves in particular facilitated the occupation of conquered land and the development of an agrarian capitalism. The political insurrection, led by the Gracchi brothers, was nothing but a protest against this development, and its failure actually meant the further decline of the remainder of the peasant class.

Henceforth, a new social class became dominant. Its members lived in cities and based their life on overseas commerce and rent from rural land. The latter was rented to coloni, who were provided with the necessary inventory by the owner, or it was cultivated by slaves. These slaves were bought in the slave market. They were often worked to the point of exhaustion under overseers. They lived

TABLE 3

Theories Concerning Rural Life in Classical Antiquity

Theories	Accepted by Weber after elaboration by the following	Countries of these men	Elab-orated by Weber	Men influenced by Weber	Countries of these Men	mutual influence of Weber and these men
1. Greeks						
Culture based on conversion of woodland into arable land	-	-	x	Oppenheimer	Germany	-
Culture a seashore culture rather than an inland culture	-	-	x	Oppenheimer	Germany	-
Structure and central role of the sib	Eduard Meyer	Germany	-	-	-	-
Sib as rudiment of city and state	-	-	x	Oppenheimer	Germany	
Shifting from infantry warfare to cavalry and chariot combat	Maspero	France	-	-	-	-
Importance of the development of cavalry for the change in the structure of rural life	-	-	x	Schmoller	Germany	-
Policies of expansion that of being able to live a life based upon the labor of subjected peoples	-	-	x	Hazebroek	Germany	-
Life of equites as a life of *rentiers* without capitalistic mentality	-	-	x	Hazebroek	Germany	-
Lack of power of handicraft groups in cities	-	-	x	Hazebroek	Germany	-
Social struggle centering around land rent	-	-	x	Hazebroek	Germany	-
2. Hellenistic Age:						
Ostraka and papyrus sources regarding everyday rural life	Mitteis / Wilcken	Germany / Germany	-	-	-	-
Particulars concerning everyday rural life	Mitteis / Wilcken / Rostoutzeff	Germany / Germany / Russia and United States	x / x	Mitteis / Wilcken / -	Germany / Germany / -	x / x / -
Structure and uninterrupted continuance of the latifundia and their bureaucracy from ancient Egypt to Alexander's Empire, the Hellenistic Age, and the Roman Empire	Rostoutzeff	Russia and United Slates	-	-	-	-

TABLE 3 (cont.)

Theories	Accepted by Weber after elaboration by the following	Countries of these men	Elaborated by Weber	Men influenced by Weber	Countries of these Men	mutual influence of Weber and these men
3. Romans:						
Patricians as castle owners	Mommsen	Germany	-	-	-	-
Plebeians as allotment owners	Mommsen	Germany	-	-	-	-
Ager publicus originally state land	Mommsen	Germany	-	-	-	-
Social struggle primarily occurring over fallow land	Mommsen	Germany	-	-	-	-
Rise of plebeians by becoming hoplites	-	-	x	Oppenheimer Below Louis Gras Westermann	Germany Germany France United States United States	-
Increasing participation of plebeians in land partition	-	-	x	Oppenheimer Louis Gras Westermann	Germany France United States United States	-
Interest of plebeians in the conquest of non-Roman land	-	-	x	Oppenheimer Louis Gras Westermann	Germany France United States United States	-
Social unimportance of the peasant class after the Gracchi	Mommsen	Germany	-	-	-	-
Predominance of bourgeois class after overseas expansion	Mommsen	Germany	-	-	-	-
Existence and importance of *coloni*	Mommsen	Germany	-	-	-	-
Socio-economic status of coloni	Rostovtzeff	Russia and United States	-	-	-	-
Particulars concerning rural life in the later Roman Empire	Mitteis Wilcken Gummerus Rostovtzeff	Germany Germany Germany Russia and United States	x	Mitteis Wilcken Gummerus Rostovtzeff Oppenheimer	Germany Germany Germany Russia and United States Germany	x x x x
Life of slaves in the slave barracks after oversea expansion	-	-	x	Openheimer Gras	Germany United States	x

TABLE 3 (cont.)

Theories	Accepted by Weber after elaboration by the following	Countries of these men	Elab-orated by Weber	Men influenced by Weber	Countries of these Men	mutual influence of Weber and these men
Hypothesis concerning shifting of the center of life from city to rural es-tate in the later Roman Empire	Seebohm	England	-	-	-	-
New viewpoints sup-posed to support See-bohm's hypothesis noted above	-	-	x	Oppenheimer Sombart Below Gothein Dopsch	Germany Germany Germany Germany Austria	-
Hypothesis concerning uninterrupted continu-ance from the Roman villa to the early medie-val feudal estate	Möser Eichhorn Roth	Germany Germany Germany	-	-	-	-
New viewpoints supposed to support Roth's hy-pothesis noted above	-	-	x	Oppenheimer Sombart Below Gothein Dopsch Vinogradoff	Germany Germany Germany Germany Austria Russia and England	-

as unmarried men in barracks and reproduced themselves through a kind of regulated prostitution. But again changes occurred especially near the very end of the Roman Empire, that is, after the wars of con-quest.

The center of life next shifted from seashore and city life to inte-rior and estate life, that is, to the villa. The landlord and his family lived on the latter; here they were surrounded by coloni, who had to pay fixed charges in kind, and by *servi*. The latter were forced to do an unlimited amount of skilled handicraft work to satisfy the needs of the landlord and dependents. That meant dominance of socage estates, decay of cities, shifting to an economy based on kind, and the beginning of the Middle Ages. Conquering tribes of Nordic origin, speaking Teutonic languages, settled down in these self-suf-ficient villas of the late Roman Empire and began there their own medieval feudalism.

Where does this Weberian synthesis of the Roman agronomico-historical development stand in the development of knowledge of the history of agriculture?

Mommsen had elaborated the following points: (1) the patricians as castle owners; (2) the plebeians as allotment owners; (3) the *ager publicus* as state land; (4) the social struggle as a struggle primarily over fallow land; (5) the unimportance of the peasant class after the Gracchian reform: (6) the predominance of the bourgeois class after overseas expansion; and (7) the existence and importance of *coloni*.

To these statements by Mommsen, the following additions were made. Rostovtzeff elaborated on the socioeconomic status of the coloni. Mitteis, Wilcken, and Herman Gummerus contributed particulars concerning rural life in the later Roman Empire. Frederic Seebohm put forth his hypothesis about the shifting from seashore life to interior life—a hypothesis that lacked convincing proof. Paul von Roth presented a hypothesis (in contrast to the formerly dominant catastrophe theory of the complete break between later antiquity and the Middle Ages) which pointed to the uninterrupted continuance from the Roman villa to the early medieval feudal estate, a hypothesis put forward without convincing proof.

Weber accepted these theories of Mommsen and Rostovtzeff and the hypotheses of Seebohm and Roth but added the following new parts to the whole system mentioned above: (1) the rise of plebeians by becoming hoplites; (2) the increasing participation of plebeians in land partition; (3) the interest of plebeians in the conquest of non-Roman land; (4) particulars concerning rural life in the later Roman Empire; (5) the life of slaves in barracks, a description based on an analysis of Latin writings in the field of agronomy hitherto little used in connection with this problem; (6) new material and reasons supposedly supporting Seebohm's sypothesis; and (7) new material and reasons intended to substantiate the hypothesis of Roth.

Of these Weberian ideas, all seven were accepted by Franz Oppenheimer, numbers 1 and 2 by scholars' varied philosophies, including the Americans N.S.B. Gras and W.L. Westermann, and the Frenchman, Paul Louis, number 4 in part by Ulrich Wilcken, Ludwig Mitteis, and their continuator, Herman Gummerus, number 5 by the American historian of agriculture, N.S.B. Gras, numbers 6 and 7 by scholars of varied philosophies, including the Austrian Catholic medievalist, Alfons Dopsch, the nationalistically minded German medievalist, Georg von Below, the economic historians Eberhard Gothein and Werner Sombart, and Paul Vinogradoff (perhaps with slight modifications).

In Roman rural history Weber was strongly influenced by earlier scholars. Moreover, there was some mutual influence between Rostovtzeff, Wilcken, Mitteis, and Weber but also a very strong influence by Weber on scholars of various kinds. By way of recapitulation, Weber's participation in the development of the history of agriculture in classical antiquity is summarized in table 3.

To understand the importance of Weber's theory concerning the uninterrupted continuance of the self-sufficient large estates from the late Roman Empire to medieval feudalism, it is necessary to deal with Weber's synthesis of rural life in the Middle Ages.

Weber became interested in the agriculture and rural life of the Christian world when he was dealing with the later Roman Empire. His thesis for his doctorate in law dealt with an economic problem which involved the uniqueness of the medieval city. In his treatment of the various Christian cultures some peoples and eras deserve a somewhat more exhaustive discussion than others.

Celtic Peoples

Speaking languages and having forms of life which were different from the surrounding world, the Celtic peoples had continued to exist in remote parts of the occidental world. These included Ireland, the Highlands of Scotland, the Isle of Man, Wales, Brittany, and up to the end of the eighteenth century, Cornwall. The existence of such remnants supplied the inspiration for many persons and groups to deal with the Celts, and Weber stood within the continuity of these groups.[14]

The earliest of these groups were the antirationalists of the eighteenth century. James Macpherson edited a translation of Gaelic songs supposedly old High Scottish in origin, which, he asserted, were written by Ossian. An extended discussion of their authenticity began, in which Johann Gottfried von Herder, a forerunner of German Romanticism, the young Johann Wolfgang von Goethe, and Samuel Johnson and James Boswell were involved. Both Boswell and Johnson had traveled in the Highlands and the Hebrides and doubted the authenticity of these songs. Their writings were widely read and contributed much to the development of an interest in Celtic matters.

The German Romanticists always hoped to discover an incarnation of the true life in the remote past or in a remote district, and in this case, starting with Macpherson, Herder, and Goethe, they began to deal with the Celtic past.

After French Romanticism developed, Hersart de la Villemarque and others began to be interested in the Bretons and to edit Breton songs, supposed to be old and original. In spite of the proximity of Brittany, the French Encyclopedists, including Jean Jacques Rousseau, had shown almost no interest in Celtic peoples.

The Irish nationalists, influenced by the Romantic movement, began to edit Irish sources.

The Celtic philology, strictly speaking, originated, like so many of the special philologies, largely out of German Romanticism. Based on and in continuance of Franz Bopp's discovery of the unity of the Indo-European languages, the southern German, Johann Kaspar Zeuss, elaborated the comparative and historical grammar of the Celtic languages. Based on his work, Whitley Stokes in England, Henry Gaidoz in France, Hermann Ebel, Christian Wilhelm von Gluck, Ernst Windisch, Heinrich Zimmer, Ludwig Christian Stern, and Kuno Meyer in Germany built up a Celtic philology in central Europe. It is true that there was only one full professorship for Celtic philology in Germany, the one at the University of Berlin, in the second half of the nineteenth century, but in some of the other universities, such as Leipzig, Bonn, and Heidelberg, professors of comparative Indo-European linguistics occasionally taught classes in Irish and Welsh grammar and literature. There was therefore an uninterrupted continuance in Celtic studies also in Germany, but the main interest of these scholars (like almost any interest which originated in German Romanticism) centered around the comparative history of Celtic languages and literatures.

The socioeconomic development of the Celtic peoples had been studied to a smaller degree. The impulse to do so came from two sources. The American evolutionist, Lewis H. Morgan, believed that the Celtic gens was similar to an institution which he found among the Iroquois Indians. With regard to this and many other assertions put forward by Morgan, the Marxists, especially Friedrich Engels and August Bebel, followed the American anthropologist and by doing so made the Celtic gens popular in many countries. Sumner Maine, the evolutionist, incorporated Irish institutions into his system of rural collectivities which he argued existed everywhere in the beginning.

Frederic Seebohm's original interest centered around the English village, but his attempt to find the causes of the phenomena that he investigated led him from Anglo-Saxon and English studies to the comparative study of the Irish, Scotch, and Welsh rural past and laws. Based on all this material he argued as follows. The Celts originally lived the nomadic life of the tribal system just as the Germans did at the time of Tacitus and as almost every people in the world had once done, for his tribal system was an inevitable stage in the development of every people. Even after settling down, the Celts maintained much land for pasture. The other land was divided equally among the families. Thus the latter were in a similar economic situation to a large extent. Even the tribal chiefs were not much different from other persons, and the chief's status was not hereditary. Often the family shifted from one dwelling to another when the extinction of one family made a new partition inevitable. They were so accustomed to land partition that they maintained this custom even centuries later. All this was a pure autochthonous Celtic development. In contrast the manorial system in the Celtic islands as in Gaul and Germanic lands originated by a combination of autochthonous and Roman elements.

August Meitzen, the German rural historian and statistician, attempted to define the German settlement in its characteristic traits. That meant an elaboration of its differences from the Celtic and Slavic settlement. Thus, Meitzen had also to define the Celtic settlement in its essential traits. In order to do so he combined the results of the investigations made in France, Great Britain, and Ireland with those made in Germany and elaborated a new synthesis.

Meitzen accepted the following five theories of Seebohm: original Celtic nomadism; the predominance of animal husbandry for a long time over the cultivation of crops; equal partition of land among the families belonging to the tribe; the nonhereditary character of the chief's position; and the maintenance of the custom of partition of land for a long time. To these theories of Seebohm, Meitzen added two: Christian monasticism especially contributed to the sedentary life, and in this way the chief shifted to the position of a manorial lord; and the results of Seebohm's Irish investigations must be combined with observations made among the Westphalians in Germany.

In the eighteenth century Justus Möser had studied the Westphalians. He was an antirationalistically minded emphasizer of rural life, independent farmers, local traditions, and especially the old Westphalian farmhouse. The latter was different from the farmhouses in surrounding German districts. It contained the human dwelling and the stable under the same roof. It was isolated from other farmhouses and was surrounded by its own fields. At the end of the nineteenth century it was still in existence in some Westphalian districts. This old Westphalian settlement as described by Möser was, according to Meitzen, the same as the old Irish settlement described by Seebohm; for both, the Westphalian and the Irish could be traced to the same common ancestor, the original Celtic settlement, which in Westphalia was then accepted and continued by the German conquerors. This view, elaborated by Meitzen, is for us of great importance.

Weber admittedly was a pupil of Meitzen, and except for the fact that he considered the Irish-Westphalian equalization as not completely proven, he accepted and propagated the whole Seebohm-Meitzen synthesis about Celtic rural economic development. He expressly denied that he himself had added anything positive of his own to it. Thus it is understandable that in the Celtological field almost no one refers to Weber, but almost everyone to Meitzen. The American historians of agriculture, N.S.B. Gras, Melvin M. Knight, and Nellie Neilson, the Austrian Catholic, Alfons Dopsch, and Paul Vinogradoff, originally a Russian, accepted Meitzen's theory of the Irish development, the two former even his Irish-Westphalian equalization, while Neilson, Dopsch, and Vinogradoff, just as did Weber, considered this Celtic-Westphalian theory as unproven. The Meitzen-Weber relationship was similar as far as the Slavic peoples are concerned.

Slavic Peoples

The Slavic peoples and their agricultural past especially attracted Weber's attention because of two phenomena, the Russian mir and the southern Slavic zadruga.[15] The mir had been brought to the attention of Weber's generation in the following ways. August Ludwig von Schlozer, one of the founders of the science of statistics in Germany, had lived for years in Russia and had described the Russian rural collective, the mir, at the end of the eighteenth century. August von Haxthausen, a conservative and feudal German Romanticist, had traveled through Russia and praised the mir as an institution which merited survival.

The Slavophile movement of Ivan Kireevsky and his followers went even further. In general this movement accepted the emphasis given by German Romanticists, such as Friedrich Wilhelm von Schelling and Franz Xaver von Baader, to the uniqueness of every nation in contrast to the internationalsim of the enlightenment and the French Revolution. Moreover the Slavophiles glorified the collectivism of the past in contrast with the individualism of the eighteenth century. Furthermore, this movement strengthened the admiration which Haxthausen had expressed for the mir. It also combined Schelling's emphasis on national uniqueness generally and Haxthausen's special emphasis on the mir. In this way they came to a glorification of the mir and the rural collective as a true Russian and Greek Orthodox form of life.

Feodor Dostoevsky and Count Leo Tolstoy, the well-known Russian fiction and religious writers, had actually lived somewhat earlier than the Weberian generation, but they were not discussed in Germany until a short time before the First World War. They were especially comprehended and used with respect to the simple Russian peasant as the true Christian man, even the ideal man himself.

The Narodniki movement of Peter Lavrov, Victor Tchernov, and their followers, who later were called Social Revolutionaries, gave this idea another twist. This group was familiar with Haxthausen's ideas and accepted the theory of the especially Russian character of the mir. But out of this conviction they drew conclusions in conflict with those of the Slavophiles. First of all, the poor Russian peasant should accomplish a Russian revolution, eliminate private landownership, and realize a land nationalization program. Such a program was meant to embody the basic principles of the mir.

The evolutionists, especially Sumner Maine, had claimed that the same stages succeeded each other automatically and necessarily within the independent and parallel development of the various peoples. They placed special emphasis on the idea that every people, independent of influences received from others, had passed through the stage of original communism. Accordingly they incorporated the mir into this system and regarded it as nothing but a remnant of the rural collective stage, through which every people, including the Russians, had to pass. The Marxists in general and especially Friedrich Engels did the same.

The Russian Marxists, especially George Plekhanov and Peter Struve, certainly accepted the Engels system, including the past of the Russian rural collective, but they were impelled to defend their own political program and visualize the future against the Narodniki. In doing so they asserted that Russia would not remain rural but would of necessity develop in a capitalistic direction. Such development would then also destroy the rural collective.

Russian anarchists, especially Prince Peter Kropotkin, used the rural collective as an example of the inborn tendency of man to live a life of mutual help and as a proof that a society without any legal compulsion is possible.

Under such circumstances Russian economists, sociologists, and philosophers were forced to participate in the controversy. Some of them were J. von Keussler, Konstantin Kavelin, Maxim Kovalevsky, Isaac Hourwich, Vladimir Simkhovich, Pavel Milyukov, Nikolai Oganovsky, Alexis Yermolov, and the Scandinavian Knud Asborn Wieth-Knudsen.

The German youth movement held the ideal of a simple and natural life in contrast with urban life. The latter was supposed to be unnatural and hyperintellectual. Moreover, this youth movement advocated a return to a life which should be based on mutual help in contrast to present-day competition. This new youth movement rediscovered Dostoevsky and accepted his glorification of the simple Russian.

August Meitzen attempted to define the German settlement in its characteristic traits. That meant an elaboration of its differences from the Celtic settlement. With that we have dealt above. But it meant the same with regard to the Slavic settlement. Because the mir was declared by some of the writers mentioned above to be the typical Slavic settlement rather than just one of the many kinds of Russian settlements, Meitzen had to deal with it intensively.[16]

Meitzen characterized the essence of the mir as follows. The fields were the property of the rural corporation. Every family in the village was, ipso facto, a member of the latter and was entitled to an equal allotment of land; this could be managed independently according to the decisions made and orders given by the father of the family. But new repartitions always occurred because the younger generation had the same right to allotment as the older one.

The origin of this institution was explained by Meitzen as follows. Since the beginning of the Mongolian rule in Russia land became more and more chartered real property. At the same time peasants began to cede their land to the church or to the feudal lords. They did so to escape the arbitrary actions of functionaries. By doing so the formerly independent peasants changed their status and as the next step became tenants for a time with the right of the tenant to withdraw from the tenancy. But increasingly the right of recalling diminished because in the case of withdrawal and removal the tenant had to pay increasingly high forfeit. He often was unable to raise it. Furthermore, the feudal lord became increasingly entitled to refuse the notice made to him by his tenant. In many laws in the sixteenth and seventeenth centuries the state sanctioned this development; moreover it entitled the feudal man to sue the fugitive peasant without superannuation and to have him brought back. Finally the law abolished the last remaining difference between peasant serfs and slaves and comprised both under the term bondsmen. At the same time the community of the latter became jointly responsible for exaction and delivery of the imposts. Thus the bondsmen's community became interested in the settlement of people who would be capable of working. Accordingly it encouraged them to do so, by showing them the advantage of settling within a community where they would be entitled regularly to participate in the new allotment of land. Out of this interest the mir originated. In this manner and in contrast to the theory which had been put forward by earlier authors, the mir was declared by Meitzen to be a relatively recent institution, and he was one of the chief teachers of Weber.

What was the attitude of Weber toward all these theories concerning the origin, essence, and development of the mir?[17]

Weber was connected with at least five of the twelve groups which have been enumerated. Apart from being an admiring pupil of

Meitzen, Weber was in his last years personally connected with some groups of the German youth movement. He liked them but warned them against becoming romantic. Furthermore, he was personally acquainted with some Russian Social Revolutionaries and Marxists who studied in Heidelberg, many of whom he directly protected. He did so for two reasons. Although he certainly was not an adherent of either one of the ideologies, he felt ethically bound to protect his adversaries. Moreover, these Russian revolutionary students were to his mind idealists, persecuted and willing to die for their convictions. In this respect he found some similarity between them and himself and therefore protected them. Besides he was deeply affected by Dostoevsky and Tolstoy, whom he wanted to make the subject of a special study. Under all these circumstances it would have been a miracle if this rigorous Neo-Kantian Protestant had not dealt with the mir and with Russian rural life in general. Although a middle aged man, Weber learned the Russian language in order to study these problems. He also studied many books which did not deal explicitly with Russian agricultural history but rather with Russian economic development generally. Such were the publications of the moderate Marxists, Mikhail Tugan-Garonovsky, and of Pavel Milyukov, one of the leaders of the so-called Cadets, i.e., the Constitutional Democrats.

Like Meitzen and the majority of the Russian scholars, except the Slavophiles, Weber considered the mir not a primitive Russian institution, but rather a product of the taxation system and serfdom of the post-Mongolian epoch and especially the seventeenth and eighteenth centuries. Moreover he largely accepted the explanation given by his teacher Meitzen. But at the same time he insisted on the importance of some other traits. These he contrasted with the admiring description given among others by the Social Revolutionaries and with their belief that the mir could and should be maintained in contrast with an individualistic rural organization as the salvation of the economic life of present times. To them Weber's answer was as follows. Equality of the members, democratic character, and community of interests in the mir existed on paper only. That was due to two reasons. The allotment took into account how much labor force a dwelling mustered. Thus every family which had increased in a large ratio was in favor of re-division; but there were other interests arrayed against that. Many members needed implements and to be able to buy them became indebted to the kulaks, the well-to-do and independent middle-class farmers in the village. Accordingly they held the mass of the propertyless members of the mir in their power through money lending. According to whether they were interested in keeping their debtors poor or allowing them to acquire more land, they controlled the decision of the village when re-division was asked for by the heads of enlarged families. Thus the decision in this nominally collectivistic institution was actually often determined by individualistic economic interests. Indeed the right to the land pertained to the individual and accordingly was perpetual. Even after the abolition of serfdom the worker, whose forefathers had emigrated from the mir generations before, might go back and assert the right if he found it to his interest to return unsolicited. On the other hand, the village reciprocally held an unquestionable claim to his labor, even when he had gone away with the permission of the headman of the village and taken up an entirely different profession. The mir of course was inclined to use this right when a relatively small number of persons had remained behind and the tax burden was increased for them since it was a joint obligation. Consequently, the same collective, whose decisions, as demonstrated above, were actually often determined by individualistic economic interests, limited the members' freedom of movement. For both reasons Weber did not deplore the actual abolishment of the mir through the agrarian reform accomplished by the Russian minister, Peter Stolypin, although he did not like the way it was accomplished. But this conviction was completely involved in Weber's whole social program concerning the rural organization of the present and future. Accordingly, it does not come within the scope of this study.

Weber was much concerned with Russian agriculture, but actually only his ideas concerning the present and future have been noted. More recent authors dealing with the mir, as the American, Gerald Tanquary Robinson, cite neither Weber nor Meitzen. Others such as Alfons Dopsch did just the same as they did in dealing with the Celtic rural past, that is, they cited Meitzen but not Weber. In this case the glory of the master has overshadowed that of the pupil. The same is true with regard to the other supposedly Slavic rural collective, the zadruga.

In the history of the investigation of the zadruga,[18] many names already noted in dealing with the mir reappear; evolutionists (among them Sumner Maine, Carl Bucher, and Emile de Laveleye), anarchists, Marxists, and Meitzen. To them must be added many southern Slavic writers such as Milan Markovich and Dragolioub Novakovitch and some Austrian writers including Dopsch. The interest of both groups was, of course, at least in part, a practical one. The institution existed until recent times in parts of Serbia as well as in those districts of the former Turkish Empire which the Austria-Hungarian Monarchy occupied in 1878, annexed in 1908, and lost in 1919.

The argument about the origin of the zadruga centers around the problem: is the phenomenon especially Slavic in character or is it nothing but a remnant of the general agricultural communism every people has to pass through? The latter is the theory of evolutionists and Marxists; the former was formulated in its most pronounced from by Meitzen.

Meitzen described the zadruga in the following way. Land had originally been occupied by the whole clan, that is, by the unit of all families related to one another by blood on the male side, under leadership of the head of this clan. No partition of land among the individual families of the clan occurred. On the contrary, all the land was managed in common according to the orders given by the head of the clan. The latter also nominated one of his sons or nephews as his successor. Everything acquired by the individual became property of the community, except for war plunder and bridal attire, or if a member renounced his partnership and withdrew from the zadruga.

Weber accepted, for the most part, this description given by his teacher. In addition, however, he pointed out that, although some anarchists cited the zadruga as proof of their theory that a society without legal compulsion is possible, they are wrong. It is true that in the zadruga there was no legal compulsion administered by the state, but nevertheless coercion was carried out by the village community. Thus, he argued that the existence of the zadruga contradicted both the theories of the anarchists and the state worshippers. However, the existence of the zadruga indeed proves that a stateless legal coercion is possible.

As to the problem concerning the origin of the phenomenon, it is scarcely necessary to indicate Weber's attitude. This Neo-Kantian had always in principle opposed the belief in automatically occurring parallel developments as conceived by evolutionists. In this case he also denied the possibility of considering this phenomenon as a remnant of a universal rural collectivism of an earlier stage. There still remained in his day, however, the yet unsolved question of the date and special causes of the origin of this institution, and the geographical, political, or social factor could have been the essential one. But again the Heidelbergian social historian took the character of the sources, the amount of knowledge available in his day, and his own unfamiliarity with the language into account, and accordingly abstained from making a final decision.

Under such circumstances Weber's remarks on southern Slavic collectives passed almost unnoticed. Also in this case Dopsch cited the teacher and not the pupil. In his studies of the German rural past Weber had to face a completely different situation.

The Germans

The rural past of the Germans had been the object of scientific interest in Germany since the time of the pre-Romanticists such as Justus Möser, mentioned previously in connection with the Irish-Westphalian equalization. On the history and especially the beginning of German agriculture, many special problems and controversies developed, and the following description is subdivided according to them.

1. Were the Germans at the time of Christ primarily animal husbandry people, as for example the Celts, or were the Germans already growing crops?[19] Both theories had often been advocated. The interpretation of certain passages in the writings of Julius Caesar played a part in these discussions. Some investigators insisted that Caesar contradicted himself. They asserted that he once described the ancient Germans as a sedentary people who grew crops and again as an unstable people who migrated with their animals and only occasionally lived long enough in one place to raise some crops. Others consid-

ered the passages under consideration as only seemingly contradictory and tried to reconcile them. Some scholars, therefore, were proponents of German nomadism. In this group were many of the earlier scholars, Weber's teacher, August Meitzen, and Weber's contemporaries, Georg Friedrich Knapp and Werner Wittich. Others were proponents of the sedentary character of the early German life. Wilhelm Fleischmann made a new distinction. He argued that Caesar described the Suebi as a migratory people with almost no tillage but that this was the description of an exceptional situation. Weber accepted this suggestion, incorporated it into a more universal concept, and argued as follows. At the time of Caesar, agriculture in Northern Europe was not a recent invention; it had spread to and was practiced by every Indo-European linguistic people, including the majority of the Germanic tribes. Caesar had the latter in mind when he wrote that the Germans were crop raisers. The Suebi, on the other hand, were a migratory martial tribe; accordingly they only occasionally grew crops. This Weberian interpretation was accepted by Alfons Dopsch and Eberhard Gothein.

2. Did the Roman writers, Caesar and Tacitus, mean that the Germans shifted from one locality to another every year or merely that they plowed fresh portions of land in the same locality?[20] Some investigators, especially Frederic Seebohm, decided on the latter interpretation. Here Weber made a second distinction. Caesar and Tacitus were not contemporaries, and reasonably enough they had different phenomena in mind. Caesar meant change of locality, and Tacitus the two-field system. This was also accepted by Dopsch and Gothein.

3. Was the method of using land among the Germans after Christ the wild field grass husbandry system or already the three-fallow system?[21] A few Romanticists, such as Carl Friedrich Eichhorn and his followers, believed the latter, while more recently Seebohm, Fleischmann, Dopsch, Gothein, Georg von Below, and N.S.B. Gras accepted the former. To this last group, Weber also belonged. Moreover, he expressly insisted that he neither knew nor had written anything new on this subject. Accordingly the matter of Weberian influence does not require consideration.

4. What was the origin of the type of land partition, village location, and structure of rural houses?[22] The history of this particular problem is relatively short. Georg Hanssen was the first who dealt with it. He was a German who lived and worked for a short time in Denmark. At the beginning of this career in the 1870s, Meitzen elaborated a classification of settlement forms according to nations. His main types were the following. As to the structure of the settlement, the Celts had isolated farms surrounded by their fields, the Germans had long villages with the land strips immediately behind the farmyard, and the Slavs had radial settlement. As to the form of the fields, the German settlements had long strips, the Romans rectangular strips, and the Slavs block strips. Meitzen's classification of settlement forms was widely accepted soon after its publication, first by Seebohm and later by Below and Gothein. Between them stood Meitzen's pupil in Heidelberg. Weber had his doubts, mentioned above in connection with the Celts, about the possibility of correlating the Westphalian with the Irish house. The latter had been done by Meitzen in connection with his classification of villages and field strips. But except for this he accepted the system elaborated by his teacher.

5. Was land among the Germans once collective property?[23] The German Romanticists notoriously were strictly opposed to the economic individualism of laissez-faire and the French Revolution. Accordingly they emphasized any kind of non-individualistic economy and were interested in an original communism which was supposed to have existed among early Germans. Johann Kaspar Zeuss, the founder of the comparative Celtic grammar, and the brothers, Jacob Ludwig and Wilhelm Karl Grimm, who became known as editors and investigators of old German texts, supported this idea. It was supported even more widely since the theory of an original universal rural communism had been expounded by socialistic writers such as Friedrich Engels and by nonsocialists such as Sumner Maine and Emile de Laveleye. Weber considered the source material cited, and especially that regarding the original German communism, just as unconvincing as the theory of original universal rural communism. But later some

land, owned in common, the Markgenossenschaft, was to be found among certain German groups.

6. What was the origin of the Markgenossenschaft, the land obviously owned collectively by the rural community in the epoch of the Carolingians and which remained outside the feudal system?[24] Needless to say German Romanticism had especially cherished this phenomenon for obvious reasons. Eichhorn and Zeuss and their followers, Georg Ludwig von Maurer and Otto von Gierke, as well as the Marxists and Meitzen were interested. In contrast with these men Weber and Dopsch were cautious. The latter denied the existence of the Markgenossenschaft in the era of Tacitus, while the former asserted that we know only about the existence of the phenomenon in the epoch prior to the rise of the Carolingians and not earlier. At any rate, privately owned land existed in the period of Tacitus, but the question of who owned the land is very difficult to answer.

7. Was the privately owned land owned by seigniors or free peasants?[25] Since the time of the Romanticists, from Eichhorn and Maurer to Meitzen and Below, the latter alternative was the most popular. The seignorial manor theory had been advocated by Seebohm. Knapp and Wittich latter combined Seebohm's theory with an older idea. They gave impetus to the idea that the original animal husbandry nomadism had been the dominant form of life. Combining both suggestions they argued as follows. Chieftains owned herds and disdained crop raising and related work. This work was done by dependent and impoverished people. Out of this combination of conditions the manorial system originated.

    Weber was opposed to this synthesis. He applied the two distinctions concerning Caesar and Tacitus, mentioned above, to the new situation. He argued that Caesar recognized the big difference between the Gallic Celts, who in his day lived in an already developed feudalism, and the Germans. Moreover Caesar distinguished between the Germans who had already settled on the banks of the Rhine and the Suebi who were still migrating. But even the latter did not show the typical aristocratic patriarchalism of herdsmen but rather the communism of a warrior tribe; they showed aristocratic traits even less than the others; they were a society of free men with the right to equal hides and with few if any serfs or slaves. Tacitus, in contrast to Caesar, described an already differentiated society. But even the latter consisted of free owners rather than manorial seigniors. Slowly changes began to occur and led to feudalism.

8. How did feudalism originate?[26] In continuing his theory Weber argued as follows. Leaders in war and conquest began to become owners of great portions of land, and in this connection they had clients dependent upon them. But this was just one of the factors which brought feudalism. The other was the rural situation in the late Roman Empire which was mentioned at the end of the earlier section on classical antiquity.

9. Did there exist an uninterrupted continuance from the Roman villa into the rural estate of the Middle Ages?[27] This problem has previously been treated from the viewpoint of the later Roman Empire, but it must now be considered from the viewpoint of medieval history. In the 1870s Paul von Roth made some comments on the continuance of the Roman villa, and Seebohm considered the possibility as probable. But as early as 1891 Weber asserted that the Roman villa changed into a self-sufficient large estate, based upon an economy of kind. Thus everything was prepared for the chieftain of the Germanic tribes to settle down on these "villas," make himself owner of them, and to evolve the medieval socage farm. Some authors like E. Lipson, Sir William Ashley, Helen Douglas-Irine, and Charles Seignobos considered the dependence of the Germanic manor upon the Roman villa as unproven. On the contrary, others, like Franz Oppenheimer, Alfons Dopsch, Werner Sombart, Eberhard Gothein, and Paul Vinogradoff (perhaps with slight modifications) accepted the theory and made it popular. But Weber who brought up this question opposed the use of this theory in a unilateral sense.

10. Was the manor with its dependencies prior to the high Middle Ages the only kind of rural settlement, or did there still exist, at least in some German districts, independent peasants up to the High Middle Ages?[28] Knapp and Wittich insisted on the former alternative, but Below especially brought forth new material in opposition to them. Weber followed the latter with-

out claiming to add anything new, and Oppenheimer incorporated Below's viewpoints into his system. The same situation was true of the two following viewpoints.

11. What was the status of the peasants from the eighth to the twelfth century?[29] It steadily improved. There were not many wars, and accordingly there was not much slave trade. On the other hand the lord needed peasants to clear land and colonize eastward. Accordingly he had to deal well with the peasants.

12. Which factors were conducive to the predominance of the manor?[30] This came about primarily by using the political means of appropriating territorial power, that is, political rights by usurpation and feoffment. As to these particulars Weber neither claimed nor was supposed to have been original. This is not true of his synthesis concerning the essence of the Middle Ages.

13. What made the difference between the rural life of the Middle Ages and that of antiquity?[31] According to Weber the latter was exactly the opposite of the former. In antiquity, colonization was by sea, the culture was seashore, the urban feudals owned land outside the city, and there was no urban social struggle between urban feudals and powerful guilds. In the Middle Ages, colonization was by land, the culture was inland, the rural feudals lived on the manor, and the urban social struggle was between landowning feudals organized handicraftsmen out of which originated capitalism, the factory, and industry. This Weberian antithesis of antiquity and the Middle Ages was almost completely accepted by Below, Johannes Hazebroek, and Oppenheimer, and through them became popular. The antiquity-Middle Ages antithesis has been considered by many writers to be the climax of the Weberian historico-agricultural system.

Modern Western and Central Europe.

Weber has small claim to originality in his treatment of the cultural unit known as modern Western and Central Europe.[32] Rather he reproduced the well-known ideas elaborated by the schools of Gustav Schmoller and Georg Friedrich Knapp. The latter has already been mentioned in connection with the theory of the predominance of the manor in the early Middle Ages. Weber, as we have seen, disagreed with that school as far as this special concept is concerned. In contrast, he completely accepted their concept about the dissolution of the manorial system. Accordingly, later writers referred to the schools of Schmoller and Knapp rather than to Weber. We can, therefore, omit further consideration of the origin and spread of these theories.

Two phenomena that especially attracted the interest of Weber were the capitalistic development of the manor and the dissolution of the manorial system. The manor became powerful capitalistically as explained above. It produced for the market rather than remained self-sufficient. The development was different in the various parts of Europe. The more Slavic a district or the nearer to Slavic-speaking peoples, the more hereditary dependency developed as in Prussia, for example. To this situation in which the nobility gained power, the state rulers and especially centralized absolutism opposed. This was particularly true in Prussia and Austria. But this situation was merely one of the causes of the dissolution of the manorial system.

The essential causes of the dissolution of the manorial system were the interest of the centralized government, the increasingly complicated system of interdependency, and the interest of the newly established bourgeoisie. The latter promoted the disorganization of the manor because it limited the marketing opportunity of the bourgeoisie. Moreover, the not yet completely developed capitalism desired a so-called free labor market. These obstacles were supposed to be opposed by the manorial system through the attachment of the peasant to the soil.

Out of the convergence of these various factors originated the liberation of the peasant. This occurred in three different ways. The peasants were expropriated. This happened in a few parts of eastern Germany and especially in England. Though no legal emancipation of the peasants ever actually took place; rather the mere fact of the development of a market as such destroyed the manorial system from within. The peasants were expropriated in favor of the proprietor and became free without land.

The overlords were expatriated. This occurred in some parts of southern Germany and in a more rapid and radical way in France.

TABLE 4

Theories Concerning Rural Society in the Christian World

Theories	Accepted by Weber after elaboration by the following	Countries of these men	Elaborated by Weber	Men influenced by Weber	Countries of these Men
1. Cells:					
Origin, essence, and development of rural life	Seebohm	England	-	-	-
Christian monasticism contributing to non-nomadic life	Meitzen	Germany	-	-	-
Undemonstrability of Meitzen's Irish-Westphalian equalization	-	-	x	-	-
2. Slavs:					
Particulars concerning feudal development	Milyukov	Russia	-	-	-
Origin, essence, and development of the mir	Keussler Simkhovitsch Meitzen	Russia Russia Germany	-	-	-
Nonexistence of democratic character and community interest in the mir	-	-	x	-	-
Mir limiting the members freedom of movement	-	-	x	-	-
Origin, essence, and development of the zadruga	Meitzen	Germany	-	-	-
Zadruga administered by the village under legal compulsion	-	-	x	-	-
3. Germans:					
(1) Caesar's description of the Suebi as an exceptional situation	Fleischmann	Germany	-	-	-
New viewpoints concerning Caesar's distinction between the Suebi and other German tribes	-	-	x	Dopsch Gothein	Austria Germany
(2) Difference between Caesar and Tacitus; Caesar: migration; Tacitus: Two-field system	-	-	x	Dopsch Gothein	Austria Germany
(3) Use of the wild field grass husbandry system at the time of Christ	Seebohm	England	-	-	-
(4) Classification of forms of land partition, village location, and structure of rural houses according to nations	Meitzen	Germany	-	-	-
(5) New viewpoints concerning the undemonstrability of an original German rural communism	-	-	x	-	-

TABLE 4 (cont.)

Theories	Accepted by Weber after elaboration by the following	Countries of these men	Elab- orated by Weber	Men influenced by Weber	Countries of these men
(6) New viewpoints concerning the undemonstrability of an existence of the *Markgenossenschaft* earlier than the pre-Carolingian epoch	-	-	x	-	-
(7) New viewpoints concerning the theory of Caesar and Tacitus that the Germans were peasants rather than manorial lords	-	-	x	-	-
(8) Chieftains conquering land as one of the factors leading to feudalism	-	-	x	-	-
(9) New viewpoints concerning the theory of continuance of the Roman estate as one of the causes leading to feudalism	-	-	x	Oppenheimer Sombart Below Gothein Dopsch Vinogradoff	Germany Germany Germany Germany Austria Russia and England
(10) Independent peasants still in existence at the end of the early Middle Ages	Below	Germany	-	-	-
(11) Steadily improving status of tlse peasants from the 8th to the 12th century	Below	Germany	-	-	-
(12) Factors conducive to the Predominance of the manor	Below	Germany	-	-	-
(13) Essential differences between Antiquity and the Middle Ages. Colonization: Antiquity, by sea; Middle Ages, by land. Location: Antiquity, seashore; Middle Ages, interior. Feudalism: Antiquity, urban; Middle Ages, rural. Social struggle: Antiquity, land rent; Middle Ages, guilds vs. feudal lords	-	-	x	Oppenheimer Below Hazebroek	Germany Germany Gemnany
4. *Modern Western and Central Europe:*					
Capitalistic development of the manor	Schmoller's school	Germany	-	-	-
Dissolution of the manorial system	Knapp's school	Germany	-	-	-

The latter development was possible because the French landlord was a courtier noble who made his living in the army or in civil service positions. Thus no productive organization was destroyed but only a rent relation.

The peasant became free with a part of the land. This took place mostly in Prussia but not as far as the crownland peasants were concerned. Already in the eighteenth century the peasants on private holdings had largely become liberated. Here the state was compelled to lean upon its landed proprietors because it was too poor to replace them with salaried officials. Thus the kind of regulation was very favorable to the proprietors, and the peasants actually became rural proletarians. The situation of the Prussian peasants of his day as well as the status of the Russian peasants and even North American tenants greatly concerned Weber. He considered these interests and activities as belonging not to a theoretical and objective science of the history of agriculture but rather to practical rural economics and sociology. Accordingly it has been described by the author in two special articles.[33]

In recapitulation, Weber's participation in the development of the history of agriculture as far as the Christian world is concerned is summarized in table 4.

Weber's dependence on others, his originality, and his influence, and the reasons for these relationships, as summarized in the four recapitulation tables, show the following.

Weber made original contributions regarding every cultural group except the Etruscans, the Celts and modern Central and Western Europe.

With the exception of the Chinese, the Hindus, and the Slavs, his contributions have found adherents somewhere. His original contributions concerning the Hebrews, the Romans, and the Germans have been most widely accepted.

Weber accepted ideas elaborated by many more scholars than he himself influenced with his own theories. He unilaterally influenced some Americans such as N.S.B. Gras and W.L. Westermann and the Frenchman, Paul Louis. As to mutual influence he probably accepted more than he gave, and this is especially true of Ulrich Wilcken and Ludwig Mitteis. With Gustav Schmoller, Herman Gummerus, and most of all, Rostovtzeff, Weber's giving and accepting was about equal.

Weber received influences from many countries, especially British India, France, Italy, Imperial Russia, and Switzerland, which did not accept anything from him. He accepted much more from England than it did from him. He accepted as much from as he gave to Germany, Austria, and the United States.

With regard to the relationship between special cultures and the home countries of the scholars, Weber had mutual interrelationship with German scholars concerning almost every culture. His mutual influence with Austria was limited to classical antiquity and the Christian world. From the United States he accepted ideas concerning primitive peoples, the Hindus, Hellenism, and Rome, and gave theories concerning the latter.

The fact that Weber did not make original contributions concerning the Etruscans and the Celts is due to his feeling that he was not entitled to judge about matters when he was insufficiently familiar with the sources. As to modern Central Europe others had already completed historical work which he appreciated. Moreover, he felt compelled to deal with some recent phenomena from a political rather than a historical viewpoint. That his original contributions concerning the Chinese, the Hindus, and the Slavs did not receive attention may be attributed to the fact that other publications, written from other viewpoints, appeared a short time after his death or that the interest shifted to other aspects of the subjects. That his original contributions concerning the Hebrews, the Romans, and the Germans found the greatest acceptance is understandable. It was known that he conducted completely new investigations in which he made use of original sources. In many of these his approach or viewpoint was completely original.

With regard to other scholars, the fact that Weber was influenced by more than he himself influenced is self-evident. While his work was based on the results of the thinking of more than one century, only a little more than a quarter of a century has elapsed since his death. The special unilateral influence is explained by the age relation. The special mutual interrelationship is explained by the special interests of and studies made by the authors under consideration.

The nonacceptance of Weberian ideas in countries from which he had derived ideas may be explained in the following way. British India collected material for practical purposes but was less interested in theories. France was much positivistically and evolutionalistically minded and therefore not much interested in the ideas of a Neo-Kantian who denied the possibility of automatically occurring parallel development. In Italy and Russia a short time after his death independent and objective science disappeared. In England the number of scholars working in the field is relatively small. On the other hand, Weber scarcely dealt with England but rather with the Celtic-speaking districts of the British Isles. The mutual influence with Germany and Austria is self-evident. After the impoverishment of Europe and the rise of totalitarianism, the leadership in scientific studies shifted to the United States. This country, which had already given something to Europe, accepted many influences from the Old World.

The interrelationship between special cultures and the particular countries of the authors may be summarized as follows. German scholars during the epoch under consideration were active in the historical investigation of many cultures. Weber likewise was interested in many of them. Accordingly an interrelationship for many of them was inevitable. Austria was a country without colonies or much sea navigation. Interest in oversea cultures was accordingly not developed to a large extent. In contrast, Catholicism as well as its spiritual adversary, liberalism, let the intellectuals deal with the classic antiquity and the Middle Ages, and conforming to the relations existing with Germany they gave and accepted impulses from and to that country. The United States, a country where many intellectuals had an evolutionistic background, had a positive and productive interest in many cultures and made original contributions. Moreover American universities gave professorships to many outstanding Europeans in the historico-sociological fields, among them the refugee Rostovtzeff. The latter worked in the precise field in which Weber was considered especially outstanding. Before Rostovtzeff's emigration, these men had held each other in mutual esteem. Accordingly the continuance of Weber's influence on and through him into the United States is understandable.

These influences, exercised in many countries and especially in the United States, justifiy this extensive treatment of Max Weber as a historian of agriculture.

Notes

1. After the death of Weber almost all of his publications were collected by his widow, Marianne Weber, and published by J.C.B. Mohr at Tübingen. Those thus published are: *Wirtschaft und Gesellschaft (Grundriss der Sozialökonomik*, Abt. 3, 1922); *Gesammelte Aufsätze zur Religionssoziologie*, 3vols., 1921; *Gesammelte Aufsätze zur Sozial- und Wirtschaftsgeschichte*, 1924 (in this volume note especially Weber's *Agrarverhaltnisse in Altertum*, and his *Der Streit um den Charakter der Altgermanischen Sozialverfassung in der deutschen Literatur des letzten Jahrzehnts*); and *Gesammelte Aufsätze zur Wissenschaftslehre*, 1924. This last volume includes writings of an epistemological and methodological character which give the background of the man and provide the bases for some of our introductory remarks.

   Not included in the posthumous editions are *Die romische Agrargeschichte in ihrer Bedeutung für das Staats- und Privatrecht* (Stuttgart, F. Enke, 1891); and *Wirtschaftsgeschichte* (München, Leipzig, Duncker & Humblot, 1923), translated into English by Frank H. Knight under the title *General Economic History* (New York, 1927).

   The excellent translations of publications by Weber, *The Protestant Ethic and the Spirit of Capitalism*, by Talcott Parsons (New York, 1930), *The Theory of Social and Economic Organization*, by A.M. Henderson and Talcott Parsons (New York, 1947), and *From Max Weber: Essays in Sociology*, translated and edited by H.H. Gerth and C. Wright Mills (New York, 1946), are not of much importance with regard to Weber as a historian of agriculture. For Paul Honigheim's review of and objections to the latter book, see the *American Journal of Sociology*, 52:376-378 (1947). Paul Honigsheim, "Max Weber as Rural Sociologist," *Rural Sociology*, 11:207-218 (1946), includes a list of 21 other books and articles dealing with Weber. See also Marianna Weber, *Max Weber, ein Lebensbild*, (Tübingen, Mohr, 1926); *Lebenserinnerungen* (Bremen, 1948), and Paul Honigsheim's review of this book in the *American Journal of Sociology*, 55:102-104 (1949); Paul Honigsheim, "Max Weber as Applied Anthropologist," *Applied Anthropology*, 7:27-35 (1948).

   In this article citations to other authors are made only when the similarities and dissimilarities between their viewpoints and those of Weber appear distinctly.

   The following authors seemingly deal with the same matters in some of their books as Weber, but actually they do not mention him, even in their footnotes and bibliographies, and accordingly they can be omitted: Albert Edward Bailey, George A. Barton, Charles Bemont, Alexander D. Bilimovich, George C. Brodrick, P. Hume Brown, John Lossing Buck, Valentine Chirol, W.H.R. Curtler, A.V. Dicey, DeWitt-Mackenzy, Samuel Dill, H.H. Dodwell, Eleanor Shipley Ducket, W.E. Durret, George Dunbar, Joseph Dunn, Henry Courtenay Fenn, Gustave Glotz, Alexander Goldenweiser, L. Carrington Goodrich, Marcel

Granet, Howard L. Gray, Stephen Gwynn, Francis Hackett, Wolseley Haig, Chen Han-Seng, Leonard Egerton Hubbard, George Robert Hughes, Tom Ireland, Charles Foster Kent, Alexander F. Kerenskij, A.L. Kroeber, P.I. Lennox, Ralph Linton, Kate L. Mitchell, Gabriel Monod, H.V. Morton, George O'Brien, Albert Ten Eyck Olmstead, Lois Olson, Charles Oman, Walter Allison Phillips, John E. Pomfret, Marjorie and C.H.B. Quennel, Robert S. Rait, H.G. Rawlinson, P.E. Roberts, Geroid Tanquari Robinson, Abraham Leo Sacher, Grant Showerman, Alexander M. Sullivan, Edgar T. Thompson, Vladimir P.Timoshenko, Chi Tsui, Edward Raymond Turner, Lazar Volin, Milton Whitney, and Francis Yeats-Brown. The same is true of articles in the *Encyclopedia Americana*, the *Encyclopaedia Britannica*, the *Encyclopaedia of Religion and Ethics*, and the *Dictionary of Religion and Ethics*.

2.   For Weber's conclusions on pre-state society, see his *General Economic History*, 24-25, 28-39, 51-54, *Agrarverhaltnisse im Altertum*, 35, *Wirtschaft und Gesellschaft*, 205-207, and *Der Streit um den Character der Altgermanischen Sozialverlassung...*, 524.

For the pertinent views of others, see Sir Henry Sumner Maine, *Village-Communities in the East and West* (New York, 1880), 1-203, *Ancient Law* (Amer. ed. 3 from the London ed. 5, New York, 1888), 251, and *Lectures on the Early History of Institutions* (New York, 1878), 81; Adolf Bastian, *Die Völker des öslichen Asien*, 5:viii (Jena, 1869), *Das Bestandige in den Menschenrassen und der Spielweite ihrer Veranderlichkeit* (Berlin, 1868), *Der Papua des dunkeln Inselreiches* (Berlin, 1885), *Der Buddhismus als religions-philosophisches System* (Berlin, 1893), 9, and *Ideale Welten nach uranographischen Provinzen in Wort und Bild* (Berlin, 1892), 2:254; Carl Bucher, *Industrial Evolution* (New York, 1901); Eduard Hahn, *Von der Hacke zum Pflug* (Leipzig, 1914), 11-23, and "Waren die Menschen der Urzeit zwischen der Jagerstufe und der Stufe des Ackerbaus Nomaden?" *Das Ausland*, 64:485-487 (Stuttgart, 1891), and *Das Alter der Wirtschaftlichen Kultur der Menschheit* (Heidelberg), 1905), 91-99, 131; Lewis H. Morgan, *Ancient Society* (New York, 1877), *passim*; Friedrich Engels, *Der Ursprung der Familie, des Privateigentums, und des Staats* (ed. 11, Stuttgart, n.d.), xi-xv, 1-47, 105-131; August Bebel, *Die Frau und der Sozialismus* (Stuttgart, 1919), 9-14, 28-56; *Doctrine de St.Simon*, nouvelle ed. par C. Bougle et E. Halevy (Paris, 1924), 214-216; C. Bougle, *Proudhon* (Paris, 1930), 122-124; Robert H. Lowie, *An Introduction to Cultural Anthropology* (New York, 1940), 45-53 and "Subsistence," in *General Anthropology*, ed. by Franz Boas (Boston, 1938), 282-322; Gladys A. Reichard, "Social Life," in ibid., 416-417;, Ludwig Gumplowicz, *Ausgewahlte Werke*, (Innsbruck, 1926-28), 2:94-105, 4:225-227; Franz Oppenheimer, *System der Sociology*, 2:212-303, 321-328 (Jena, 1926), 3:146-152 (ed. 5, Jena, 1923). See the review of and the objections to this concept by Paul Honigsheim, "Viehzüchternomadismus, Bodenrente, Reichtumsbildung, Staatsgründung," *Kolner Vierteljahrshefte für Soziologie*, 9:38-86); J.J. Backofen, *Der Mythus von Orient und Occident* (München, 1926), *passim*;

Ludwig Klages, *Vomkosmogonischen Eros* (ed.2, Jena, 1926), 236-246, and *Der Geist als Widersacher der Seele*, 3:888-923 (Leipzig, 1932); Bernhard Ankermann,"Kulturkreise in Africa," *Zeitschrift für Ethnologie*, vol. 37 (Berlin, 1908); Fritz Graebner,"Ethnologie,"*Anthropologie: Die Kultur der Gegenwart, ihre Entwickelung und ihre Ziele*, 3(5):447-521 (Leipzig, 1923); Wilhelm Schmidt and Wilhelm Koppers, *Gesellschaft und Wirtschaft der Volker* (Regensburg, 1924), 256-297, 539-589; Oswald Menghim, *Weltgeschichte der Steinzeit* (Wein, 1931), 498-499, 510-514, 523-526; and Sylvester A. Sieber and Franz H. Mueller, *The Social Life of Primitive Man* (St. Louis, 1941), 192-258, 369-398. On this last book see Paul Honigsheim's review and objections in the *American Sociological Review*, 6:898-902 (1941).

3. For recent discussions of evolutionism and antievolutionism, see Paul Honigsheim, "The Problem of Diffusion and Parallel Evolution with Special Reference to American Indians," Michigan Academy of Science, Arts, and Letters, *Papers*, 27:515-524 (Ann Arbor, 1942); Leslie A. White,"History, Evolutionism, and Functionalism," *Southwestern Journal of Anthropology*, 1:221-248 (Albuquerque, 1945), "Morgan's Attitude toward Religion and Science," *American Anthropologist*, 46;218-230), and"Diffusion vs. Evolutionism, an Anti-Evolutionist Fallacy," ibid., 47:339-356 (1945); Robert H. Lowie,"Evolution in Cultural Anthropology,"ibid., 48:223 (1946).

4. For the history of the theories, see A. Bauemler, "Einleitung," in Bachofen, *Der Mythus von Orient und Occident*, xc-ccxciv; Karl Albrecht Bernoulli, *Johann Jakob Bachofen und das Natursymbol* (Basel, 1924), 95-177, 364-377; Georg Schmidt, *Johann Jakob Bachofens Geschichtsphilosophie* (München, 1929); Peter Heinrich Schmidt, *Wirtschaftsforshung und Geographie* (Jena, 1925), 117-130; Wilhelm Koppers,"Die ethnologische Wirtschaftsforschung,"*Anthropos*, 10:627-645 (Wein, 1915), 11:975-981 (1916); and the following articles by Paul Honigsheim,"Eduard Hahn und seine Stellung in der Geschichte der Ethnologie und Soziologie," ibid., 24:597-601 (1929),"Die geistes geschichtliche Stellung der Anthropologie, Ethnologie, Urgeschichte und ihrer Hauptrichtungen," *Festschrift, Publication d'hommage offerte au P.W. Schmidt*, ed. by W. Koppers (Wein, 1928), 851-855,"Adolf Bastian und die Entwicklung der ethonolgischen Soziologie," *Kölner Vierteljahreshefte für Soziologie*, 6:61-76 (München, 1926),"Soziologische Fragestellungen in der gegenwartigen prähistorischen und ethnologischen Literatur,"ibid., 7:331-343, 427-446 (1928-1929),"Ein Wort zu Adolph Bastians 100. Geburtstag," *IPEK; Jahrbuch für prähistorische und ethnographische Kunst* (Leipzig, 1927), 2:28-91, "Kulturkreislehre, prähistorisch-ethnologische Zusammenhänge und primitive Kunst,"ibid., 123-132 (1929), and"The Philosophical Background of European Anthropology,"*American Anthropologist*, 44:376-387 (1942). In these historical articles otherpublications under consideration are listed.

5. Weber, *Gesammelte Aufsätze zür Religionssoziologie*, 1:20, 350-351, 379; Franz Heinrich Reusch, *Der Index der verbotenen Bücher* (Bonn, 1883-85), 2:771-774; Jacques Crétineau-Joly, *Histoire religieuse, politique et littéraire de la Compagnie de Jesus* (Paris, Lyon, 1845-46), 3:141-178, 5:39-68, 320-328; C.L. Montesquieu, *Oeuvres completes* (Paris, 1875-79), 3:279-82, 333, 4:334-335; Francois Marie Arouet de Voltaire, *Oeuvres completes* (nouvelle ed., Paris, 1877-85), 11:54-59, 164-81, 12:58, 167,431,432,13:167, 18:156-58, 360, 19:368, 40:304, 41:402, 47:292; Denis Diderot, *Oeuvres completes*, ed. by J. Assezat (Paris, 1875-77), 4:45-47, 6:697-446, 14:122, 126, 141; "Gablentz," *Allgemeine Deutsche Biographie*, 8:286-288 (Leipzig, 1878), and 50:548-555 (Leipzig, 1905); J. Lessing "F.W.K. Müller," *Zeitschrift der deutschen morgenländischen Gesellschaft* (Berlin), 62:344-345; Richard Wilhelm, *Ostasien* (Potsdam, 1928), 11-38; Karl August Wittfogel, *Wirtschaft und Gesellschaft Chinas* (Leipzig, 1931), 73, 101-103, 110, 395, 495, which cites the passages in the publications of Karl Marx and Engels concerning Chinese agriculture; Schmidt and Koppers, *Gesellschaft und Wirtschaft der Völker*, 341-342, 350, 596, 604-606, 610-611, 620; Sieber and Muller, *The Social Life of Primitive Man*, 425-427, 449, 464-468; Oswald Menghin, *Weltgeschichte der Steinzeit*, 475, 524-526, and "Zür Steinzeit Ostasiens," *Festschrift, Publication d'hommage offerte au P.W. Schmidt*, 908-942; Paul Leser, "Westoestliche Landwirtschaft," ibid., 416-484, and *Entstehung und Verbreitung des Pfluges* (Münster, 1931), 384-411, 503-515, 540, 565. See also Paul Honigsheim's evaluation of Leser's book in *Zeitschrift für Sozialforschung*, 1:232-233 (Leipzig, 1932).
6. Weber, *General Economic History*, 62, and *Gesammelte Aufsätze zur Religionssoziologie*, 2;297-300.
7. Weber, *General Economic History*, 22-23, and *Gesammelte Aufsätze zur Religionssoziologie*, 126-130, 160 n.4, 215-216, 280-287; Reusch, *Der Index der verbotenen Bücher*, 2:774-777; Crétineau-Joly, *Histoire religieuse, politique et littéraire de la Compagnie de Jesus*, 1:152-193, 398-374, 5:1-38; Montesquieu, *Oeuvres complètes*, 5:218; Voltaire, *Oeuvres complètes*, 15:325-326, 21:430, 29;484, 45:468, 49:458; Diderot, *Oeuvres complètes*, 13:378; Georg Wilhelm Friedrich Hegel, *Vorlesungen über die philosophie der Geschichte*, Tiel I, Abschnitt 2 in every edition, and Vorlesungen über die Geschichte der Philosophie, Orientalische Philosophie, B, Indische Philosophie, in every edition; Arthur Schopenhauer, *Die Welt als Wille und Vorstellung* (ed. 8, Leipzig, 1891), 1:333, 419-421, 450-454, 458, 470, 487, 2:529, 558, 576-578, 582-583, 697-699, 702, 705, 716-718, 728-729, 733; Maine, *Village-Communities*, 1-175; C. Bouglé, *Essais sur le régime des castes* (Paris, 1927), *passim*; J. Hertel, "Eugen Hultsch," *Zeitschrift der deutschen morgenländischen Gesellschaft* (Berlin), 82:49-54.
8. Weber, *Agrarverhältnisse im Altertum*, 45-83, 283; Theodor Mommsen, *The History of Rome* (New York, 1868), 2:16-30; Fustel de Coulanges, *The Ancient City* (Boston, Many ed.); Gaston Maspero, *History of Egypt, Chaldea, Syria, Babylonia and Assyria* (London, 1901), 2:56-57, 62-64,

76-77, 3:267, 4:313-317, 7:13-14; Sir John Gardner Wilkinson, *The Manners and Customs of the Ancient Egyptians* (Boston, 1883), 1:279, 372, 2:388-389; Oppenheimer, *System der Sociologie*, 2:620, 4:364, n.9 (Jena, 1929); M. Rostovtzeff, *A History of the Ancient World*, 1:17-20 (Oxford, 1926).

See also the articles on"Albanier,""Hettiter,""Indogermanen,""Karer," "Kreta,""Ligurer,"" Lydia,""Mykenae,""Raeter,""Skyten," and"Traker" in *Real-Encyclopedia der classischen Altertunwissenschaft*, ed. by A.F. Pauly And G. Wissowa (Stuttgart, 1894-1940), and in *Reallexikon der Vorgeschichte*, ed. by M. Ebert, vol. 1-15 (Berlin, 1924-1932). See also Honigsheim,"Viehzeuchternomadismus...,"279.

On the history of the excavations, deciphering, and theories, see Fritz Hommel, *Geschichte Babyloniens und Assyriens* (Berlin, 1885), 59-146; Johannes Duemichen and E. Meyer, *Geschichte des altem Aegyptens* (Berlin, 1887), 267-317; Morris Jastrow, *The Civilization of Babylonia and Assyria* (Philadelphia and London, 1925), 1-119; and J. Friedrich, "Hethitisch und kleinasiatische Sprachen," *Grundrisse der Indogermanischen Sprach- und Altertumskunde, Abteilung Geschichte der Indogermanischen Sprachwissenschaft* (Berlin, 1931), II, Teil 5, Band 4. 9. Weber, *Agrarverhältnisse im Altertum*, 83-93, *Gesammelte Aufsätze zur Religionssoziologie*, 10, 15-16, 21, 44, 76 n.i, 77, 293-294, 360, and *Wirtschaft und Gesellschaft*, 352; Werner Sombart, *Der moderne Kapitalismus* (ed. München, Leipzig, 1921), l: 898-919, *Die Juden und das Wirtschaftsleben* (Leipzig, 1911), 183-434, *Der Bourgeois* (München, Leipzig, 1913), 299-302, 337-348; and Paul Honigsheim,"The Roots of the Nazi Concept of the Ideal German Peasant,"*Rural Sociology*, 12:11-12 (1947), where other publications under consideration are listed. Weber's letters concerning Protestant orthodoxy and liberalism are in his *Jugendbriefe* (Tübingen, n.d.), 20, 44, 52, 66, 106, 170, 196, 204, 224, 300, 334, 343, 348. See also Paul Honigsheim,"Max Weber: His Religious and Ethical Background and Development,"this volume.

10. Weber, *Agrarverhaltnisse im Altertum*, 190-191.

The scholars who advocated the Indo-European and especially the Italic character of the Etruscans are: Mommsen, *The History of Rome*, 1:166-169; Wilhelm Paul Corssen, *Uber die Sprache der Etrusker* (Leipzig, 1874-75), esp. 2:566-568, 577-579; and George Hempl, *Mediterranean Studies No. IV* (Stanford University Publications, University Series, Language and Literature, vol. 3, no.3, Stanford, 1932).

Those advocating the non-Indo-European, and especially the eastern Mediterranean, origin are: Karl Otfried Müller, *Die Etrusker* (Breslau, 1828), 69, 75, 100-101, 375, 403-404; Bachofen, *Der Mythus von Orient und Occident*, 539-560, 595, 599; Wilhelm Deecke, *Corssen und die Sprache der Etrusker* (Stuttgart, 1875), and *Etrusker Forschungen*, n. 1-6 (Stuttgart, 1875, and later), esp. no.l, p. 36-37, 77, no.2, p. 144-145, no.3, p. 389; Carl Pauli, *Etruskische Studien* (Göttingen, 1879-1880), esp. no.3, p. 5-6; Fritz Weege, *Etruskische Malerei* (Halle, 1921), 62, 67; Hans

Mühlestein, *Die Kunst der Etrusker* (Berlin, 1929), 13-39, and *Uber die Herkunft der Etrusker* (Berlin, 1929); Fritz Schachermeyr, *Etruckische Frühgeschichte* (Berlin, 1929), 88-89, 114-115, 202, 216-217, 252; Oppenheimer, *System der Soziology*, 2:274, 4:95-96, 105-106, 112-113, 169; David Randall-MacIver, *The Etruscans* (Oxford, 1927), 11; Léon Homo, *Primitive Italy and the Beginnings of Roman Imperialism* (London, 1926), 55-57; Howard H. Scullard, *A History of the Roman World from 753 to 146 B.C.* (New York, 1939), 17; and Honigsheim, "Viehzeuchternomadismus...,"79-80. In doubt was Bartolomeo Nogara, *Les Étrusques et leur civilisation* (Paris, 1936), 16.

For the history of the theories, see Corssen, *Uber die sprache der Etrusker*, Introduction in vol. 1; Eva Fiesel, "Etruskieche," *Grundrisse der Indogermanischen Sprach- und Altertumskunde, Abteilung Geschichte der Indogermanischen Sprachwissenschaft*, Teil 2, Band 5, no. 1 (1931); "Corssen," *Allgemeine Deutsche Biographie*, 4:504-505 (Leipzig, 1876); "Deecke," *ibid.*, 47:636-637 (Leipzig, 1930); G. Deeters, "Gustav Herbig," *Zeitschrift der deutschen moegenländischen Gesellschaft* (Berlin), 5:189-201.

11. Weber, *Agrarverhaltnisse im Altertum*, 3, 12-16, 32, 93-154, and *Wirtschaft und Gesellschaft*, 555, 562, 566, 572, 583-601; Oppenheimer, *System der Sociologie*, 2:623-624; J. Hazebroek, *Griechische Wirtschafts- und Gesellschaftsgeschichte* (Tübingen, 1931), vii, 586, 589; Georg von Below, "Agrargeschichte," *Handwoerterbuch der Staatswissenschaften* (ed. 4, Jena, 1927), 49; Rostovtzeff, *A History of the Ancient World*, l:218-226; Gustav Schmoller, *Grundrisse der Allgemeinen Volkswirtschaftslehre* (Leipzig, 1904), 2:500.

12. Weber, *Agrarverhältnisse im Altertum*, 154-190, especially 185.
Weber considered the following basic: Ulrich Wilcken, *Griechische Ostraka aus Aegypten und Nubien* (Leipzig, Berlin, 1899); Rostovtzeff, "Kornerhebung und Transport im griechisch-roemischen Egypten," *Archiv für Papyrusforschung*, vol. 3 (Berlin, 1916), and "Der Ursprung des Kolonats," *Klio*, vol. 1 (Berlin, 1901). Weber's concept was accepted by Oppenheimer, *System der Sociology*, 4:364, n.8; and Ludwig Mitteir and Ulrich Wilcken, *Grundzuege und Chrestomatie der Papyruskunde*, 1:255, n.l (Berlin, Leipzig, 1912). Weber's concept was rejected in ibid., 1:184 n.4, 258 n.2, 336 n.l, 339; and Rostovtzeff, *Studien zur Geschichte des römischen Kolonats (Beiheft zum Archiv für Papyrusforschung*, Leipzig, Berlin, 1914), 403. The publications by Rostovtzeff which do not mention Weber and which are not mentioned by him are: "Angariae," *Klio*, vol. 4 (1906); "Alexandria and Rhodos," *ibid.*, vol. 36 (1936); *Caravan Cities* (Oxford, 1932); *Out of the Past of Greece and Rome* (New Haven, 1932); "Zur Geschichte des Ost- und Suedhandels im Ptolemaeischen Egypten," *Archiv für Papyrusforschung*, vol. 4 (1908). Tenney Frank, *An Economic History of Rome to the End of the Republic* (Baltimore, 1920), 379-387, is based on Rostovtzeff. On the whole problem, see William Linn Westermann, "Egyptian Agricultural Labor under Ptolemy Philadelphus," *Agricultural History*, 1:34-47 (July 1927). For the history of

discovery, investigation, and theories, see Mitteis and Wilcken, *Grundzuege und Chrestomatie der Papyruskunde*, i-xxvii; and Wilcken, *Observations ad historiam Aegypti provinciae Romanae* (Dissertation inauguralis, Berlin, 1885), 5-7.

13. Weber, *Die römische Agrargeschichte*, 3, 10, 49-52, 119-121, 140-141, 219, 227-275, *Agrarverhältnisse im Altertum*, 191-278, *Der Streit um den Charakter der altgermanischen Sozialverfassung...*, 296-311; Mommsen, *The History of Rome*, l:256-258, 564, 3:489.

Weber considered (*Agrarverhältnisse im Altertum*, 286) basic the theories developed by Rostovtzeff in his "Der Ursprung des Kolonats," *Klio*, vol.1 (Berlin, 1901), "Geschichte der Staatspacht in der roemischen Kaiserzeit," *Philologus*, supplement 9 (Leipzig, 1901), and *Studien zur Geschichte des roemischen Kolonats*, 133.

Weber's concepts as explained in *Die römische Agrargeschichte*, 119-21, 128, 135-259, were accepted by Rostovtzeff, *Studien zur Geschichte des roemischen Kolonats*, vi, n.1, 306, 313 n.1, 317 n.1; Herman Gummerus, *Der römische Gutsbetrieb als Wirtschaftlicher Organismus nach den Werken des Cato, Varro und Columella (Beiträge zur alten Geschichte, Beiheft 5, leipzig, 1906)*, 9-11, 18020; Mitteis and Wilcken, *Grundzuege und Chrestomatie der Papyruskunde*, 1:257 n.1, 259, 265 n.1.

Weber's concepts as explained in *Die römische Agrargeschichte*, 130-132, 140, 185-186, 224, 245, 246, 252, were rejected by Gummerus, *Der römische Gutsbetrieb*, 59, Mitteis and Wilcken, *Grundzuege und Chrestomatie der Papyruskunde*, 1:283 n.4, 342 n.5; and Rostvotzeff, *Studien zur Geschichte des roemischen Kolonats*, 316, 422 n.198.

A parallel development of ideas by Weber and Rostovtzeff appears in *ibid.*, vii, and *A History of the Ancient World*, 2:98, 231, 296-297, 351-366.

Weber is not mentioned in Rostovtzeff, "Das Patrimonium und die Ratio Thesaurorum," *Mitteilungen des Kgl. Deutsch. Archaeologischen Instituts* (Roem. Abt. vol. 13, Rome, 1893).

The theories of Weber and Rostovtzeff were accepted to a large extent by Oppenheimer, *System der Sociologie*, 4:325-406; Below, "Agrargeschichte," 50-52; Sombart, *Der moderne Kapitalismus*, 1:41-42; Alfons Dopsch, *The Economic and Social Foundations of European Civilization* (New York, 1937), 137, 337; N.S.B. Gras, *A History of Agriculture in Europe and America* (New York, 1940), 56-57, 65, and his "Agriculture in Antiquity and the Middle Ages," *Encyclopaedia of the Social Sciences*, l:574-576 (New York, 1930); Paul Louis, "Agrarian Movements: Classical Antiquity," *ibid.*, 494' André Pigariol, "Latifundia," *ibid.*, 9;186-188 (1933); William Linn Westermann, "Slavery: Ancient," *ibid.*, 14:75 (1934); Paul Vinogradoff, *The Growth Of the Manor* (London, 1920), 37-87, 103, 106; Tenney Frank, *Roman Imperialism* (New York, 1921), 93, 108, 236, 241.

Although Weber is not mentioned, the theories of Rostovtzeff are accepted, although in part with some restrictions, in the following:

E.G. Hardy, *Some Problems in Roman History*, (Oxford, 1924); H.J. Haskell, *The New Deal in Old Rome* (New York, 1939), 202-204, with restrictions; Bernard W. Henderson, *Five Roman Emperors* (Cambridge, England, 1927), 228-245; Thomas Rice Holmes, *The Architect of the Roman Empire* (Oxford, 1928-1931); Frank Burr Marsh, *The Reign of Tiberius* (Oxford, 1931); H.St.L.B. Moss, *The Birth of the Middle Ages, 395-814* (Oxford, 1935), A.M.D. Parker, *A History of the Roman World* (New York, 1929), 119-128, 288-289; Edward Kennard Rand, *The Building of Eternal Rome* (Cambridge, Mass., 1943); Scullard, *A History of the Roman World*, 371-365.

Neither Weber nor Rostovtzeff are cited in Homo, *Primitive Italy and the Beginnings of Roman Imperialism*, 219-226, and Frank Burr Marsh, *The Founding of the Roman Empire* (Austin, Texas, 1922), 33-38, notwithstanding the fact that they formulate similar ideas.

14. Weber, *General Economic History*, 11, 15-16; Samuel Johnson, *Letters of Samuel Johnson*, ed. by George Birkbeck Hill (New York, 1892), 1:255-260; James Boswell, *Boswell's Life of Johnson*, ed. by Chauncey Brewster Tinker (New York, 1933), 1:442, 547, 549, 551, 557, 582-582, 2:34, 83, 179-180, 438, 469, 519, and *Boswell's Journal of a Tour to the Hebrides with Samuel Johnson* (New York, 1936), *passim*, and *Letters of James Boswell*, ed. by Chauncey Brewster Tinker (Oxford, 1924), 1:204, 208-211, 228; Johann Gottfried von Herder, *Herders sämmtliche Werke*, ed. by Bernhard Suphan (Berlin, 1877-1913), 4:231, 320-325, 5:159-208, 330-334, 416-420, 8:391-392, 9:317, 542-543, 11:296, 14:261-266, 16:88, 18:450-462, 27:301-306; Johann Wolfgang von Goethe, *Dichtung und Wahrheit*, Teil w, Buch 13, in every ed.; Albert Bielschowsky. *Goethe* (ed.23, München, 1911-12), 1:117, 120; Richard M. Meyer, *Goethe* (ed.3, Berlin, 1905), 1:46, 144-145; Herman Grimm, *Goethe* (ed.2, Berlin, 1880), 152; Voltaire, *Oeuvres complètes*, 6:160-161, 18: 106-108, 19: 178; Diderot, *Oeuvres complètes*, 6: 433; "Zeuss," *Allgemeine Deutsche Biographie*, 45: 132-136 (Leipzig, 1900); Heinrich Zimmer, *Sprache und Literatur der Kelten im Allgemeinen*,"Die Kultur der Gegenwart, Teil I, Abt. xi, 1 (Berlin, Leipzig, 1909), 74-75; K. Meyer,"Die irisch-gaelisch Literatur,"Ibid., 78-95; C. Stern,"Die schottisch-gaelisch und die Manx-Literatur,"Ibid., 99-102, and"Die kornische und die bretonische Literatur,"Ibid., 134-137; Morgan, Die Urgesellschaft, 301-303; Engels, *Der Ursprung der Familie*, 132-135; Maine, *Village-Communities*, 186-187 and *Ancient Law*, 5-6, 12; Frederic Seebohm, *The English Village Community* (London, 1915), 118-119, 236-237, 244, 369, 422, 428; August Meitzen, *Siedelungen und Agrarwesen der Westgermanen und Ostgermanen, der Kelten, Römer, Finen, und Slaven* (Berlin, 1895), 1: 174-232; 3: 236-237, 557; and "Beobachtungen über Besiedelung, Hausbau und landwirtschaftliche Kultur," *Anleitung zur Deutschen Landes und Volksforschung*, ed. by A. Kirchhoff (Stuttgart, 1889), 481-496; Dopsch, *The Economic and Social Foundations of European Civilization*, 110-112, 122-123; E. Gothein,"Agrargeschichte," *Die Religion in Geschichte und*

Gegenwart, ed. by Friedrich Michael Schiele, 1: 238 (Tübingen, 1909), 288; N. S. B. Gras, *The Economic and Social History of an English Village* (Cambridge, Mass., 1930), 3, *An Introduction to Economic History* (New York, 1922), 65, and "Agriculture in Antiquity and the Middle Ages," *Encyclopaedia of the Social Sciences*, I: 574-5777; M. M. Knight, "Serfdom," Ibid., 670; E. Lipson, *An Introduction to the Economic History of England* (London, 1926), 75-76; Vinogradoff, *The Growth of the Manor*, 18, 24, 35-36, 91 n. 20; Nellie Neilson, *Medieval Agrarian Economy* (New York, 1936).

15. Christian von Schlözer, *August Ludwig von Schlözers öffentliches und Privatleben*, 2: 249 (Leipzig, 1828); Ferdinand Frensdorff, "Von und über Schlözer," *Abhandlungen der Kgl. Gesellschaft der Wissenschaft zu Göttlingen* (Philos.-Hist. Klasse, Neue Folge, v. 11, Berlin, 1909), 98-101; Friederike Fürst, *August Ludwig von Schlözer* (Heidelberg, 1928), 191, esp. n. 1; August von Haxthausen, *Die ländliche Verfassung Russlands* (Leipzig, 1868), and *The Russian Empire*, I: 93-115, 120-140, 2: 202 (London, 1856); J. Kirejewski, *Drei Essays* (München, 1921), 129-139; *Gesellschaft und Staat im Spiegel deutscher Romantik*, ed. by Jacob Baxa (Jena, 1924)), 177, 431, 483-485; Friedrich Wilhelm von Schelling, *Schriften zur Gesellschaftsphilosophie* (Jena, 1926), 206-251, 375-389, 463-464, 716-720, 777-802; Franz von Baader, *Schriften zur Gesellschaftsphilosophie* (Jena, 1925), 1-452; F. M. Dostojewski, *Politische Schriften* (München, 1923), 134-153, 177, 189, 199-200, 221-232, 282-287; the following titles and volumes in *The Complete Works* (Boston, 1914) by Count Leo Tolstoi, *Moral Tales*, 12: 327-519, *My Confession*, 13: 3-90, *The Four Gospels*, 14: 207-302, esp. ch. 4, *What Shall We Do Then?* 17: 3-340, *On Life*, 20: 318-405, ch. 21-34, and *Resurrection*, v. 21-22.

On the Narodniki movement and the Social Revolutionaries, see Lancelot A. Owen, *The Russian Peasant Movement* (London, 1937), 89, 122 n. 2, 182, 246; Vladimir J. Gurko, *Features and Figures of the Past* (Stanford, 1939), 590 n. 8, 618 n. 6, 623 n. 2; and Alfred Levin, *The Second Duma* (New Haven, 1940), 34-37.

Maine, *Ancient Law*, 125, and *Lectures on the Early HIstory of Institutions*, 2, 7, 81; Engels, *Der Ursprung der Familie*, 45; P. Kropotkin, *Mutual Aid: A Factor in Evolution* (New York, 1925), 97, 99, 137, and *Ideas and Realities in Russian Literature* (New York, 1919), 266-270, 276; J. von Keussler, *Zur Geschichte und Kritik des bäuerlichen Gemeindebesitzes in Russland* (Riga, St. Petersburg, 1876-1887); Konstantin D. Kawelin, *Der bäuerliche Gemeinbesitz in Russland* (Leipzig, 1877), *passim*; Maxime M. Kovalevsky, *Modern Customs and Ancient Laws of Russia* (London, 1891), 730118; Isaac A. Hourwich, *the Economy of the Russian Village* (New York, 1892), 19-27, 37-42, 90-103; Wladimir G. Simkhowitsch, *Die Feldgemeinschaft in Russland* (Jena, 1898), 11-70; Paul N. Milyoukow, *Russia and Its Crisis* (Chicago, 1905), 366-423; Nikolai P. Oganowski, "Die Agrarfrage in Russland seit 1905," *Archiv für Sozialwissenschaft und Sozialpolitik*, vol. 37 (Tübingen, 1913); Alexis S. Yermoloff, *La Russie agricole devant la crise agraire* (Paris, 1907), 9-20; Ferdinand von Wrangel, "Die agrare Neugestaltung Russlands," *Jahrbuch für Gesetzgebung, Verwaltung und Volkswirtschaft*, 36: 11-25 (München, Leipzig, 1912); Knud Asbjorn Wieth-Knudsen, *Bauernfrage und Agrareform in Russland* (München, Leipzig, 1913).

On the German youth movement, its relation to Dostoevsky, etc., see Howard Becker, *German Youth: Bond or Free* (New York, 1946). This book is reviewed by Paul Honigsheim in the *American Journal of Sociology*, 53: 159-160 (1947), and in *Die Friedenswarte*, 47: 209-210 (Zürich, 1947). See also Honigsheim, "The Roots of the Nazi Concept of the Ideal German Peasant," 16-19, where other publications under consideration are listed.

On the whole problem of the mir and the zadruga, see Honigsheim, "Rural Collectivities," in Charles P. Loomis and J. Allan Beegle (eds.), *Rural Social Systems* (New York, forthcoming), and "Roots of Soviet Rural Social Structure: Where and Why It Spreads," forthcoming.

16. Meitzen, *Siedelungen und Agrarwesen...*, 2:141-269, 3:341-354, 575, "Beobachtungen...," 495-496, "Kulturzustände der Slaven in Schlesien vor der deutschen Kolonisation," *Abhandlunger der Schlesischen Gesellschaft für vaterländische Kultur* (Philos.-Hist. Abteilung, v.2, Breslau, 1861), and "Die Ausbreitung der Deutschen in Deutschland und ihre Besiedelung der Slavengebiete," *Jahrbücher für Nationalökonomie*, v. 22. See the objections to Meitzen's concept concerning the boundaries between the Slavic and German rural settlement in Paul Honigsheim, "Der limes Sorabicus," *Zeitschrift für Thüringische Geschichte und Altertumjunde*, 24:303-332 (1906); this article lists the sources and other publications under consideration.

17. Weber, *General Economic History*, 17-21, and *Wirtschaft und Gesellschaft*, 720. See also Honigsheim, "Max Weber as Rural Sociologist," 214-217, where the publications of Weber concerning his attitude toward Social Revolutionaries, Stalypin, etc., are listed.

18. Weber, *General Economic History*, 11-12; Émile de Laveleye, *The Balkan Peninsula* (New York, 1887), 57, 227; Engels, *Der Ursprung der Familie*, 44; Meitzen, *Siedelungen und Agrarwesen...*, 2:213-218; Milan Markovic, *Die Serbische Hauskommunion* (Leipzig, 1903), *passim*; Dragolioub Novakovitch, *La Zadruga* (Paris, 1905), passim; Dinko Tomasic, *Personality and Culture in Eastern European Politics* (New York, 1948), 11, 149, 156. On this last book see Paul Honigsheim's review and objections in *Rural Sociology*, 14:182-183. (1949).

19. Weber, *Der Streit um den Charakter der Altgermanischen Sozialverfassung...*, 513, 522-523, 526, 529; W. Fleischmann, "Über die Landwirtschaftlichen Verhältnisse Germaniens um den Beginn unserer Zeitrechnung," *Journal für Landwirtschaft*, 51:92, 99 (Berlin, 1903); Dopsch, *The Economic and Social Foundations of European Civilization*, 82.

20. Weber, *Der Streit um den Charakter der altgermanischen Sozialverfassung...*, 543-544; Seebohm, *The English Village Community*, 344, 369; Dopsch,

The Economic and Social Foundations of European Civilization, 38-39; Gothein,"Agrargeschichte,"239.

21. Weber, *Der Streit um den Charakter der altgermanischen Sozialverfassung...*, 545; Seebohm, *The English Village Community*, 411; Fleischmann,"Über die landwirtschaftlichen Verhältnisse Germaniens...," 96; Below, "Agrargeschichte,"53; Dopsch, *The Economic and Social Foundations of European Civilization*, 38; Gothein, "Agrargeschichte," 240; Oppenheimer, *System der Sociology*, 4:254-262; Gras, *A History of Agriculture in Europe and America*, 96.

22. Weber, *Der Streit um den Charakter der altgermanischen Sozialverfassung...*, 520-521; Seebohm, *The English Village Community*, 371; Meitzen, *Siedelungen und Agrarwesen...*, 1:32-122, 3:236-237, 280-319, and"Das deutsche Haus in seinen volkstuemlichen Formen," *Verhandlungen des ersten deutschen Geographentages* (Berlin, 1882); Below, "Agrargeschichte," 53; Gothein, "Agrargeschichte,"240; Gras, *The Economic and Social History of an English Village*, 3; Lipson, *An Introduction to the Economic History of England*, 64-65, 75-76; Douglas-Irvine, *The Making of Rural Europe*, 19.

23. Weber, *General Economic History*, 23-24; Dopsch, *The Economic and Social Foundations of European Civilization*, 34; Engels, *Der Ursprung der Familie*, 137-146; Bebel, *Die Frau und der Sozialismus*, 65.

24. Weber, *General Economic History*, 7-8; Otto Gierke, *Das deutsche Genossenschaftsrecht*, 1:60-80 (Berlin, 1868); Meitzen, *Siedelungen und Agrarwesen der Westgermanen...*, 1:122-162; Below,"Agrargeschichte," 52-54; Dopsch, *The Economic and Social Foundations of European Civilization*, 47, 156; Engels, *Der Ursprung der Familie*, 155, 161; Bebel, *Die Frau und der Sozialismus*, 65.

25. Weber, *Der Streit um den Charkater der Altgermanischen Sozialverfassung...*, 511-554; Gierke, *Das deutsche Genossenschaftsrecht*, 1:28-60, 89-153; Seebohm, *The English Village Community*, 415; Meitzen, *Siedelungen und Agrarwesen...*, 1:4, 8, 10; Dopsch, *The Economic and Social Foundations of European Civilization*, 44-46, 112; Gothein,"Agrargeschichte,"238, 240, 246; Oppenheimer, *System der Soziologie*, 2:354, 388-89, 527, 537-539, 4:299-325; Charlotte M. Waters, *An Economic History of England*, 1066-1874 (London, 1925), introduction; Wilhelm Hasbach, *A History of the English Agricultural Labourer* (London, 1908), 1; Lipson, *An Introduction to the Economic History of England*, 10-11.

26. Weber, *Der Streit um den Charakter der altgermanischen Sozialverfassung...*, 538, 554.

27. *Ibid.*, 303-304, *Die römische Agrargeschichte*, 278, and *Agrarverhältnisse im Altertum*, 272-276; Seebohm, *The English Village Community*, 270, 314; Below"Agrargeschichte,"54; Dopsch, *The Economic and Social Foundations of European Civilization*, 54-55, 113, 164; Gothein, "Agrargeschichte," 243; Vinogradoff, *The Growth of the Manor*, 37-87; Lipson, *An Introduction to the Economic History of England*, 16-17; Douglas-Irvine, *The Making of Rural Europe*, 49; W.J. Ashley, *An Introduction to English Economic History and Theory* (London, 1923), 16-17; George

Caspar Homans, *English Villagers of the Thirteenth Century* (Cambridge, Mass., 1941), 30; Henri Pirenne, *Medieval Cities* (Princeton, 1925), 11; Ierne L. Plunket, *Europe in the Middle Ages* (Oxford, 1922); Charles Seignobos, *History of the Mediaeval and Modern Civilization to the End of the Seventeenth Century* (New York, 1907); Sombart, *Der moderne Kapitalismus*, 1: 41-42; Oppenheimer, *System der Soziologie*, 4: 325-406.

28. Weber, *Der Streit um den Charakter der altgermanischen Sozialverfassung...*, 509-510; Seebohm, *The English Village Community*, 308; Below, "Agrargeschichte," 53-54; Oppenheimer, *System der Soziologie*, 2: 549; Vinogradoff, *The Growth of the Manor*, 307-365.

29. Weber, *General Economic History*, 69; Below, "Agrargeschichte," 53-54; Oppenheimer, *System der Soziologie*, 2: 753.

30. Weber, *General Economic History*, 65-73; Below, "Agrargeschichte," 53-54; Oppenheimer, *System der Soziologie*, 2: 531.

31. Weber, *General Economic History*, 131, *Agrarverhältnisse im Altertum*, 3-6, 13, and *Der Streit um den Charakter der altgermanischen Sozialverfassung...*, 293; Below, "Agrargeschichte," 49; Oppenheimer, *System der Soziologie*, 2: 410 n. 1; Hazebroek, *Griechische Wirtschafts- und Gesellschaftsgeschichte*, 166. For the history of the theories, see Dopsch, *The Economic and Social Foundation...*, 1-29, and *Die Wirtschaftsentwickelung der Karolingerzeit* (Weimar, 1912), 1: 1-24; and Gustav Schmoller, *Deutsches Staedtewesen in älterer Zeit* (Bonn, Leipzig, 1922), 1-38.

32. Weber, *General Economic History*, 87-94, 98-106; Schmoller, *Grundriss der Allgemeinen Volkswirtschaftslehre*, 2: 518-531.

33. Paul Honigsheim, "Max Weber as Rural Sociologist," *Rural Sociology*, 11: 207-218 (1946), and "Max Weber as Applied Anthropologist," *Applied Anthropology*, 7: 27-35 (1948), where the publications of Weber concerning his attitude toward the Prussian, Russian, and North American peasants of his time are listed.

4

Max Weber: His Religious and Ethical Background and Development

In the last few decades, and especially since the excellent translations by Parsons and Gerth appeared, considerable discussion of Max Weber has taken place. Since only a few of his publications have been made accessible, the result has been an incomplete and oftentimes incorrect concept of the man. He is sometimes regarded as emphasizing almost exclusively the importance of the spiritual factor with regard to changes in the socioeconomic sphere. More frequently, he is regarded as one who deals with religious phenomena only in a rationalistic way. Both concepts of the man are equally wrong. Thus, it is my purpose to outline his basic religious, philosophical, and ethical convictions as well as the possible interrelationship between such ideas and his investigations.

An understanding of Weber's religio-ethical personality is to be sought in four kinds of sources: (1) remarks in letters and correspondence; (2) remarks in the last two speeches delivered a short time before his death; (3) information given by Weber's widow, Marianne Weber in her publications dealing with her husband; and (4) reminiscences of the writer, who knew Weber intimately. The present paper is based on these sources. Weber's philologico-historical investigations of religious documents (e.g., the Old Testament) do not enter the scope of this paper, due to lack of space. This paper, therefore, restricts itself to the religious convictions and the ethical principles inextricably connected with them. Since we are dealing with a complex personality—a human being with concern for his own development—a short biographical sketch of Weber's environmental influences, as well as his intellectual, professional, and literary development is indispensable. Only those biographical features, of course, which have a bearing upon our central problem will be outlined here.[1]

Biographical Background

Weber was the son of an academically trained municipal politician and Reichstag deputy. His father was a member of the national-liberal party, a movement which represented the right wing of economic liberalism. This party was supported largely by the powerful industrialists, and it supported Bismarck's anti-Catholic and anti-socialist policies as well as his foreign policies. But the Weber household also was frequented by members of the progressive parties. The "progressives" were liberals who refused to support Bismarck, and advocated, in part, a combination of democracy and state socialism. This political antagonism between Bismarckian and anti-Bismarckian liberals was one of the first antagonisms which young Weber had to face. Another antagonism was to be found within the family itself. Weber's mother, compared with the average wife of an intellectual of that generation, was relatively orthodox religiously. Weber's father, like other national liberals of the time, was little interested in religion and at best could be called an indifferent "liberal" Protestant.

The same political and religious antagonisms had to be reconciled by Weber when he became a student of law, economics, history, and philosophy of the Universities of Strassburg, Heidelberg, and Berlin. He was a pupil of Mommsen,[2] at that time the best known historian of Roman antiquity and simultaneously a strong anti-Bismarckian politician. At the same time, he was a frequent guest of his uncle Hermann Baumgarten, an outstanding national-liberal writer and admirer of Bismarck. He discussed religious problems with his cousin Otto Baumgarten and with another uncle, Adolph Hausrath, professor of church history at the University of Heidelberg. Both Hausrath and Otto Baumgarten were pronounced bibliocritical, "liberal" Protestants. Weber definitely turned to their position at this time, but he did not yet buttress it epistemologically. This he began to do somewhat later, in Freiburg.

After a short period when he earned his living as a lawyer in Berlin and simultaneously taught Roman law and its history as an unsalaried instructor (*Privatdozent*) at the University of Berlin, he was called to Freiburg as full professor of economics. The teaching load of a German professor being small, he now had time to finish his work on the history of agriculture and rural life,[3] which another teacher, August Meitzen, had urged him to undertake. Here in Freiburg (as well as in Heidelberg[4] where he was soon called to a similar position) he came into contact with adherents of the South German Neo-Kantian school. Among them were Rickert, the son of an outstanding deputy of one of the "progressive" parties, and Lask, primarily epistemologists and logicists; Jellinek and Radbruch, philosophers of law; Windelband, historian of philosophy; and finally Troeltsch, historian and philosopher of religion. At this time Weber formulated his own philosophy, which was a synthesis of Protestant religiosity, Neo-Kantian epistemology and ethics, and left-wing, socially minded liberalism. Due to a nervous breakdown precipitated by overwork, Weber was obliged to withdraw from teaching and political activity in Heidelberg and to concentrate on writing. Consequently his main works in the fields of epistemology, general sociology, and sociology of religion were written at this time[5]. Although he did not teach, he continued to have younger friends and students around him. Among them were many Russian revolutionaries. They had been persecuted in their own country but were accepted in the University of Heidelberg, which at that time was among the most liberal universities of Germany. The fact that Russians of various points of view constituted an important element in the atmosphere of Heidelberg of these days is significant, as we shall see later.

When the First World War started, Weber felt ethically compelled to serve his country. For some time he was a captain in the army, but was not sent to the battlefield, due to poor health. During the last part of the war and after the collapse, which he always predicted, of Wilhelminian Germany, he participated as a freelance writer in political discussions.[6] Here he fought on two fronts. On the one hand he opposed the militarists, who wanted to incorporate conquered lands into Germany. On the other hand, he opposed those pacifists who considered Germany alone guilty or who insisted that Germany should now behave according to the Sermon on the Mount. Having partially recovered his health, he accepted a professorship at the University of Munich. In addition to economics, he taught courses in sociology and general economic history. From the latter came the book bearing the same title.[7] Shortly thereafter, still weak physically, he died from pneumonia.

This sketch shows us that Max Weber's own development was determined, at least to some extent, by the necessity of choosing between the conflicting philosophies outlined. His development reveals an unmistakable shift from national-liberalism to a left-wing and pronounced socially minded liberalism. It is outside the scope of this paper to deal with this line of change, but it represents at the same time a shift from a more conservative to a more liberal Protestantism, from a more heteronomous to a more autonomous ethic, from a more emotionally conceived philosophy to a conscious and self-willed combination of Protestantism and Neo-Kantianism. That is the reason that the entrance of the latter philosophy into Weber's life represents the essential landmark in this paper. Thus, the article is separated into two unequal parts. The first deals with the pre-Neo-Kantian Protestant, the second with the Neo-Kantian Protestant. The first, due to the scarcity of materials, will be shorter and not further subdivided. The second part, however, will deal with the following topics: the atmosphere in which Neo-Kantianism originated and developed; the Neo-Kantian systems which are either different from or are forerunners of Weber's system; Weber's own concept of Neo-Kantianism, but only insofar as important for his own religious and ethical attitude; the atmosphere out of which the interest in Tolstoy and Dostoevsky, and their concepts of the Sermon on the Mount originated; and finally Weber's answers to these problems by means of Neo-Kantianism as a tool.

The Pre-Neo-Kantian Protestant[8]

In dealing with this epoch of Weber's life, it seems preferable to start with those elements which play a lesser role in his life and then to proceed with those which became more important.

The forms of ritual[9] entered the range of Weber's interests only slightly and incidentally. Otto Baumgarten, Weber's cousin, as a young theological student, preached occasionally in and around Heidelberg. Weber often listened to and discussed his sermons with him. This experience provided the impulse for the young Weber to describe various preaching methods and compare the different forms of ritual which he had opportunity to observe during his many trips through Germany. He preferred those forms of ritual in which the minister was bound as little as possible by ritualistic precepts. The ritualistic question was of primary interest to him since it involved the problem which always troubled him, namely, the problem of the independence of the individual within the Protestant church and the sociological structure and situation of the Protestant church in Germany.[10]

The question of the independence of the individual concerned Weber even as a high school boy. At his own confirmation as well as at that of relatives, he was aware of the fact that entrance into the Christian community carried obligations with it. Even at this time, the conviction began to grow within him—a conviction which plagued him his entire life—that the official German Protestant church and in effect German Protestantism itself was moving in the wrong direction. It was not primarily the antagonism of the theological "liberal" against the "orthodox," but rather the opposition of the advocate of the autonomous religious conscience to the ecclesiastical mechanism of the State Church, indissolubly tied to conservative, feudal, and militaristic interests. Weber attacked many adversaries but the man whom he most heartily disliked was the "crowned dilettante" Wilhelm II,[11] who claimed to be an instrument of God and who each day made a new show of his theatrical and spurious religiosity. Weber also condemned the German "cowards"who lacked the courage to be "Protestants" in the boldest and ethically obliging sense of the word. Even when he did not agree with the content of their thought, Weber admired those who had the courage to be such "Protestants."

Among the religious rebels with whom Weber dealt were some very heterogeneous personalities. The one who meant the least in Weber's life was Baron von Reichlin-Meldegg.[12] He originally had been a Catholic priest and a professor of theology at the state-supported divinity school at Freiburg. But he left Catholicism and embraced Protestantism. As frequently occurs in such situations, the government, whose permanent employee he was, transferred him into the School of Liberal Arts as professor of philosophy. In his classes, to Weber's deep regret, he used every opportunity to ridicule dogma and orthodoxy. On the other hand, Weber, as a student, had great admiration for David Strauss.[13] This interest, however, was probably due in large part to the fact that Weber's uncle Hausrath had a few years before completed a book dealing with this radical biblical critic. Much more significant and pointing to the character of the future religious and political struggles was Weber's interest in, and sympathy for, Moritz von Egidy.[14] He was a Prussian officer who had attempted to make Christianity primarily an ethical religion with a minimum of dogma. As a result, von Egidy had been dishonorably dismissed from the Wilhelminian army which was closely connected with the official Protestant church. In this instance, as well as subsequently, Weber attacked the Protestant church because of the political methods which the powerful and dominant orthodox conservatives used to crush their powerless liberal enemies in the struggles over dogma during these days.

In this period Weber had definitely become a biblio-critically minded liberal.[15] In contrast to such men as Reichlin-Meldegg, however, he understood the feeling of the orthodox believer, and, on at least one sad occasion, he referred to the biblical text—"And as thou hast believed, so be it done unto thee"—in anything but conventional form. But even this conservative-liberal antagonism was unimportant in comparison with the religio-ethical problem.

The religio-ethical problems[16] which involved the relation between autonomy and law already were dominant in Weber's thinking. Christianity was considered as obligatory for all members of the community, but everyone, according to young Weber, was entitled and even obliged to interpret it individually and to try to solve its enigmas. By so doing, the individual was responsible only to God and to his individual conscience. But this obligation to make decisions was not enough; the "calling"—the knowledge through some inner voice of the conscience that one has been called for a particular duty by the superior power—had a role to play. Weber's respect for the conscience and for this individual calling was very great. Indeed, throughout his life, Max Weber considered Catholicism to constitute one of the gravest threats to the autonomous decision of the individual conscience and to the independence of scientific investigation. Nevertheless, during the struggle which was called the "Kulturkampf," the young scholar denounced Bismarck's anti-Catholic laws and practices.[17] Thus, the limits of the state with regard to the individual conscience, and the duties of the individual toward his country were already problems to Weber. One can also see the problem as to the religious right of the conscientious objector entering the picture. At this stage the young German Protestant perceived only a seemingly Christian precept pointing in that direction and not yet a basic antagonism between Christian precept and the claim of the modern state.[18] In the second part of his life, however, he changed his mind and gave another answer.

In summary, we may make the following statement. Certainly Max Weber as a young man was already interested in many problems. Nevertheless, nothing had so deeply affected him as the religio-ethical problem concerning the relations between the individual and the state and between the individual and the church. This problem occupied him from the day of his own confirmation, and especially from the day he congratulated his brother at confirmation, to the day when, as a professor in Munich, he planned to write a book on Tolstoy and struggled with his colleague, Friedrich Wilhelm Foerster. That is to say, this problem concerned him from the beginning of his independent thinking about the world up to the very last days before his premature death. The problems already faced and tentatively answered in the first period were considered again and treated in a more systematic and epistemologically grounded way after the encounter with, and the changes introduced by, the Neo-Kantian philosophy.[19]

The Neo-Kantian Protestant

More so than any other Neo-Kantian group the southern German school of Windelband, Rickert, Jellinek, Troeltsch, and their followers influenced Weber. These scholars directed their main interest to problems which played only a smaller role in the thought of the other Neo-Kantians, that is, to the epistemological background of the cultural sciences and to the philosophy of history. To the distinction between the sphere of scientific knowledge and the sphere of religious and ethical perception and action, they added a new way of distinguishing between objects and methods of natural sciences, on the one hand, and of cultural sciences, on the other. Especially Windelband and Rickert elaborated a system of classification of sciences. History, they argued, deals with reality insofar as the uniqueness of the particular is concerned; natural sciences, on the contrary, are interested in and capable of perceiving, at least to some extent, general rules of automatically occurring changes. With this dominant viewpoint they tried to locate the various special sciences, but they did not deal to any extent with the essence, limitations and methods of sociology. It was at this point that Max Weber entered the picture.

It is outside the scope of this paper to deal extensively with Weber's concept of the essence and limits of science in general and the special sciences in particular. Accordingly only those basic concepts of Weber which directly played a role within the development, explanation, and justification of his own religious and ethical concept can be mentioned. These fundamentals, in part coming from Windelband and Rickert, in part purely Max Weber's own thought, are as follows. [21]

There is one fundamental division, namely, that between statements of facts and judgments of value. The former can be made in the sphere of special sciences and are the main content of such sciences; in contrast, judgments of value are of autonomous and subjective character, independent of authorities, and essential in the sphere of ethics and politics where the responsible decisions must be made by the individual at his own risk. Within the particular sphere of special sciences, which deals with statements of fact, there is a further essential division, that between natural and cultural sciences. The former to some extent are able to perceive general rules about an automatically necessitated process occurring within the sequence of forms. In contrast, cultural sciences are not able to go as far as that. To understand the meaning of this assertion, we must have the next essential division in mind. For, within the sphere of cultural sciences, there exists, among others, the difference between the historical and the sociological approach. The term history is used here in the broadest sense to include the history of every sphere of life and thinking. History primarily deals with the uniqueness of the particular object observed. Thus, within the sphere of historical investigations, general terms such as animal husbandry, nomadism, feudalism, bureaucracy, state, etc., can and must be used; but in so doing, one must have in mind that such terms actually are nothing but abbreviations. They are used to denote the sum of all these particular historical subjects, which have the same characteristic traits in common. There is no possibility of knowing about the existence or nonexistence of an entity in the metaphysical sense corresponding in reality to these terms. Moreover, within the sphere of historical investigations, it is impossible to make statements concerning automatically occurring changes. But even within the cultural sciences by applying the sociological approach and by using the result of historical investigations made before within the field, it is not possible as far as in the natural sciences. There is no more than the possibility of making some statements concerning the probability that some forms of social systems, for example, may succeed one another in the same sequence in more than one case. Accordingly, man cannot and never will be able to predict the future. He may calculate only to some degree the probability of the effects recurring in a given situation. However, historical knowledge can be used for practical purposes, especially in choosing the means which are supposed to be useful if one wants to realize a special socioeconomic goal. The realization of such a goal is then supposed to represent a good, which is supposed to be of higher value than the nonrealization of the goal under consideration. But we must repeat again, at the end of this digression into Weber's epistemology, what has been said at the beginning: the decisions concerning value-systems, value-differences, and value-hierarchy are not derived from the scientific sphere but rather from considerations based on the autonomous religio-ethical conscience of the individual.

Weber combined these epistemological solutions with his Protestantism. This combination of Protestantism and Neo-Kantianism provided him with the tool to solve his own religious and ethical problems. These problems increasingly concerned the compatibility of the precepts of Jesus with the demands of modern society.

The Rise of the Problem Concerning the Sermon on the Mount

Our pre-Neo-Kantian Protestant had insisted upon the right of the individual to decide autonomously, and, at the same time, denied the existence of an antagonism between Christian precept and the challenge of the modern state. What then about the person who, making use of the right of autonomous decision, would insist upon such an incompatibility? This person is not a character of fiction but one who lived in Weber's day—namely, Tolstoy. Hence

Tolstoy, and with him Dostoevsky, as well as the Russian form of Greek Orthodoxy, enter the picture.

Various factors facilitated the entrance of that world into prewar Germany and, accordingly, into Max Weber's horizon. First, we must mention the general discontent of many Germans with the institutionalization of the Protestant church, the specialization of science, and the nonexistence of an all-embracing universalistic system. Therefore, some Germans turned to Roman Catholicism, oriental mysticism,[21] or became disciples of the extremely anti-democratic Catholic poet, Stefan George. George preached to his small, esoteric group of followers the gospel of a world-escaping, "elite" life, similar to that of the early-medieval Benedictine monks.[22] Even more Germans were impressed by Dostoevsky's vision of the Russian peasant life of brotherly love. Along with Dostoevsky, Tolstoy also entered the picture. Second, the situation in prewar Heidelberg made this place especially susceptible to this influence. For, as already indicated in the biographical sketch, more so than in other German universities, students who had political, racial, or other difficulties in their own countries were admitted, among them Russians of almost all political and social convictions. Max Weber, although no longer a young man, had learned the Russian language in order to follow and to judge the changes occurring in Russia. He protected these Russian students just as he did all persons persecuted for their convictions. This encounter with Russian students was another stimulus for him to deal with Tolstoy. Finally, there was still another impetus. After the collapse, Germany underwent a bloody revolution. Some of the leaders emphasized the right to use violence in the revolution but simultaneously denied its use in war. Other Germans escaped from a supposedly evil world into romantic youth-movement[23] groups, or Christian-socialist rural collectivites.[24] Moreover, in contrast to the militaristic mentality of the prewar epoch, many Germans insisted on Germany's war guilt. Among the most important was Friedrich Wilhelm Foerster, who appealed to a Christian concept of natural law.[25] Since Max Weber had accepted a call to the University of Munich, he became the colleague of Foerster. The classes of the latter were disturbed by rioting students, and Weber could not refrain from taking part in the struggle. He respected Foerster's integrity and courage but sharply differentiated his own views from those of his colleague.[26] Weber's own development as well as impulses coming from the surrounding world converged, and, using the tool provided by Neo-Kantianism, Weber gave his answer to the complex of problems. His premature death prevented him from giving his answers in a systematic fashion, but his answers can be found in his "swan-songs," the lectures on "Science as a Profession" and "Politics as a Profession." These recall the epistemological details already indicated. We now restrict ourselves to their application to religion and ethics.

The Tragic Religio-Ethical Dilemma[27]

According to Weber's basic conviction, there is no possibility of making statements concerning the existence or nonexistence of an entity in the metaphysical sense which corresponds in reality to words such as state, church, family, economic institutions, and so on. These indeed are nothing but words, used in the boldest nominalistic sense to denote nothing but special kinds of continuing collective activities performed by a more or less large number of individuals. Accordingly, if any of these institutions claims to be more than a word used to denote such collective activity, then it exceeds its rights: even more so, if it claims to be entitled to make decisions within the religious or ethical sphere and to bind the individual by them. The latter is a reality. If no group has the authority to formulate orders within the religious and ethical sphere, and if no branch of philosophy or science is able to formulate judgments of value, then only the autonomous individual remains. His conscience tells him what to do. The conscience says if and to what extent the individual is entitled to work, even to sacrifice itself for an institutionalized group, such as one's native land. Thus this conscience may direct man to decisions which are in opposition to man's vital interests. Its existence is the evidence of the reality of a higher order and a superior being. Max Weber's personal friends know that this relation to God, by radically and exclusively following the voice of the individual conscience, was basic to all his decisions and actions. But this did not mean a disregard for the group; quite the contrary. For here is one of the tragic antagonisms of life. Man cannot live exclusively by voluntary cooperation without compulsory forces; anarchistic society is impossible. Accordingly, there originates the antagonism between an institution which is able to use compulsory force, on one hand, and the value judgment which is made by the individual conscience and which is opposed to the vital interests of the group, on the other. The individual may decide: "Here I stand, I cannot do otherwise, so help me God." By doing so the individual takes the risk of being persecuted, even of being killed. But that is not the worst; for in choosing between two alternatives the individual takes the even greater risk of becoming an even greater sinner than by choosing the opposite alternative. This is true since the two ethics stand in discordant antagonism. Conduct can be directed by a radical ethic, that is, it can be oriented exclusively toward ends considered absolute values, or conduct can be directed by an ethic of responsibility. The former is that of the religious prophet who "knows the one thing that is needful" and of his followers who act according to the precept: "The Christian does rightly and leaves the result with the Lord." In the opposite case, that is, in the case of a conduct directed by the ethics of responsibility, one is expected, even bound, to give an account of the foreseeable effect of his action. This basic difference manifests itself in antagonistic attitudes toward at least five phenomena. These are as follows.

First of all as to man's dignity, the radical ethic gives the unconditioned order: "Turn the other cheek," and gives no consideration to the consequences. The ethic of responsibility will insist upon the individual's dignity and upon the dignity of the group which the individual represents. Therefore, the ethics of responsibility will reject this precept. The same is true with regard to the selection of means generally. The radical ethic will reject all actions involving means which this ethic considers ethically dangerous. The adherent of such principles will act according to the commandment: "Resist not him that is evil by force." But by acting according to such a principle he will let evil triumph in the world. On the other hand, the follower of the ethic of responsibility, because he feels responsible for the effect, will resist evil by force. He knows that if he does not do so, he will be responsible for the victory of evil. By doing so, however, due to his own feeling of ethical responsibility, he will charge himself with ethical guilt for using unethical means. Similarly the radical ethic will reject aesthetic and scientific values, if they endanger arriving at the "one thing that is needful"; the ethic of responsibility will insist on the obligation of preserving and de-

veloping these values. The same is true as to property. The radical
ethic will insist on the biblical precept: "Give what thou hast,"and
will not ask about the effect, that is, who will enjoy these economic
goods and how they will be distributed. The politician will act otherwise. He may or may not favor private property. Nevertheless, he
will feel responsible for men and goods and accordingly will investigate the possibilities, means, and calculable effect of the various
ways of distributing property. Finally as to war and revolution, the
radical ethic simply says: "All they that take the sword shall perish
by the sword. "The followers of the radical ethic will accept the
status of an oppressed national or social group and refuse to resort
to war and strikes, while the adherents of the ethic of responsibility
will feel bound to use them.

In a word, the radical ethic is oriented toward the image of the
saint; the ethic of responsibility toward that of the hero. The individual must choose between the two, and, by deciding for the one,
the individual inevitably sins against the other precept.

What then about the man who is obliged to live in an epoch such
as ours in which no prophet appears who knows the "one thing that
is needful," a man who himself feels unable to make autonomous
decisions? The answer is neither the loveless contemplation of the
world as Schopenhauer taught, nor suicide, conceived by Weber as
uncharitableness toward one's fellow men and condoned in one single
case, that of an irreparable mental derangement. The answer to those
who are unable to live and to decide autonomously is: go back to
church. If one can make the "intellectual sacrifice," Weber will not
rebuke him. The simple confession of an incapacity to live autonomously and of a willingness to make the intellectual sacrifice has
greater intellectual integrity than ignoring the limits of philosophy
and science and claiming to be able to make, by philosophical or
scientific methods, general religious and ethical precepts.[28]

Under such circumstances, is there any possibility of dealing scientifically with religion, and is there any ethical precept for the one
who attempts such work?

The Ethos of the Investigator of Religious Phenomena[29]

Again we must omit all details of Weber's concept concerning
epistemology as well as with regard to the ethics of the scientists.

Only three basic attitudes will be mentioned. First, that which occurs in time sequence and which is characterized by man's interference belongs to history and not to faith. Thus, every phenomenon which supposedly is connected with revelation falls into the sphere of history. Sociology of religion, just as every special branch of sociology, presupposes that all the phenomena to be considered have already been investigated in a comparative historical way. Accordingly, every phenomenon which claims to be connected with revelation must also be the object of comparative historical and sociological investigation. Second, the same imperative which may cause a given individual to work as politician and another to sacrifice himself for his radical preaching, may stimulate another, and indeed stimulated Weber himself, to deal scientifically with religion. The essential quality then is to have the courage to deny oneself. For the historical and sociological investigator in the field of religion must know that he may undermine traditional beliefs which may be precious to many and perhaps even to himself. Nevertheless, if he enters that field which his own personal imperative has obliged him to enter, he must be willing to face the consequences. This attitude helps us understand Weber's attitude toward theological schools. The theological schools in Germany of Weber's day were part of the state-supported universities and accordingly were objects of uninterrupted conflicts, not only between orthodox and liberal schools of theological thought but also between state and church as well as between the various political parties. Weber often took part in the controversies. He followed the literature in the field of biblical theology and church history as closely as possible. Especially, he always tried to become familiar with the ideas of, and the publications written by, the men who were considered as candidates for theological professorships. He strongly advocated the calling of liberal scholars rather than the orthodox candidates who were usually supported by the government, the feudal aristocracy, the army offices, and other conservative powers. He also vigorously opposed the "neo-romantic" believers of all kinds who played a role in prewar and an even larger role in postwar, Germany. He did not find fault with orthodox Protestants and Neo-Romanticists with reference to the special content of their concepts, such as transubstantiation, divinity of Jesus, and so on. Rather he found fault with them for what he considered a lack of intellectual integrity;[30] namely, that of failing to elaborate epistemologically the basis of their statements and obliterating the limits between the spheres of thought. Phenomena appearing within the sequence of time for him belonged to history and not to faith; and the university to him was one of the few places where pure science, within the narrow limits of its capacity, was pursued, rather than politics and religious preaching. He considered both religion and politics as having enough opportunities to propagate their programs outside of the universities.[31]

The scientist who deals historically and sociologically with religion, even more so than other scientists, must suffer a threefold unhappiness. The unhappiness of undermining beloved traditional creeds, of being limited in elaborating general laws, and of having to refrain from passing judgments of value on that which is essential in the sphere of religion. Just as human life in general, so also is the life of the scientist tragic in itself.[32] Nevertheless, Max Weber chose this life. The two words "tragic" and "nevertheless" provide us with the key to our concluding comparison.

Conclusion

By comparing the statements in the last section with those made in the preceding section, Max Weber's originality stands out in bold relief against the background of forerunners and contemporaries. We shall start with a comparison which actually concerns one trait, but which is indeed a very characteristic one. Weber often was compared with Emile Zola. Of course not with Zola as the author of naturalistic novels (although Werner Sombart recommended him to his students as one of the best analysts of modern social life) but the Zola of the Dreyfus Affair who threw his "J'accuse" into the face of the French leaders to protect an innocent individual against the persecution of a powerful group. This stand was one which Max Weber also could have taken. Not only did Weber definitely feel a kinship with Zola but he did not deny the comparison just made. As mentioned previously in a different connection, Weber deplored the fact that his own beloved German people had produced so few men like Zola and Voltaire.

But we must turn to the camp of the Kantians if we wish to encounter individuals who can be compared with the Heidelbergian sociologist under more than just this viewpoint.

Kant not only had been the climax of the Enlightenment; he advanced beyond it. He denied the basic optimism with regard to man's perceptive capacity as well as with reference to man's inborn goodness.[33] But he went no further. In his adolescence, Kant had shifted from the pietism of his home and his university teachers.[34] This kind of pietism had already separated the sphere of emotional religiosity from the natural sciences which were in high esteem.[35] Thus, there was actually no sharp break; the tragic finds no place in Kant's own personal existence nor in his conception of the world. Here, more so than in epistemological detail, rests the fundamental difference between Kant and Weber. This dissimilarity is even more deeply rooted than that between Kant and the other Neo-Kantians.

As to the latter, the similarity of Friedrich Albert Lange and Max Weber is indeed striking. Both set the whole sphere of religion and ethics outside of the sphere of philosophy and science; moreover both were pitiless in their ethical challenge toward themselves and inexorable strugglers for what their autonomous imperatives told them to struggle for. Unlike that of Kant, Lange's life was a chain of persecution, illness, martyrdom, and tragedy; but he neither considered life as tragic in itself nor ethics as anti-nomistic in itself. This also coincided with the thought of the revisionist socialists. After the collapse of Germany in 1918 it is true that the revisionists and Max Weber were so close politically that Weber said: "We are so much alike that we could be taken for one another." Indeed they had eliminated Marxist determinism, but nevertheless maintained progressivism and were, if not anti-religiously, then surely a-religiously, minded.

Such a-religiosity, indeed, does not apply to the next Kantian group, Ritschl and his forerunners, the various "Vermittlungstheologen." But they all projected into the domain of faith phenomena which, according to Weber, belongs to history. Such an accusation Weber, to be sure, did not make of Southern German Neo-Kantianism. Indeed, Rickert and Troeltsch especially have many traits in common with Weber. They struggled against the same adversaries; they suffered from the same developments in Germany and within Protestantism; they limited man's sphere of knowledge and suffered from this restriction. Nevertheless, there remains the basic difference: the non-existence of a concept of world, life, ethics, and science as tragic in themselves. Consequently, both Rickert and Troeltsch were "terrified" when the concept of the tragic aspect of existence appeared in Weber's swan song,"[36] and behind it—the true Weber. This attitude of Weber, on the other hand, may have pleased many neo-romanticists, followers of Tolstoy, religious socialists, members of the German Youth Movement, and settlers in rural collectivities, as well as Stephan George and his followers. Max Weber had many discussions with the "master" and his disciples. He even helped the best known among George's followers, Friedrich Gundolf and Arthur Salz, in their academic careers. But he did so, as always, guided by his ethical imperative which ordered him to protect the adversary. At the same time, many neo-romanticists were criticized by Max Weber for not having the courage and integrity to be scientists within the sphere of science. What then remains? A pure philosophical and scientific contemplation of a senseless world, withdrawal from it, without relation to it and without interference? Such was the thought and life of Schopenhauer. Indeed he had considered Kant his forerunner; but at the same time he laughed at the *Critique of Practical Reason* as well as the categorical imperative.[37] Is Max Weber's further elaboration of Kant, in last instance, nothing but a hopelessness similar to that of Schopenhauer? At this point appears the importance of the other element which, next to the term "tragic," differentiates Weber from his forerunners and contemporaries; namely, the imperative introduced by the word "nevertheless!" Schopenhauer's answer means pessimism; Weber's answer means "tragicism." Although the world is tragic, the ethic indissolubly connected with contradiction, and the domain of science limited, nevertheless, do your work in accordance with that demanded by your imperative!

After reading these pages is would be strange indeed if Dostoevsky did not flash before the reader's mind. After having shown that Tolstoy meant to Weber only one of the possible attitudes, but just the one which Weber did not choose, certainly a comparison of Dostoevsky and Max Weber is inevitable and necessary in order to provide the key to Max Weber's innermost self.

Both Dostoevsky and Max Weber suffered from the tragic aspect of life and felt man's inescapable inferiority and culpability to a degree experienced by very few persons before them. Nevertheless, both shouldered their yoke: they faced reality, especially in their conviction that politics is inescapable and that it is the individual's duty to become involved in politics in order to work for his people. Both were conscious that by so doing they became involved in sin and guilt. Although they were similar in this respect, the two men were different in almost all other respects. Their attitudes toward the state, the church, the nation, and human reason were diametrically opposed.

As a true Russian, Dostoevsky rationalistically conceived neither the czarist state nor the Greek Orthodox Church to be a juridical institution as the state and church in the West increasingly had been since the day of the rationalistically structured Roman law. Nevertheless, for Dostoevsky, both the czarist empire and the Greek Orthodox Church remain mystically embraced metaphysical entities. And life can be brought to the highest possible degree of fulfillment, only if it runs its course within both. Moreover, the Greek Orthodox Russians are not just a nation; they are a people, chosen by God, the collective Messiah who in this capacity feel bound to save the world by bringing it under their control, just as the secularized successors of the Greek Orthodox czarism, the Soviets, who everywhere appear in the role of a collective Messiah using violence. Dostoevsky insisted especially that Constantinople, and thereby the Balkans, should come under czarist Russian control to protect the Balkan peoples from being perverted by European influences,[38] again just as the contemporary Soviets assert they are obliged to do. Indeed, Dostoevsky respects and sometimes even loves murderers and prostitutes as his brethren in Christ. But the same Dostoevsky does not regard as brothers those among his fellow prisoners in the Siberian "House of the Dead" who were Polish insurgents against czarism.[39] To him the Poles remain those Slavs who became traitors by way of their Roman Catholicism, which to him meant Western rationalistic intellectualism and European bureaucracy.

Max Weber also loved his nation. Next to his religiously grounded categorical imperative, the feeling of being rooted in and bound to his nation determined his attitude toward life and social groups. Nevertheless, he never considered his people as the ethically superior nation or as the chosen people in a religious sense. Accordingly, he never would have tried, ethically or religiously, to justify subjection and conquest on the part of his people. He also never tried scientifically to justify his feeling of being bound to his fellow

Germans. For his science remained separated from the religious and ethical sphere, and only in a very special way was it possible to bring them into relationship. Nevertheless, work in the special sciences continued to represent for him an inescapable duty.

Science, even in the restricted sense of a tool used to realize religiously or ethically conceived goals, was, for Dostoevsky, always a senseless enterprise and an a-religious western attitude. This basically different attitude cannot be attributed to the fact that Dostoevsky was a "novelist" and Max Weber a "scholar," but rather to the fact that Dostoevsky was a non-European Russian and Max Weber a European. In this difference also is rooted the difference between the basically heteronomous ethics of the Greek Orthodox and the basically autonomous ethics of the Protestant. For Max Weber was not just a Protestant by birth; he was one by emotion and feeling. To be sure, he strongly criticized German Lutheranism, but he distinguished carefully between German Lutheranism conceived as an historically explainable aberration from the basic attitude of the founder, and the young monk from Wittenberg himself. If anyone is entitled to be brought into the neighborhood of Luther, it is Max Weber. His tragic-consciousness has manifested itself not just in a theory emphasizing the tragic but also in a life determined by his own religiously-conceived categorical imperative. This means nothing other than the realization of a life conforming to Luther's words: "Here I stand. I cannot do otherwise, so help me God."

Notes

1. The main sources for the following are Marianne Weber, *Max Weber* (Tübingen, 1926) and *Lebenserinnerungen* (Bremen, 1948), 51-58; Max Weber, *Jugenbriefe* (Tübingen, n.d.) and *Gesammelte Politische Schriften* (München, 1921); Paul Honigsheim, "Max Weber as Rural Sociologist," *Rural Sociology*, XI (1946), 207-209 includes a list of 21 other books and articles dealing with Weber.
2. As to the role which Mommsen and his concept of antiquity played in Weber"s life, see Paul Honigsheim, "Max Weber as Historian of Agriculture," *Agricultural History*, XXIII (1949), 191-199.
3. After the death of Weber almost all of his publications were collected by his widow, Marianne Weber, and published by J.C.B. Mohr at Tübingen. The volume which contains the works in the field of history of agriculture is: *Gesammelte Aufsätze zur Sozial-und Wirtschaftsgeschichte* (Tübingen, 1924). Not included in the posthu-

mous edition is *Die römische Agrargeschichte in ihrer Bedeutung für das Staats und Privatrecht* (Stuttgart, 1891).

4. As to the Heidelbergian atmosphere of that time and the individuals with whom Max Weber came in contact, see Wilhelm Windelband, *Kuno Fischer* (Heidelberg, 1907); idem, "Zum Geleit," in Georg Jellinek, *Ausgewählte Reden und Schriften*, I (Berlin, 1911), 5-11; Heinrich Rickert, *Wilhelm Windelband* (Tübingen, 1915); Ernst Troeltsch, Review of Georg Jellinek, *Ausgewählte Reden und Schriften in Zeitschrift für das Privat- und öffentliche Recht der Gegenwart* (Wien, 1912); Paul Honigsheim, "Veit Valentin," *Die Friedens-Warte*, XLVII (Zurich, 1947).

5. Those volumes which contain the works in the field of epistemology, general sociology, and sociology of religion, which mostly were written in Heidelberg, are: *Gesammelte Aufsätze zur Religionssoziology*, 1-3, (Tübingen, 1920-1921), *Gesammelte Aufsätze zur Wissenschaftslehre* (Tübingen, 1922), *Wirtschaft und Gesellschaft* (Tübingen, 1922).

6. The most important political publications of this epoch are collected in *Gesammelte Politische Schriften*.

7. *Wirtschaftsgeschichte* (München, 1923): translated into English by Frank H. Knight under the title *General Economic History* (New York, 1927).

8. The main source for the following in Max Weber, *Jugendbriefe*.

9. Ibid., 20f., 24, 45, 52, 55, 211f.

10. Ibid., 64, 106f., 212.

11. Ibid., 294, 334; Marianne Weber, *Max Weber*, 408. As to the constant disdain of Max Weber for William II, see Max Weber, *Gesammelte Politische Schriften*, 75, 187, 193, 343, 456, 477, 480.

12. *Jugendbriefe*, 59-60.

13. Ibid., 44, 205, 208.

14. Ibid., 334.

15. Ibid., 60f., 196, 229.

16. Ibid., 22, 86, 106f., 213, 268.

17. Ibid., 204, 234, 311.

18. Ibid., 191f.

19. An explanation of the atmosphere out of which Neo-Kantianism originated may be found in O.A. Ellisman, "Biographisches Vorwort" in Friedrich Albert Lange, *Geschichte des Materialismus*, I (Leipzig, 1905), 12-14.

20. The following articles which are reprinted in *Gesammelte Aufsätze zur Wissenschaftslehre*, contain Weber's basic epistemological theories: "R. Stammler's Überwindung der materialistischen Geschichtsauffassung," 291-359, "Die Objektivität Sozialwissenschaftlicher Erkenntniss," 146-214, "Zur Auseinandersetzung mit Edward Meyer," 215-265. "Der Sinn der Wertfreiheit der Soziologischen und ökonomischen Wissenschaften," 451-502. The last three mentioned among these four articles have been translated under the title *Max Weber on the Methodology of the Social Sciences*, translated and edited by Edward H. Shils and Henry A. Finch

(Glencoe, 1949). See also Max Weber, *The Theory of Social and Economic Organizations*, translated by A.M. Henderson and Talcott Parsons (New York, 1947), 87-157. Consult also Paul Honigsheim, "Max Weber als Soziologie," *Kölner Vierteljahrshefte für Soziologie*, I (1920).

21. For further details about these movements, see Paul Honigsheim, "Romantische und religiös-mystisch verankerte Wirtschaftsgesinnungen," *Die Wirtschaftswissenschaft nach dem Kriege*, ed., M.J. Bonn and M. Palyi, I (München, 1925), 298-312, and "The Roots of the Nazi Concept of the Ideal German Peasant," *Rural Sociology*, XII (1947), 16-19.

22. See the collected works of George, entitled *Gesamtausgabe der Werke* (Berlin, 1927-1934). Especially, consult Vol. III, *Bücher der Sagen und Sänge* (1930); Vol. V, *Der Teppich des Lebens*; Vol. VI-VII, *Der Siebente Ring* (1931); Vol. VIII, *Der Stern des Bundes* (1929). See also the English translation of a selection of his writings entitled *Poems rendered into English* (New York, 1943). The main publications of the adherents of George may be found in the review, "Blätter für die Kunst (Berlin, 1892-1919). Consult F. Gundolf, *George* (Berlin, 1920).

23. The best characterization of the German youth movement and survey on its most important groups may be found in Howard Becker, *German Youth: Bond or Free* (New York, 1946).

24. For further details, see Paul Honigsheim, "Rural Collectivities," in C.P. Loomis, and J.A. Beegle, *Rural Social Systems* (New York, 1950), 839-846, and Georg Becker, *Die Siedlung der deutschen Jugendbewegung* (Hilden, 1929), 11-41, 60-80.

25. The ideas of Foerster and his adherents were mainly propagated in the review *Die Menschheit* (Weisbaden).

26. Max Weber, "Politics as a Vocation," from *Max Weber, Essays in Sociology*, translated by H.H. Gerth and C. Wright Mills (New York, 1946), 122, 124.

27. The basic religious and ethical ideas of Max Weber may be found in: "Politics as a Vocation," 119-127; "Science as a Vocation, Ibid., 133, 146, 149-156; Die Objektivitat Sozialwissenschaftlicher Erkenntniss,' 153; and "Zwischen zwei Gesetzen," *Gesammelte Politische Schriften*, 60-63.

28. "Science as a Vocation," 155f.

29. Ibid., 153f.

30. Ibid., 137.

31. Ibid., 143f., 150.

32. Ibid., 143.

33. This viewpoint of Kant appears most clearly in his book *Religion Within the Limits of Reason Alone*, translated by Theodore M. Greene and Hoyt H. Hudson (Chicago, 1934), 15-49.

34. As to the interrelationship between Pietism and Kant, see, for example, Johann Casper Lavater, *Ausgewählte Schriften*, eds., Johann Kasper von Orelli (Zürich, 1841, 1844), II, 175, VIII, 309, and Johann Heinrich Jung-Stilling, *Sämmtliche Werke*, VIII (Stuttgart, 1841), 453.

35. As to the interest of pietists in natural sciences, see for example, Jung-Stilling, *Werke*, I, 448ff., II, 31, IX, 866; Johann Christian Edelmann, *Selbsbiographie*, ed., Wilhelm Klone (Berlin, 1849), 103, 201, 314f., and Friedrich Christoph von Octinger, *Selbsbiographie*, ed., Julius Hamberger (Stuttgart, 1845), 85.
36. Heinrich Richert, "Max Weber und seine Stellung zue Wissenschaft," Logos, XV (Tübingen, 1926), 231.
37. Arthur Schopenhauer's attitude toward Kant's ethic can be found in his main work *The World as Will and Idea*, translated by R.B. Haldane and John Kemp, 8th ed. (London, n.d.), 133, 152.
38 Dostoevski's attitude toward other Eastern Peoples can be found in *Politische Schriften* (München, 1928), 174-184, 355-397, 437-454.
39. F. Dostoevski, *The House of the Dead*, The Novels of Fyodor Dostoevski, V (New York, 1923), 23, 26, 62-3, 143, 264-268.

Part 2

On Max Weber

5

Memories of Max Weber

Max Weber in Heidelberg

Whoever would have a picture of Max Weber, the scholar and the man, must see it against the background of the Heidelberg of his time. Its university was then not only the most liberal but also the most international in Germany. People who would have been excluded in other places on grounds of race, nationality, politics, or religion were acceptable in the city on the Neckar. And so they were all there, the representatives of national minorities from Austria, Hungary, and the Balkan countries, and, last but not least, the Russians. These latter were there in all their varieties, from Greek Orthodox mystics to those most leftist *Narodniki* who didn't want to wait any longer, but would have had the revolution start today rather than tomorrow.

It was the same with respect to contemporary German movements: the Stefan George circle as well as Friedrich Naumann's National-Social Association (a combination of leftist liberalism with monarchic social reform and patriotism), and all sorts of other ideologies—they all had their representatives in Heidelberg and they found a ready audience.

The situation was similar, although not exactly so, with respect to the faculty. It was remarkable that faculty members could have an

Paul Honigsheim, "Erinnerungen and Max Weber," *Kölner Zeitschrift für Soziologie und Sozialpsychologie*, 15 (1963), pp. 161-271.

appointment in more than one faculty. Jellinek, for example, was officially an *Ordinarius* in public law in the law faculty, but one could take a Ph.D. under him with a dissertation in the philosophy of law, political theory, or the history of political ideas. One could also choose him as an examiner for a minor in government and politics. Students made good use of both opportunities. Troeltsch's position was similar in that he belonged to the theology as well as to the philosophy faculty. Both Jellinek and Troeltsch, therefore, exercised a strong influence, but nevertheless it was small in comparison with that of another man. Although only a limited number of people were able to meet him face to face, everyone knew about him, and when he spoke his remarks were transmitted to others by go-betweens. For this was the voice of the "legend of Heidelberg," the voice of Max Weber.

He had lectured in Heidelberg for only a few years. The nervous disturbance that had set in relatively early had brought his teaching activities to an unexpectedly early end. Following the onset of his illness he had spent many months in seclusion, several of these in Italy. During an extended period of convalescence, years followed during which he was not able to teach, but he did research, he wrote, he offered a weighty opinion on public affairs and controversies, and above all, he gathered a circle of friends and acquaintances around him. And who could count the people or name the names who gathered together here. In order to understand the broad range of Weber's interests, it is necessary to name only a few of this heterogeneous group: the politician Friedrich Naumann and his associate at that time, Theodor Heuss (later president), the poet Stefan George and several members of his circle, a whole host of philosophers and economists, and finally natural scientists and medical men such as the botanist Klebs, the psychiatrist Gruhle, the anatomist Braus, and the gynecologist Eymer (who later was well known and recognized in America as a cancer researcher). At first they came alone to visit the Webers. But as the continuation of this custom threatened to take too much time and energy, a Sunday afternoon open house was instituted. But that soon led to a consequence that had not been anticipated. The guests were numerous, and they often had things to say that they wanted to say only to the master and not to the company at large. So on Sundays they would make an appointment for the following week, and the result was that the Webers had single visitors in the house during the week, as in the beginning, or, instead of having just the Sunday open houses, as later in the middle Heidelberg period, they had both: on Sundays the house was full of guests and on work days one or another would be there for a private discussion. Both the Sunday teas and the private discussions shall be reported here insofar as they express Max Weber's attitudes.

Certainly Max Weber showed a golden sense of humor at times and he had a deep sense of charity; surely Marianne was goodness personified. But in spite of this, dark clouds overshadowed everything. They were not caused by Max Weber's illness; he was much too selfless to allow his suffering to show or to complain about it. Something else oppressed him much more and had the same effect upon his friends. Weber really loved Germany and felt ethically obligated to work for his country to the extent of risking his life for it. But he saw it taking a course that would lead to destruction. In Bismarck's lifetime almost everyone had jubilantly praised the unifier of Germany for the completed unification. The socialist and Catholic opposition had entirely different roots and were scorned by the so-called patriots; the lone voices of isolated federalists such as Constantin Frantz and Planck were ignored. But Max Weber raised his voice in the interest of the German nation: Bismarck's solitary rule may have fostered worthy bureaucrats but this was not always the case. "In each little city there is a house with a sign saying 'Royal Police Court'; and in it there is a man who, in case of doubt, is a nincompoop." And even worse: " The government likes to make presiding judges out of erstwhile prosecuting attorneys." Weber didn't care for them very much, as might be gathered from such a conversation. For their careers depended on how successful they were in condemning the largest number of poor devils, particularly if they could put them in prison for contempt of the crown. By the time he had been on the throne for only two years, Wilhelm II had managed to have not less than 1,600 people put in prison for this reason. And the Junkers from east of the Elbe were no better. Even the less restrained Troeltsch called them, in my presence, the "worst hucksters." As for Weber, he commented scornfully: "They might be all right in a card game or a hunting party, but otherwise they don't amount to anything." In addition there was the lie by which they maintained their power position in the army, the government, and the diplomatic service, as patent protectors of the Fatherland. For the crassest economic motives, they employed Polish farm laborers who were cheaper than German, thereby slowly filling the eastern areas with a Slavic population.

The person whom Weber hated most was Wilhelm II. Weber called him "this crowned dilettante," and he jeered when Wilhelm rather pathetically had given another "nice sermon"; it made Weber furious when Wilhelm, in spite of all the warnings on the part of his Reichschancellor Bülow, told his jovial jokes right in front of the stiff-necked and pedantic Czar, for the Czar didn't like that sort of thing and Wilhelm really harmed Germany in this way. Weber had commented on the proclamation expressing the Emperor's personal commitment to social welfare *(Soziale Kaisertums)* with especially biting scorn: "I had said at the time it would last only three years, and it didn't even last that long. "Weber hated the "Stumm era, which followed the "social welfare era," just as much. It is true that Max Weber was the son of a National Liberal delegate who, following Bennigsen, had supported the politics of Bismarck. The same party had offered the son the Reichstag seat for Saarbrücken, that is, in Stumm's industrial empire. Weber turned it down, however, for a highly characteristic reason: "I had just been called to Heidelberg and to go away so soon—I really can't do that to the people here." He had also informed himself about the political situation and he reported it in this way: "I went there, ate lunch in a restaurant, but I felt as though I were being spied upon by the other guests there—obviously engineers and higher bureaucratic officials; they believed that I belonged to Stumm's spy system." Having heard him express himself in this way, one felt justified in considering the question as to whether or not the nationalization of the mines would remedy the situation. But he was skeptical about this because of his aversion to state bureaucrats. His wife then reminded him that he had been embittered when the state had abandoned its plan to socialize the"Hibernia." But he replied,"That was because at that time the government had once again knuckled under to big business." Otherwise he remained skeptical about state socialism. I once asked him directly, "What would you decide if there were only two alternatives—state socialism or trusts?" Without hesitating for a second, he replied, "For the latter, because when there is domination by trusts, one can still fight against them."

This basic position was the origin of another statement. At the time of our first conversation in June, 1909, in the garden of the legendary cafe called the "Stiftsmühle," he explained, "It may surprise you to hear this from me, but I don't put any great weight on our social welfare politics *(Sozial Politik)*; what good is it if the workers have a little comfort in their old age if they have to obey when their bones are young and healthy? "But this reservation about German social welfare politics did not prevent him from veering from the National Liberal Party of his father to the left, to work with Friedrich Naumann to found the *Nationalsoziale Verband.* Joined in this party were ideas of nationalist power politics with social welfare politics and with cultural liberalism. With respect to the Reichstag, it certainly received no recognizable mandate; it joined with the *freisinnige Vereinigung* and became the yeast of leftist liberalism. All of this is too well known to need repeating here. I should like only to report a few facts. One of Weber's first opportunities for a public appearance after his long retirement was at a panel discussion before a meeting at Heidelberg of a *freisinnige* group. Furthermore, he told me that he had the greatest respect for Naumann as a human being, and he said admiringly, "This man lives completely by his pen."

Finally, it might be mentioned that Weber also took an interest in the internal political life of other German states. One Sunday, Heuss, one of Naumann's closest collaborators, was a guest in the Weber house on the Ziegelhäuser Landstrasse. The elections in Württemberg had just taken place. For the Left, in comparison with the preceding *Lantag,* things had gone very badly. "It's really terrible; how could it have happened?" asked Weber. Heuss replied, "The incumbents governed for a long time, and after something like that people feel the need for a change." But Weber was still displeased.

The preceding makes it understandable that Weber kept his distance from Schmoller, the chief originator of the social welfare legislation of Germany. This man, born in Württemberg, had made a life-long but vain attempt to lose his Swabian accent. In this he was like Treitschke, who was born in Saxony. They both glorified Prussia and the Hohenzollerns, particularly the bureaucracy. Schmoller argued like this: formerly, in the age of absolutism, the monarch (and especially the Prussian monarch), together with an academically trained bureaucracy, had protected the lower strata, the urban citizenry and the peasants, against the middle stratum, the all-powerful feudal nobility. Now, although the relationships may appear quite different, in fact they are the same. Thus, the monarchy, and especially the German emperor, together with a university-trained bureaucracy, should defend the workers, the new lower stratum, against the all-too-powerful high bourgeoisie, by means of the social welfare laws. Schmoller had considerable success in interesting socially prominent circles in social welfare politics, and in influencing, in various ways, the structure of the labor laws. His influence reached beyond the borders of Germany as far as Uruguay, which reflected the notions of social welfare politics more than any other Latin American country. And last but not least, through his personal contacts in the Prussian ministry of education, he got his students into influential positions in the government and the university, and in this way became a university pope such as no other university professor had been since the time of Hegel. Weber was highly opposed to this kind of favoritism.

I can still hear two characteristic remarks on this situation; we had been talking about the career of Robert Michels of whom I shall speak in another connection. A particular question had arisen in the debate, namely, whether it might not be better to change the system by which one qualified for academic teaching. It might be better for the candidate to seek permission from a central commission rather than to seek the approval of the current faculty of a particular university. A central commission could at least confer the right of formal admission to a particular discipline. Weber's answer to all of this was: "Then Schmoller would be even more powerful and we would see only his students in teaching posts." Another time he angrily made a remark when he was alone with me, and I can therefore produce no witnesses: "Everyone talks as though I were Schmoller's student; I certainly was not; I had other teachers, Meitzen, for example." This is not unimportant; it will interest us later in a discussion of Weber's attitudes toward historians, and this may serve to lift this man from an undeserved obscurity.

In general, in the larger circle, there wasn't too much talk about politics. An incidental remark will reveal the reason for this better than a whole chapter of theoretical explanations. Gundolf, whom we will discuss later when we take up Stefan George, was sitting at a table with the host and me, and something was said about politics. The door opened and two new guests, who happened to be students, came in and sat down with us. After an informal greeting, Gundolf said to Weber, "You were interrupted, and were saying...," whereupon the master answered, "I must stop; there are students here now, and naturally I don't have the right to talk about politics in front of them; it might influence them." So great was his respect for the sanctity of autonomous decision and so great his sensitivity. The following anecdote shows further evidence of this: one time he said to me, "My wife and I are going to Berlin for two weeks." I understood, however, "for two months." Therefore for six weeks I didn't go to see the Webers. But Jellinek stopped me and asked, "Why aren't you going to the Webers? He can't understand it." And so I went there immediately. Weber met me with the words, "You were as good as dead." I explained that I had misunderstood. He gave a sigh of relief and said, "Oh, so that's how it is; my wife and I racked our brains to think what we might have done to you." And I was just a young greenhorn then. His sense of empathy was so acute and his fear that he might hurt someone so great.

One can imagine what the man suffered when he, obliged by his love for Germany, climbed down into the political arena only to get covered with the mud there—he knew this was unavoidable if one were involved with politics. And, in addition, there was his almost demonic feeling for justice. This had interfered right at the beginning of his career. Weber was, of course, the son of a Reichstag deputy, and because of that even powerful persons in the ministry of education might consider it wise to advance him. Although they weren't blatant about it, they hinted that he might get an academic appointment. And who was opposed to it? None other than Max Weber himself; and for what reason? "Professor Zeuner deserves it more than I." He was referring to the Berlin historian of law who was later well known in his discipline for his work on German constitutional history in the Middle Ages and in modern times. Now Zeuner may have deserved this recognition one hundred times over (and he certainly earned it) and one may also say that this opportunity for Weber's advancement was somewhat less meaningful because of the call to a teaching post at Freiburg. But in spite of this, it remains that Weber belonged to the category of professors that one can count on the fingers of one hand: those who are willing to step back in favor of colleagues and rivals. I would not have been able to believe it had not Weber told me about it after I had urged him to do so.

There is another incident in this same context. His reservations about socialism, mentioned above, did not prevent him from defending socialists with vigor and outrage if he felt an injustice had been done them. Thus he always became upset when the conversation turned to Adolf Wagner. He was certainly not as powerful as Schmoller, but he had quite a lot of influence. He was an *Ordinarius* at Berlin and a sympathizer of Stoecker's Christian Socialism, and at one time served as a deputy to the Reichstag for the Conservative Party. He had, however, lent a hand in removing the right to teach from a *Dozent* at the University of Berlin, because, among other things, the *Dozent* was a Socialist." And now no Socialist will so much as take a piece of bread from his hand," said Weber, and he gave the Socialists credit for actually behaving this way.

Weber was not less embittered that Robert Michels was refused permission to teach for the same reason. Werner Sombart was the cause of even more severe conflict. Sombart was the *enfant terrible* of the social and economic historians, and at that time had strong Marxist views. Weber was convinced that he himself would not be able to teach for some time. First they offered him an unlimited leave, and finally a full pension. He declined both for a reason analogous to the reason he had given for declining the National Liberal Party's offer of the parliamentary seat for Saarbrücken, and he told me about it in these words: "I really cannot do that to the people at Heidelberg. I taught there for only a few years and now they want to give me a pension. For this reason I have resigned from my position. "This was a noble thing to do, but it left the chair unfilled, and there was therefore a question of finding a successor, and this would not happen without some fighting. Weber wanted Sombart to be his successor, probably because he liked the work that Sombart had published, and also because he thought it unjust that Sombart was still just an *Extraordinarius*. And now there was an opportunity to see and hear Sombart in Heidelberg. The German Historians' Congress met there in 1903, and it was known that Georg von Below would attack Sombart at the meeting. Von Below was a recognized authority on medieval German agrarian and city history as well as on economic origins of contemporary German states. Physically, however, nature had been a wicked step-mother to him. He was embittered for this and for other reasons. (During the first World War, he had favored a politics of expansion, and for this reason he had caused his younger colleague at Freiburg, Veit Valentin—whom we will discuss later as the chief student of Erich Marcks'—to be expelled, not only from Freiburg but from the academic world altogether. Valentin was a Bethmann-Hollweg man, that is, an opponent of von Tirpitz; this latter was the chief proponent of submarine warfare and was thus responsible for the sinking of the Lusitania and thereby for the entry of the United States into the ranks of Germany's enemies.) Von Below scorned everything that was even remotely connected with Schmoller, and he therefore scorned Sombart and spitefully criticized his book, *Moderner Kapitalismus,* which had just appeared in its first edition. (Later editions of the book were very different.) In general, von Below's criticism was unfavorably received. It would therefore have been easy for Sombart to win sympathy with factual arguments. But instead of this he assumed the role of a cynic. The representative of the ministry at Baden therefore told Max Weber, "The impression Sombart has made is terrible, and there is no possibility of considering him as your successor."

At that time I was just a young whippersnapper, a fresh-baked Gymnasium graduate. At our local Gymnasium in Düsseldorf, Theodor Kückelhaus was one of the history teachers. In spite of his early death, he was well known for his historical works on French absolutism, particularly on Sully, Richelieu, and Richelieu's associate, Fanean; and he deserves not to be forgotten. Kückelhaus took me along to this meeting of the Historical Congress. I went there with a pounding heart, because I still believed that university professors were demigods, and I was painfully disappointed at the style and form of the debate between Sombart and von Below. At that time I saw only what was obvious; many years later Weber gave me insight into the background.

Some of the people to whom Weber gave his support gave him little thanks for it. Sombart, the Proteus of German social scientists, who had just as many Weltanschauungen as women (and that's really saying something), landed in the vicinity of Hitlerism after a lot of changes; Robert Michels died an honorary member of Mussolini's party; the breast of this superannuated socialist was decorated with a fancy fascist medal.

It was otherwise with Simmel. I shall not discuss in detail why he failed to be appointed to a chair. I have already explained this in Landmann's book, *Dank an Simmel*. But this much might be said: certainly Simmel's Jewishness was a negative factor in the situation, and this embittered Weber deeply.

Races and Nationalities

With regard to Weber's views on race, nationalities, and peoples, there is a certain amount of misunderstanding that must be cleared up. Certainly he was dedicated to the German people whom he loved and lamented so much. But that never induced him to view other nations as having less value. On the contrary, he loved to point out unambiguously those attitudes of other peoples which found an echo in his own. This was especially true of the Russians. I have already mentioned their importance in Heidelberg at that time. Max Weber loved these revolutionaries because of their readiness to die. They had built a Russian library on the banks of the Neckar; it was opened ceremonially in 1913. And whom did they get to give the official speech of dedication? None other than Max Weber. For years he had scarcely made a public appearance in Heidelberg. But the opportunity seemed well worth a great effort. His chance to speak didn't come until midnight, as was typical at these Russian student affairs. He held forth then in formal dress, with elegant gestures but in grave earnest, before an auditorium so quiet that one could have heard a pin drop. His remarks were so profound that the speeches of von Radbruch and Alfred Weber, meaningful as they were, paled in comparison. This speech revealed the whole breadth of Weber's view. He underscored the significance to world history and the human greatness of the Russian revolutionaries, but not without adding, "Should the tension between nations increase to such a point that the Russians feel obliged to support Serbia, then we shall meet again on the field of honor."

Afterwards he was so overstimulated that the two Webers, Lukács, Bloch, and I went to a coffee house for awhile. As a satiric piece follows a Greek tragedy, this deadly earnestness was followed by relaxation, and Weber told all kinds of jokes and wolfed down eight little cakes in just an hour.

Besides the Russians, the Poles, of whom there were a great many in Heidelberg then, played an important part in Weber's thinking.

For him they were not only, as noted above, cheap labor for the Junkers and thereby a danger to the preservation of the German character of the eastern provinces, they were also something quite different. They were people whom Bismarck and Wilhelm, with their "silly language policies," had tried forcefully, but naturally without success, to deprive of their mother tongue. They were driven thereby into the arms of the Czar, even though they were his natural enemy. No less important to Weber was this consideration: they are people whom we are trying to rob of their culture, and yet they fight against it, heroically and ready for death. He loved them for this.

If not to the same extent as the Russians and Poles who were always visible in Heidelberg, other peoples played a role in Weber's thinking and perception. This was true, although little known, of the French. In no way did he regard them as the arch-enemy before the first World War; on the contrary. Certainly this South German sociologist was not a partisan of the rights of man in the sense of the natural law theorists from the Stoa to the French Enlightenment, however much he took an interest in Jellinek's and my work along those lines. But he loved the French for their support of the rights of the persecuted, even though they had produced only two persons whose views characteristically reflected this idea. The first was Voltaire. Certainly Weber did not share Voltaire's views on Deism, which had originally been quite optimistic. But Voltaire, who hated Calvinism, had supported—in spite of this or perhaps because of it—Calas, the persecuted reformer from southern France. This reminds one of a similar attitude of Max Weber's. He had taken an interest in my studies of Voltaire, even though he asked me almost pityingly, "Do you have to read those countless articles of Voltaire's?"

The second was Zola. Weber didn't have too much in common with his views on naturalism, heredity, or faith in the future. But this French anti-militarist had interceded for the army captain Dreyfus when he was unjustly accused and sentenced, and Zola had written *J'accuse* on behalf of Dreyfus. Could not this article have been written by Weber?

Since his trip there in 1904, the United States was prominent in Weber's field of vision. It is well known that this served as a precipitant to the investigation and discussion of ascetic Protestantism. I shall say only this much: he opposed the snobbish deprecation of the Americans as a materialistic people. On the contrary, he remarked in admiration, "In spite of opposing business interests, the Methodists have managed to have the Exposition in St. Louis closed down during the hours of Sunday services; what would happen if we tried that?" He also said, "The Americans don't have any state metaphysic, à la Gierke, but what difference does that make?" His attitude on the southern states of the Union was quite different. He thought that they constituted a different world, and even now this is the source of lasting complications.

From other sources he was well acquainted with the problems of the American southern states. Georg Jellinek, one of his most intimate friends, was not only Weber's epistemological boon companion as well as his predecessor in the formulation of the problem of the relation of ascetic Protestantism and the social world, he was also, essential in this particular context, the author of the book on the theory of international relations *(Die Lehre von den Staatenverbindungen)*. It may be outdated now, but at that time it was a sensation. However that may be, Jellinek was, aside from his importance in other fields, one of the very few Europeans who had dealt in a scholarly way with the structure of the Confederate states, i.e., with those secessionist southern states, Alabama, Georgia, etc., whose break with the Union had signaled the outbreak of the American Civil War in 1861. From his contact with Jellinek, Weber was well prepared to study the South in the United States. It is hardly necessary to say that he was extremely concerned with the Negro problem. A great difficulty was that the relatives he visited were typical Southerners, and in the ensuing arguments neither side gave an inch. Later, Weber talked about his impressions at that time. He indignantly labeled a "pure lie" the assertion that there was a "Negro scent," i.e., an odor peculiar to Negroes. He told of visiting revival meetings at Negro churches. He thought that the departure of the Negroes from the Methodist Church, which at that time had a lot of tent meetings and Pentecostal movements, to the less emotional Baptist Church indicated noteworthy progress on the part of Negroes. He underscored his conviction that some day the Negroes would be an important cultural factor in the United States.

Just as he had visited the religious services of the Negroes, the world of an oppressed people, he observed the activities of another oppressed people who lay closer to his heart. In New York he went not only to the grand opera and the theatre, as other tourists did, he went also to the Yiddish theatre. "It is true," he said, "that it is some-times hard to suppress a smile when at a deadly earnest spot the Jewish word is used, so that with our different usage it sounds comi-cal; and thus, the hero at the climax of the drama, declaims: 'How *lousy* life is.'" In spite of this, he was generally deeply impressed.

This was only one among many of his expressions of pronounced sympathy for members of the Jewish faith. I can remember two other especially meaningful remarks. In regard to the first one, he talked to me directly: "I am thought to be apart from the usual activities of the university, For this reason I am occasionally asked to give an opinion on the nomination for a chair. Instead of sending in one list, I have sent in two and have appended a note that the first list contains only the names of three Jews; the second list designates three non-Jews. The man who stands in third position on the list of Jews is superior to the man who stands in first place on the list of non-Jews. I know very well that in spite of this they will choose one of the non-Jews." And that's just what happened.

The other remark in this context is even more characteristic, and in any event is more consequential. One should remember his opin-ions of Poles and Russians as well as his relation to Jews. Keeping this in mind, one can understand how he came to say this to me:

> "If someday I am well again and can hold a seminar, I shall accept only
> Russians, Poles, and Jews, no Germans. A nation which has never
> chopped off the head of its monarch is not cultured. "This is the correct
> wording of his statement that is sometimes incorrectly cited, "A nation
> which has never deposed its monarch . . . "The importance of this inci-
> dent is centered on the combination "Russians, Poles, and Jews." He
> had used this phrase in front of other friends because, during the fruit-
> less attempt to bring Simmel to Heidelberg, the opposition had trum-
> peted that Simmel was the nucleus of a group of "Russians, Poles, and
> Jews."This was an unbelievable, silly lie, as Weber told me in a high fury.

This great empathy for other peoples and their ways, however, certainly didn't make him a pacifist. This is documented by the re-mark he made to the Russian students: "We shall meet again on the field of honor." His often repeated call to be prepared for death and his conviction that evil cannot be eradicated in the world, which goes far beyond Kant's position, helps to explain this. Two intercon-nected events are firmly imprinted on my mind. In America, money was made available to re-publish old books dealing with international law, thereby to serve the cause of peace. Jellinek had been invited to edit a book of critical essays by Pufendorf. At first he didn't want to. Later, however, Weber said to me, "Jellinek has been talked into doing it." When I charily asked about the significance of the undertaking, I received the answer, "The whole thing is senseless."

Another time I mentioned to Weber that I had gone to the Heidelberg Peace Congress. This was organized by the *Friedensbüro*. At that time it was in Bern; later it was in Geneva. Germans who were involved then were Quidde and Hans Wehberg; but one of the chief speakers at the Heidelberg meeting was the well-known French pacifist, Baron d'Estournelles. But before I could even begin to tell about it, Weber shut me off with an impatient gesture.

The reader who has thus far followed my recollection of Weber's political remarks can imagine, even without my saying so, that our political discussions were not always peaceful. He barely tolerated my activity as elected representative of the revolutionary soldiers of the Senne encampment near Paderborn, where, as a corporal, I had served during almost all of the war as a translator for the prisoners of war. What would he have said of my pacifist position from 1921 to 1933? But this lies outside the limits of these memoirs, which deal only with personal relationships before the First World War. One thing, however, must not be forgotten: he encouraged disagreement, particularly among his younger friends, and I was impressed that he did this not only in political matters but also in scholarly areas.

Philosophy and Philosophers

The next section will be devoted to a discussion of Weber's position with respect to science. An endless amount has been written about his philosophy, and especially about his epistemology. Johannes Winckelmann and I have assembled a bibliography of not less than 600 items. This will be published in the new edition of the volume on methodology, *Gesammelte Schriften zur Wissenschaftslehre*. Raymond Aron, the greatest French authority on German sociology, asked directly, "Is it possible for one to say anything essentially new about Weber's value theory?" Consequently a detailed discussion would be superfluous here.

Several characteristic positions must, however, be pointed out. Kant's epistemology is the unavoidable point of departure. In order to relieve Windelband, who was sick, Troeltsch decided to give a series of lectures on the history of modern philosophy. He spoke with Weber about it, adding that he would not lecture on epistemology. In my presence Weber responded, "A series of lectures on Kant is naturally a series of lectures on epistemology." The man whom Weber thought of as having a position at odds with his own was Hegel. My own position at that time was quite panlogistic. From this orientation I expressed myself to the Webers. This called forth a remark from Marianne that I was a "messianic young man," and Weber gave the opinion that I was "worse than Hegel," and "these notions are completely up in the clouds." He agreed completely with someone who said, "Whoever uses the word 'synthesis' today, without making the meaning explicit, deserves to be boxed on the ears."

Kuno Fischer was one of the contemporary philosophers whom Weber knew. Fischer's ponderous tomes are forgotten now but not his tremendous vanity nor the many anecdotes about him. To be quite truthful, Jellinek asserted that several of these stories had been told in the eighteenth century about Christian Wolff, who also didn't hide his light under a bushel. Weber could tell one or another of these stories to a newcomer who might not know them. Here is an example: "I made my first visit to the Fischers'; he had nothing more urgent to do than to boast about how many students he had. 'How many were there exactly?' he asked his wife who was sitting there thoughtfully. She answered admiringly and promptly, giving the exact count right down to the last student." Other Kuno Fischer jokes that circulated in the Weber circle are so well known that it would be superfluous to repeat them here. In addition Fischer had little influence on the life of Weber or members of his circle.

The situation with respect to Fischer's successor, Windelband, was almost the reverse, and is therefore worth discussing in more detail. A few years before, Windelband had given his rectorial address in Strassburg. The speech had been entitled, "History and Natural Science," which perhaps was not a happy choice. This was at a time when the methodology of natural science was still thought to be a cure-all, by quite a few people. The speech had therefore attracted attention and, moreover, it can be regarded as a starting point for much that Jellinek, Troeltsch, and Max Weber had to say about methodology. In addition, Windelband was the author of a textbook on the history of philosophy. The book had a singular structure not often found in a work on the history of philosophy: it was organized in terms of the history of problems as well as in terms of the delimitation of various schools. This made the book indispensable, and it is still used today in a new edition revised by Heinz Heimsoeth. Last but not least Windelband was also the author of a book on contemporary philosophy. This book took up simultaneously, so to speak, a consideration of all the areas that had any relation to wisdom. Thus it included, for example, mathematics, natural science, religion, and even mysticism. As Siegfried Behn has justly pointed out, Windelband was able to write with understanding even about people whose notions were very different from his own.

As the reader can see, there should be many points of agreement between Windelband and the subject of these memoirs. Actually, however, there were more points of friction. For this great historian of philosophy had a human side that simply got on Weber's nerves. One cannot overestimate the role that good food played in Windelband's life. Everyone noticed this, even his students. Some of them, as Sigsbee, had come from as far away as America to sit at the feet of the great thinker, and were then somewhat disenchanted. Even Weber was driven to making witty observations. Thus, for example, I told Windelband in 1909 that I had just returned from the Bibliothèque Nationale in Paris where I had worked for nine months. He interrupted me with the remark, "Yes, I remember my work there very well; right nearby there was a little restaurant where I could pause in my work and have Cheshire cheese and Chablis." Both Ray Addison Sigsbee, who until a few years ago was a professor at City College of New York, and Erich Franck, who later became well known in both Europe and America as a teacher and author, were students of Windelband's at that time and were present when Windelband made the remark noted above. They both said to me later, "Typical of Windelband; his first thought isn't for the treasure trove of books in the Bibliothèque Nationale, but for good eating and drinking." Even Jellinek's widow told me that, when Windelband met her husband, the friend of his youth, after years of separation, he was always talking about eating.

Max Weber made an observation in the same vein. At that time in Heidelberg they had just founded "Eranos," a small circle of researchers who took a scientific interest in religion. They intended to meet once a month at the homes of various members. There were difficulties because in some houses the rooms were very small. "No wonder," Weber said, "because Windelband alone needs two rooms for himself and his atmosphere." Nevertheless there was no unbridgeable personal difference between the two men. As barriers which could not be overcome, however, there were politics, the university, and the emancipation of women. Windelband was privy councillor and member of the upper house in the state of Baden, and unfortunately, like some professors in Wilhelm's Germany, he was the father of an active officer. This guided his judgment of the world of politics. I particularly remember one judgment of Windelband's. It is such a characteristic illustration of the difference between him and Weber that it should not be forgotten. One of the many Russian revolutionaries whom the Czar later executed, although the man was really a moderate, was in Heidelberg just then as a former student of Jellinek's. Weber offered the man heart-felt sympathy. I repeated this to Windelband and received an answer which tells something about both Windelband and Weber: "Naturally, but that's only because the man has been sitting around in prison." And in the matter of trying to get an appointment for Simmel, for which Weber fought and struggled so hard, Windelband did nothing at all. When Weber considered the possibility of allowing a woman, the social welfare politician, Maria Bernays, to be formally qualified, this was just too much for Windelband, and Weber groaned in despair, "To talk with Windelband about either politics or the position of women—it's simply impossible." And laughing scornfully as he sometimes did, he recounted an anecdote which I shall give in shortened form. Frau Jellinek was interested in protecting waitresses from moral risk, and she particularly would have liked a law that prohibited girls from working at night in establishments that sold alcoholic beverages. She therefore collected signatures for a petition to be forwarded to the proper office. The petition was also signed by Frau Windelband, who had done so without asking her husband's permission. But he thought it unfitting that the name of the wife of a full professor should appear on a piece of paper that had to do with the existence of waitresses, and he demanded that she retract her signature. Ruefully, "little mamma"—as she was called by us younger students, and even by Weber—went to Frau Jellinek. Smiling, Frau Jellinek handed a pencil to Windelband's wife, who scratched off her name and peacefully returned to her forgiving spouse.

In addition to the army officer mentioned above, Windelband had another son, a historian, and this only increased the tension. Weber simply couldn't stand him and his face turned purple with rage (such as I had otherwise never seen) when he came to speak of the historian and said, "He messes constantly in the affairs of the university; he is a completely shameless lout who ought to be constantly boxed on both ears." The object of this criticism was prone to make very outspoken remarks. As they often did, his parents had invited some young guests to dinner. Among these were Erich Franck—who was also welcome at the Weber's—and Sigsbee, as well as Hans Ehrenberg of whom we shall speak in another context, and I. On this occasion, the son made some cutting remarks about the attitudes of Alfred and Max Weber with regard to politics and the university, but he added, "At least Max Weber has proved his ability, but Alfred!" He said this latter about an economist who had already done considerable publishing on the theory of consumption but particularly on the theory of the location of industry and who later became one of the most discussed theorists of history in America. But in these memoirs we are dealing with Max Weber, not with Alfred, and so we shall return to him.

After these rather lengthy observations on the relationship with Windelband, we can be more brief with respect to Rickert, particularly since details of the relationship are widely known. This much must be added: in his unbounded selflessness and modesty, Max Weber underestimated his own independence from Rickert, and this has obscured the picture of the actual relationship of the two men. The form of the relationship between the two epistemologists was clarified first by Johannes Winckelmann's work on legitimacy and legality in Weber's sociology of authority (*Legitimität und Legalität in Max Webers Herrschaftssoziologie*), which appeared in 1952, and Dieter Henrich's book (which appeared quite independently of Winckelmann's) on the integration of Weber's scientific methodology (*Die Einheit der Wissenschaftslehre Max Webers*). Through these two publications another error was simultaneously removed and a man whose importance in this context had been overlooked, was brought into proper focus. People have justifiably wondered about the sources of Weber's scientific methodology, and one finds that one of these was Georg Jellinek. The importance of the latter as a forerunner of the Calvinism-capitalism thesis (as it is usually called in this shortened but incorrect form) is undeniable. On the other hand, if one is looking for the genesis of Weber's epistemology, then Jellinek is the wrong man. For Jellinek's conception of an ideal type is quite different from that of Weber. Because of this fact the importance of Sigwart has been obscured, if not forgotten altogether. Johannes Winckelmann has clarified Sigwart's impact, as did his friend, Jellinek. My own memories confirm the truth of Jellinek's assertions, for I was the silent witness of a conversation in which Weber spoke with great respect of Sigwart and his logic. Weber was speaking to Emil Lask and the conversation concerned special problems of logic. In terms of personal relations, Lask was probably closer to Weber than was any other contemporary philosopher. At most Weber was occasionally annoyed about "this damned Jewish decency—always in a state of anxiety lest someone's feelings be hurt." Otherwise he protected and loved this man in his touching helplessness. Lask had the sharpest logical mind of the whole circle, but he was so abstract that it was sometimes hard for him to make contact with the reality of life.

Lask was born an Austrian Jew. His fatherland at that time was very anti-Semitic. Jellinek felt this too. In Vienna, after quite a struggle, Lueger had become mayor. He was the leader of a party which was a peculiar combination of Catholicism, petit bourgeois philistinism, and anti-Semitism. The dying land of the Hapsburgs offered only neglect to this touchingly helpless man. Nevertheless, he felt obliged, in conformity with the spirit of Max Weber, to go to the front in 1914 as a volunteer. He was soon killed in the Carpathian Mountains. Weber was able to see a purpose in this death on the battlefield. Driesch and I felt quite differently about it. I feel a certain satisfaction that I could offer this lonely man a few hours—if only in a coffee house—in which he could come out of his shell. Inwardly, Lask ached to be less alone.

It might also be mentioned that Weber had great appreciation for Riehl. He once said this to me: "If Kant were to return today, he would find only Riehl's kind of philosophizing adequate." Naturally this doesn't mean that as an epistemologist Weber identified with Riehl but that Riehl's unambiguous delimitation of the content of philosophy corresponded to Weber's unyielding demand for intellectual integrity. Where he perceived a lack of integrity he could be quite harsh, as with Hans Driesch.

Even before the first World War, Driesch had attracted attention through his neo-vitalistic writings and his lectures at Heidelberg. Shortly after the Revolution, when Troeltsch was in Berlin as under-secretary of state, he told me that he didn't care for Driesch's pacifism or for his position on politics and the history of philosophy. Nevertheless Troeltsch admired Driesch not only as a natural philosopher but as a logician. Troeltsch gave Driesch a recommendation when the latter tried successfully to be appointed to a chair at Cologne. But Max Weber and Driesch just couldn't get together; an ocean of difference lay between them. Driesch operated extensively with the concept of entelechy, that is, he stressed the function of the organism in contrast to an emphasis on the mechanical, as many Darwinists had done. Proceeding from such premises, Driesch became an opponent of sociological Darwinism and as such he opposed power, force, and war.

I still have a clear memory of a discussion in his house on a hot summer afternoon. We were talking about Meinecke's book on international citizenship and national state *(Weltbürgertum und National-Staat)*. This book was characteristically dedicated to Bismark's biographer, Erich Marcks, whose work was definitely in the tradition of Treitschke. Meinecke's book is concerned with Romantic-conservative groups. Meinecke tried to show how a pronounced feeling of nationalism originally developed from the Romantic-conservative mentality and how this feeling finally culminated in a specific attitude of friendliness to Prussia. However, the basic idea which runs through the book like a red thread is this: the transformation of international citizenship to nationalism is a good thing. Except for myself, Driesch was the only one there who put his finger on this point, and he said directly to me, "Meinecke asserts that this transformation from internationalism to nationalism indicates progress; but isn't the truth of the matter just the opposite?" I certainly felt this way too; in addition, Driesch was basically inclined toward optimism and he would have liked the world to be unified in one metaphysical system, which, according to Weber's epistemology, simply couldn't be done. One can imagine that this sort of thing would be like waving a *muleta* in front of Max Weber, who stressed the tragic aspects of life and the unavoidable emphasis on power." That this man is teaching philosophy here is really a scandal. "But I am proud of having been one of Driesch's lifelong friends, and I have incorporated some of his ideas into my own view of reality.

Much later, about 1931, Marianne and I met and spoke of Driesch. This was in Leverkusen, not far from Cologne. She was there as a guest of a family we both knew. She had been in Cologne to give a lecture on her husband, as part of a series that Leopold von Wiese and Fritz Karl Mann had organized under the title, "Founders of Sociology." Without my prodding, she remarked rather sadly, "Hans Driesch was a man with whom my husband just had nothing in common."

On this occasion I heard again of Weber's position with regard to another man and another group, the neo-Romantics. "He hated Romantics," Sombart told me one time right after the first World War. Now Sombart would have asserted all sorts of things if only the day were long enough, but in this instance he was accurate. He had worked a lot with Weber, particularly in the editing of the *Archiv für Sozialwissenschaft*. His remark occurred in the course of a conversation about Scheler, and it had to do directly with him. The truth of the remark was confirmed by other evidence. Right after the end of the first World War, Marianne had given another lecture in Cologne. Afterwards I went with her to the home of the geographer Franz Torbecke and his wife, both of whom Marianne had known in Heidelberg, and I told Marianne, among other things, that I had become Scheler's assistant. I obtained the position through the mediation of Troeltsch. Because I was supporting my parents after the inflation, it was necessary for me to provide a financial base for my application for admission to a faculty. The assistantship with Scheler didn't last very long, and, as a result of a good word from von Wiese, I became director of the municipal university for adult education in Cologne. Be that as it may, Frau Weber was not pleased when she heard of my relationship with Scheler. More significant is the remark she made in 1931 after the lecture mentioned above. This was truly in the spirit of her husband: "Scheler is the impure vessel of a noble spirit." Under these circumstances it is indeed necessary to take a closer look at the man to whom these sharp words words refer; at the same time it will further illuminate Weber's attitudes.

In 1955, Leopold von Wiese and I met in Cologne after a separation of twenty-two years. He accompanied me from his home to the tram. In the course of reminiscing, we came to speak of Scheler, and we both had to agree that he was the most fantastic figure we had ever met in our lives. Countless legends circulated about this man. From time to time, more than one famous German had been cited as Scheler's natural father. Actually he was the son of a Bavarian. This man fell in love with the daughter of a rabbi, but he could marry her only by converting to Judaism. This sort of thing didn't often happen, and at that time it required a lot of courage, for anyone who did anything like that was either scorned or ridiculed. Von Wiese and I agreed that this sort of act was to be applauded. The product of this marriage was Max Scheler. Formally Scheler had been a student of Euckens', but he hadn't been particularly influenced by him. Then he embraced Husserl's phenomenology and Catholicism. Officially he became a Catholic. There were legends about this, too. Troeltsch told me that Martin Buber had mentioned this to him. Scheler then tried to combine phenomenology and Catholicism in such a way that the latter would no longer have a foundation based on Scholasticism. The result would be phenomenological in Husserl's sense. However, Husserl drew an unambiguous line of demarcation between himself and Scheler. Scheler explained that he stood in an intellectual line of descent from the church father Augustine. This isn't saying much, because who hasn't invoked Augustine, from the extreme Calvinists with their belief in the *praedestinatio ante previsa merita*, the doctrine which prevailed at the Synod of Dordrecht in the Netherlands in 1619, to the other extreme, the philosophy of the Jesuit Molina with its maximum of emphasis on the *liberum arbitrium*. This philosophy was accepted not only in the Society of Jesus but also in the Catholic Church, although there were some hard battles over it. Between these two extremes there are all sorts of formulations: systems of members of the Dominican and Augustinian orders, and of course the Jansenists with their theory that grace was essential—a doctrine that shook Catholicism for 150 years after the Council of Trent.

Now Scheler, who was interested in my studies of Jansenism for this reason, claimed to be in the Augustinian tradition. This claim was also made by other Catholics at that time, Johannes Hessen at Cologne, for example, but in general there was no mixture of elements taken from Husserl. In addition, a group of Catholic academicians had formed a club. Among the younger members there were

quite a few with a non-Scholastic orientation. They were barely tolerated by Rome and felt that they were in constant danger of being
censored, for example, by having their works placed on the Index.
That had indeed been the fate of some German Catholics in the
nineteenth century; like Wessenberg, Werkmeister, and others, they
were the intellectual descendants of the eighteenth-century Enlightenment. But a similar thing had happened to other Catholics. This
group included people like Hermes and his numerous students,
Hirscher, Baltzer, Frohschammer, Lassaulx, and others; however they
might differ from each other, all of them had been influenced either
by Kantian or post-Kantian philosophy. The members of the academic club mentioned above and many outside the club who shared
the same ideas were naturally anxious to escape such a fate. To them
Scheler appeared as just their man. A young Catholic priest of this
persuasion once told me that Scheler really had a reputation for
being able to conceptualize the Catholic faith in modern terms.

But the relationship didn't last long. A few years later Scheler
told me that he was a kind of pantheist, and he asked me directly,
"Can you understand what these Catholics want of me? I have never
been a believing Catholic. "This restless man was always poised to
take flight from himself and his own sensuality, and sought an authority that would give him a sheltering roof; for a time he believed
he would find this in Catholicism. The power of his autosuggestion
was so great that he talked himself into believing he was a Catholic,
just as later on he thought he had never been one.

The Weber circle, however, was never much influenced by Scheler.
Among other reasons, this was because Scheler's sensational conversion to Catholicism had taken place during and after the First
World War. The influence of Husserl, Scheler's temporary mentor,
was incomparably greater. There were three reasons for this. Husserl wrote for *Logos*, which was the journal for philosophy at Heidelberg. Rickert, Weber, and Troeltsch supported it and published there.
The second reason was that in 1912 and 1913 Husserl's name occurred, if vaguely, in connection with the question of a successor to
Windelband; at that time Husserl was only a *persönlicher Ordinarius*
at Göttingen. The third reason was that at that time Helmuth
Plessner began to exert an influence in Heidelberg. He came from
the discipline of biology but he belonged to the Weber circle, and
even as a student he was thought to be a literary type. He wrote me

later during the first World War to say that he rejected the rather phenomenological position he had taken as a young man. In any case, at that time he was familiar with Husserl's and Scheler's phenomenology as few of the young men were, and he kept bringing the conversation around to this subject. Later on, he became well known, particularly as a philosopher of culture both through his positions in Cologne. The Netherlands, Göttingen, and the United States, and, for a time, as the president of the German Sociological Society. Although his views were quite independent, he did show some leanings toward Scheler.

At the same time Friedrich Alfred Schmidt and Nikolai von Bubnoff worked as *Privatdozenten.* Schmidt had indisputable fame, because he, his wife, and the psychiatrist Gruhle participated in the first play that was given in the Weber house on a Sunday afternoon. Bubnoff, as his name indicates, was of Russian parentage on his father's side; on his mother's side his ancestors were German Protestants. He was known for his lectures on the history of mysticism in which he even advanced to a typology of mysticism; he was also known for his publications on Russian religious philosophers, particularly Dostoevsky. We shall discuss him later in this context.

At least for a time, the greatest influence on the Webers and their circle was the result of two incidents which had to do with the discipline of philosophy. Several of the younger academicians in Heidelberg, along with friends from Freiburg and Strassburg, had joined together for monthly meetings in Baden-Baden in order to have lectures and discussions on cultural science. Several of the more vociferous participants held an outspoken, anti-liberal position, and had just about arrived at a "new synthesis"; in fact, they were quite Hegelian. The most pronounced Hegelian was Julius Ebbinghaus, but he was not then in Heidelberg. He was the son of the strongly empirical philosopher and psychologist and, because of this, Driesch, using Hegelian terminology, called him "the idea of the father in its other being." Ebbinghaus later became strongly Kantian. However, two solid Hegelians of those days, Hans Ehrenberg and his cousin Franz Rosenzweig, did live in Heidelberg. Both were of Jewish descent but felt themselves quite outside the Jewish culture. Both demonstrated this later, Ehrenberg by turning to an orthodox Protestant religiosity, and Rosenzweig through his book on Hegel and the state *(Hegel und der Staat,)*, which caused much discussion. Friedrich

Meinecke, whom we have already mentioned as the author of a book on international citizenship and nationalism, was one of the most open-minded German historians. He was so impressed with Rosenzweig's book that he offered him a habilitation as *Privatdozent* at Freiburg. Rosenzweig, however, turned it down.

How strongly both Ehrenberg and Rosenzweig identified with Germany is demonstrated by their behavior in the first World War. Ehrenberg was, as a relative of his wrote me, "militaristically inclined"; Rosenzweig was called up as a member of the ambulance corps, but letters his family wrote me indicated that he felt obliged to seek active duty. As a consequence he became a cripple, and it was in this condition that he wrote his book, *The Star of Salvation (Der Stern der Erlösung)*, which documented his return to Judaism. Along with the writings of his friend, Martin Buber, this book is probably among the most impressive works which owe their origin to a pronounced Jewish feeling.

Because of the obviously Hegelian leanings of some of the members, the Baden-Baden group was labeled "the Hegel club" by the envious. Now there were in Heidelberg at that time some persons who were very concerned with professorial etiquette. They were indignant and complained that the entire philosophy faculty should have been invited to the opening meeting. Weber didn't feel this way at all. In spite of, or more likely, because of, his dislike for Hegel and Hegel clubs, he felt obliged to uphold the rights of others to affirm Hegel and propagate his ideas. I can still remember this genuinely Weberian position because he spoke to me about it himself.

This sort of squabble became less important, at least for a time, because of the stir caused by the appearance of two "figures from opposite poles," as Marianne called them in her biography of her husband. These were Georg von Lukács and his friend Ernst Bloch.

Lukács was then very much opposed to the bourgeoisie, liberalism, the constitutional state, parliamentarianism, revisionistic socialism, the Enlightenment, relativism, and individualism. Later, with great personal sacrifice, he became a member of the Soviet government of Hungary after the breakdown of the Austro-Hungarian Empire.

He was therefore a committed communist, but later he would incur the displeasure of Moscow. As a communist he dealt with existentialism from a Marxist standpoint, and his writings on the subject are among the most important non-Catholic critiques that have been produced in opposition to this new philosophical system.

Five of his remarks made in our Heidelberg days particularly impressed me. They are characteristic of the man who, as we shall see, really played a role in Weber's thinking. Thus it is necessary to speak of him here. Once, when we were taking a walk together, he told me, "All this individualism is just humbug; Stefan George is allowed to be a personality, but a policeman and coachman are not." Another time I spoke of the old agricultural chemist Adolf Mayer. I came to know him by chance when I was in classical school, and in the splendor of puberty I was very proud to talk to a real professor just as I did to my friends. In a warm and informal fashion he had often invited me, a mere student, to his house. I should only have felt grateful for this, and in fact I did. In spite of that I could not resist the temptation to show myself as the malicious knave I sometimes was (and perhaps still am). And so I made him the object of a nasty joke. In order to understand it, one must know that Adolf Mayer, who later lived to be almost one hundred, not only was an authority in his field, especially in the chemistry of fermentation, but also had, in his old age, published poems and philosophical and political pamphlets. I remarked that "superannuated natural scientists who can't work in their laboratories any more can suffer from three ailments: they write poetry, philosophize, or go in for politics. Adolf Mayer suffers from all three ailments." Lukács, who was standing nearby, interrupted me and said, "That doesn't make any difference so long as he is unenlightened."

Lukács' judgment concerning the following situation was along the same lines. We went quite often to the opera in Mannheim. The opera had engaged some excellent singers who had not only good voices but fine musical taste as well, for example, Baling, Felmy, Fenten, and Kromer, among others. The company was held together by the conductor Bodanzky, who had introduced the works of Mahler and Schönberg. He was often called "General Mightiness" (*Generalgewaltigen*), a name that characterized the nature of his relations with the people who worked for him. I complained about this to Lukács, but he replied, "On the contrary, that's very good; a parliamentary theatre is simply nonsense."

Another time I went with Lukács to a meeting of the Social Democratic Party. Now the Social Democrats in the model little state of Baden were not inclined to be very revolutionary, and their speaker that night was even less so. This was Ludwig Franck, the revisionist deputy to the Reichstag who had worked hard for the sanctioning of the war credits in 1914, but then volunteered for the front and was soon killed. On this evening he sharply attacked some governmental agencies because they had acted "in complete opposition to the constitution." He referred to this a number of times that evening. As we left the meeting hall, Lukács shook his head excitedly and said in a rage, " A socialist who wants to defend the constitution!"

Perhaps the fifth of the remarks he made to me is even more significant and sheds even more light on his position with respect to Max Weber. In order to understand it, it is necessary to take a backward look at the political situation at that time. The daughter of Wilhelm II had just married the crown prince of the Guelph House of Hanover. As a consequence the prince was made Duke of Brunswick, and he renounced his Hanoverian claim. A "Guelph Party" had been fighting for the re-establishment of the Kingdom of Hanover. Its demand was in the larger framework of a postulate supporting a more federalistic structure of the entire Reich. This explains why their deputies to the Reichstag, although they were Lutherans, were affiliated with the Centrist Party, whose members for the most part were Catholic. Because the crown prince of Hanover had of his own free will renounced his claim to the throne, the realization of the Guelph program was at *calendas graecas,* that is, it was put off to a far distant and improbable future, and the party had lost its reason for existence. The party's faction in the Reichstag soon dissolved. The members really didn't have much in common except for their program of restoring the crown of Hanover and their emphasis on the necessity of a more federalist structure for the Reich; although a number of them were really quite feudalistic in their views, another one, the deputy Alpers, became a member of the leftist-liberal *freisinnige Partei.* At the time all this was going on, I was for a change quite annoyed with Max Weber and thought him pedantic and dogmatic in his addiction to his principles. At the time I was given to a certain cynicism and some unpleasant persons assert that I still have not lost this tendency. We shall not investigate the extent to which this is true. In any case, I told Lukács, "The people fighting for the re-establishment of the Kingdom of Hanover are really fighting for a lost cause; therefore it should be Max Weber's task, in spite of this or even better, because of it, to support them." But Lukács replied sharply at once, "You are underestimating Max Weber!" He was quite right about this, but he was wrong when he went on to say that "Max Weber was the man who could get socialism out of the miserable relativism brought about by the work of Franck and his consorts." He referred to the same Ludwig Franck whom we mentioned above.

Lukács was really quite mistaken when he made the above remark. For after the collapse of 1918, Social Democratic party politics involved an extension of the notions of Ludwig Franck. After thinking about it, Max Weber remarked that these notions were "similar enough to appear interchangeable" with his own. The last remark by Lukács, mentioned above, shows not only his most inward feelings but also the deep impression that Max Weber had made upon him. The feeling was mutual. The two men had discussed many things, particularly esthetic problems. Lukács had originally begun with this interest, and indeed since the Second World War he has taught esthetics at the University of Budapest. His book on soul and forms *(Die Seele und die Formen)* appeared shortly before he came to Heidelberg and met Max Weber. This was one of the first places in which Kierkegaard, who was almost completely forgotten, experienced a resurrection. Kierkegaard was a Danish Lutheran who had written in the 1840s. For several decades he was known only to small orthodox Protestant groups. It was only after the First World War that he became popular, both as a presumptive precursor of Spengler (this is true only if one keeps certain reservations in mind), and as an originator of existentialism. Lukács was one of the very few who brought the notions of Kierkegaard back into view before the war.

In addition to the theoretical discussions on art, Lukács and Weber debated Marxist and epistemological questions. With regard to the reverse direction of the relationship, that is, Max Weber's position on Lukács, one should not forget one thing: Weber's ability to empathize with, and to interpret, the meaning of human action was, in a manner of speaking, unlimited; he was therefore able to understand Lukács' position or, more exactly, his turning from modern occidental individualism to a notion of collectivism. Weber explained it to me this way: "One thing became evident to Lukács when he looked at the paintings of Cimabue (who painted at the beginning of the Italian Renaissance, but who had a closer relation to the Middle Ages than to the Renaissance), and this was that culture can exist only in conjunction with collectivist values." In spite of this glaring antagonism to everything that was sacred to him, Weber immediately added, "Whenever I have spoken to Lukács, I have to think about it for days." In contrast he added these words: "When, on the other hand, I see Bloch again, I must begin by working myself back into our last conversation; this man is full of his God, and I am a scientist."

With regard to Ernst Bloch it is necessary to say that he is not the modern composer who shares that name and who is famous in America. A misunderstanding is possible because the Ernst Bloch of whom we speak here occasionally made notable remarks on musical matters. Lukács introduced him to the Weber circle. Bloch's Weltanschauung at that time was a combination of Catholic, gnostic, apocolyptic, and collectivist economic elements. He demonstrated all of this in part in his book on the spirit of utopia (*Geist der Utopie*). which appeared during the first World War. Afterwards Max Scheler called him a "Luciferian hero." As all of the Weber quotations above might indicate, Bloch did not evoke in Weber the same echo as did Lukács. I tried to put in a good word for Bloch in that what he said was really something new and independent, and he therefore deserved respect, according to Weber's principles, on the merits of autonomy. Weber simply emphasized—thereby being true to his own ideas—the obligations of "intellectual integrity." Weber then said to me, "Very well, but the man who wants to be called a philosopher is obliged, if you please, to construct an epistemology as a basis for his assertions; then we shall see if he is a philosopher or not."

On another occasion Weber became quite angry about the way that Bloch simply ignored facts which Weber considered empirically verifiable and which in his opinion constituted objections to Bloch's assertions. They had been speaking about theories of music, as they often did. Bloch made all sorts of assertions which "transcended into the metaphysical." Weber reminded him of some empirical facts concerning the music of Asiatic peoples, but this didn't impress Bloch at all. Several days later when I was alone with him,

Weber spoke about it. In this case I couldn't even attempt to justify Bloch. Weber knew my argumentative tendencies only too well and obviously feared that I would try something like this. He therefore let me say scarcely a word and said with great feeling, "You heard it yourself, you were there. Yes indeed, I remember it exactly; the man cannot be taken seriously in scientific matters." Actually it wasn't so much the content of Bloch's system as the prophetic manner of its presentation that irritated Weber so much. Weber liked good manners (which he also found lacking in the Catholic "chaplainocracy," a word he coined himself). And not only Weber but several of his friends as well saw the good fellowship of the Sunday afternoons endangered by Bloch. In fact, several people actually stopped coming because of Bloch. Friedrich Naumann who was very close to Weber politically was, on one of his rare Sunday afternoon visits, painfully disturbed by Bloch's behavior. Weber's student, the previously mentioned Maria Bernays, once told me that Weber had remarked to her, "I would like to send a porter to his house to pack his trunks and take them to the railroad station, so that Bloch would go away."

With respect to all of these quotations the accent was always on the statement, "I am a scientist." However much he dedicated himself to epistemological investigations, he did this, in the last analysis, because he felt obliged to do so for the sake of intellectual integrity. This was an important means to the end of attaining knowledge in the sphere of the special sciences. We shall now show Weber's position with regard to the various disciplines and their representatives as expressed in a number of conversations.

Disciplines and Schools

Weber agreed with Windelband that psychology was one of the special sciences. At that time the subject of psychology was a matter of some dispute. Weber had nothing against psychology, quite the contrary. He thought, for example, that an industrial psychology was both valid and possible. This is sufficiently demonstrated by his essays on the methodology of an occupational survey and on industrial psychology (*Methodologische Einleitung für die Erhebung* ...and *Zur Psychophysik der industriellen Arbeit*). The existence of this basic position is also demonstrated by a number of his remarks. He once went so far as to say to me, "I am quite in sympathy with a psychological conception of philosophy such as that of Cornelius.'" To brand Max Weber as one of the principal opponents of psychology, as is sometimes done, is just as mistaken as to brand him as the opponent of statistics. Moreover, psychiatry was represented in Weber's circle by Busch, Jellinek's son-in-law, who was killed when he was still young, early in the war, as well as by Gruhle and Jaspers. The latter went from psychiatry by way of the intermediate stage of psychology over to philosophy, and he has reported the influence Weber had on him. Jaspers' particular philosophical system was not made explicit in those conversations before the war, at least not when I was there (and these memoirs are concerned only with events that took place in my presence). The situation was the same with respect to psychoanalysis. At that time, it was in an earlier stage before its fundamental basis had been re-formed by Erich Fromm. The term "psychoanalysis" was sometimes used, by Busch, for example, but a detailed discussion of the basic principles never took place in my presence.

Now, although he accepted psychology as a valid discipline, Weber was very annoyed, as was his friend Troeltsch, by a current custom of the Prussian Ministry of Educational and Religious Affairs. If a university had two chairs of philosophy, one was sometimes filled by a Thomist as a result of pressure from the Catholic Center Party, and the other by an experimental psychologist. This situation was the cause of two jokes, which Max Weber did not invent, but which he repeated and which were circulated in the Weber circle. The point of the first is understandable only in connection with an Eastern Jewish anecdote which, in shortened form, goes like this: one of two Russian Jews gives a ten gulden bill to a Jewish woman who wants to have her child baptized. She is supposed to give the bill to the Greek Orthodox priest, who demands one gulden for the baptism, and she is supposed to return the change. She thus returns nine gulden to the first Jew. The other Jew is enraged and asks his co-religionist how he can give money for the purpose of conversion to another faith. The first answers him in Yiddish with the verbal inversion that sounds so odd to us: " Am I pleased to see happy faces all around me; is the woman happy, because her child is baptized; is the priest happy because he has received his money; and am I happy because my ten gulden bill was counterfeit."

Now the Erlangen professor of philosophy, Paul Hensel, although superannuated, was still living at that time. He had become known through his book on evolution *(Kritik des Evolutionismus)* among other things, and he was a bit of an *enfant terrible* in regard to South German neo-Kantianism. His peculiarity can be demonstrated thus: he was the descendant of a famous Jewish family, the Mendelssohns. This family gave the world more than one extraordinary personality: Moses Mendelssohn, Lessing's friend and the prototype of Nathan (in Lessing's play, *Nathan der Weise),* as well as the composer. But that didn't stop Hensel from blabbing Jewish jokes, or even inserting them in his written works, at suitable, but particularly at unsuitable, occasions. He once published a widely read article in the *Frankfurter Zeitung* concerning the fact that experimental psychologists were filling chairs of philosophy. He said that one of the chief reasons the government wanted to do this was that philosophy and experimental psychology had nothing in common and therefore there would be no friction, and "one sees happy faces all around." All the initiates knew to which Jewish joke this referred, and Max Weber told those who didn't, although not without a bitter smile. The undeniable fact hurt him deeply and caused him to be very troubled about the future of philosophy in German universities. He was also displeased when Külpe, who combined philosophy and experimental psychology, was called to the chair of philosophy at Bonn, but he never enlarged on his reasons for feeling this way.

A more biting wit than the above was introduced by the previously mentioned Emil Lask, who said, "The filling of philosophy chairs with experimental psychologists is best characterized by the [somewhat shortened] title of Kant's work, "The Attempt . . . to Introduce Negative Entities into World Knowledge.'" Max Weber gave this one his unconditional approval.

Finally it might be noted that Windelband was also embittered at the way the experimental psychologists pushed themselves to the fore. This was made obvious by his behavior toward the experimental psychologist Ebbinghaus (the father of the previously mentioned Julius Ebbinghaus, the erstwhile neo-Hegelian) at the International Congress of Philosophy in Heidelberg. In a discussion, Ebbinghaus spoke longer than the rules allowed. Finally Windelband, who was presiding at that session, felt obliged to cut him off. He did it with the words, "I regret that I must deprive our colleague Ebbinghaus of the right to speak, all the more as I have not been able to discover a connection between his remarks and the object of our discussion." I was there at the time; Max Weber repeated the story later and added, "It must have gone pretty far if Windelband was so annoyed that he felt obliged to use such words."

One discipline that Weber regarded with some skepticism, or at least the way it was conducted at that time, was geography. I had looked into it rather closely myself, just before I came to Heidelberg. Originally my major was history, but I had to consider the possibility of taking a state examination in order to be certified as an *Oberlehrer* (as a secondary school teacher was called at that time— later he was called a *Studienrat)*. Geography appeared to be an obvious minor. In addition, at the beginning of my student days, I had a strong inclination to explain historical matters as much as possible in a natural-scientific sort of way, and geography appeared to me to be one of the ways to do this. The older anthropo-geographical orientation of Peschel and his kind, represented last by Ratzel, was declining. Correspondingly, a natural scientific trend toward basing geography on geology became dominant. Richthofen, the cousin of the secretary of state, almost completely dominated the field from Berlin, and he put his students, such as von Drygalski, Passarge, and others, into influential positions. Thus von Drygalski, who had gone to the South Pole, was at Munich; Passarge, who had been in the Kalahari Desert, was in Breslau; and Philippsohn, who had done research on the islands in the Eastern Mediterranean, was in Bonn. I had attended a seminar under Philippsohn at Bonn, and because of his recommendation I was accepted in Berlin by Richthofen in his very famous and much sought-after geography colloquium. In Heidelberg I had discontinued such studies, mostly because of the heavy demands of Jellinek and his seminar. Yet I remained sufficiently familiar with the material that I could discuss it if the occasion arose. Weber, however, remained very skeptical about the subject. "These people make a Weltanschauung out of their particular discipline." When I told him about my former teacher, Philippsohn, he commented: "He's probably the worst." He spoke rather sarcastically of a geographer who had once written that history asks when something happened, geography asks where something happened, and economics how something happened. Naturally Weber wanted nothing to do with such a man.

With regard to Weber's position on history, as expressed in conversations, the reader must remember two facts that we have already mentioned before we take up the subject. Weber had begun his career as a historian of law, commerce, and agriculture; this is to say that, as a historian, he worked in a rather daring combination of areas. His wife told me a number of times that for years he had devoted a great part of his energy to empirical historical research. It may appear presumptuous to bring the great and the small into intimate relation, and to speak of Weber's basic attitudes and my own in the same breath. Nevertheless, I shall do so. I can say, without exaggeration, that my interest in historical science began when I was about twelve years old. My grandfather, whose major was ancient history, introduced me to this field and thought that I was old enough to read the Greek tragedies in German translation. But for the last twenty-five years I have lived and taught in the United States. This is the country which, in contrast to Latin America, shows the most extreme lack of ability to see things in historical perspective that the world has ever seen. And just because of this, I have become even more firmly convinced, to the extent that it is possible, that history is and remains the essential foundation of social scientific knowledge.

The reader will therefore not be surprised to learn that Weber and I talked a great deal about history, and the present discussion of history will consequently be extensive. The term "history" is used here in its most broad and general sense and will not be limited to political aspects. Indeed it was history that brought us together. Jellinek introduced me to Weber at the previously mentioned Stiftsmühle. I said openly that I had never read a line of his and knew nothing at all about his basic position; but I blurted right out, "I want to be a historian but I know in advance that this will come to mean bitter resignation." Weber replied, "Yes, that is so; it is resignation." He gave me a penetrating look, and I knew that I had his approval.

The ensuing conversations often concerned concrete historical events or individual historians or historical schools, but the theoretical aspects of history also played a part. The essence of Weber's position has been revealed in his writings, and it has often been treated in the literature. It is superfluous to go into it here, especially because not very much came up in the discussions that isn't more or less well known from Weber's works on historical methodology. It will suffice here to discuss particular historical epochs and historical schools, especially because the application of the general theory to individual researchers and to particular trends is not always immediately obvious.

Without exaggeration one dares to, indeed one must, say that he had something to say about all of these; and more than that, he was involved in all the squabbles among the various schools and he acted from a deep sense of commitment and involvement. Even those such as I and others working in the field who could not quite conform to his views (and who do not dò so even yet) were deeply impressed, if not actually awed, by his involvement. Under these circumstances, it is necessary to present an outline of the various schools and their protagonists. I shall do this here without interrupting to present Weber's position. The following discussion, therefore, constitutes a unit unto itself.

The Contemporary Historical Schools

Socialist historians were almost completely absent from German universities, whether or not they called themselves Marxists, like Kautsky, or Revisionists, like Bernstein. The German Catholics were not excluded to quite the same extent, but they still tended to be outside academic life. Their most famous representative, Johannes Janssen, had never been a university professor. The position of Catholics with respect to participation in the government was similar. This, along with other factors that had to do with the nature of Catholicism, explains why contemporary Catholic historians were less oriented to the state and took a more universalistic interest in the totality of cultural phenomena than the non-Catholic. In his work of many volumes on the history of the German people *(Geschichte des deutschen Volkes)*, Janssen focused on the various social strata as the object of his presentation. The work was heavily attacked. Finke and his school had strongly emphasized the history of ideas in their collection of research on the pre-Reformation period *(Vorreformationsgeschichtliche Forschungen)*. The Jesuit priest Ehrle and the Dominican Heinrich Denifle had done the same in their periodical which dealt with literary and church history of the Middle Ages *(Archiv für Literatur- und Kirchengeschichte des Mittelalters)*. (I shall come back to Denifle later.) This periodical also treated the history of mysticism, universities, schisms, and anti-popes in the Middle Ages. These investigations also received wide recognition in non-Catholic circles. Denifle's work on Luther, on the other hand, reminds one of the controversial literature of the days of the Kulturkampf and its aftermath. This was the epoch when, for example, Majunke paraded his evidence for Luther's suicide, which met with no approval even in Catholic circles; and members of Protestant groups such as the *Evangelische Bund* and the *Protestantenverein* repeated old tales in the style of Tümmel about the "baked God" which the Catholics carried about in their Corpus Christi Day processions or presented new evidence of the illegitimate children of Renaissance popes. Now, however, because there was little interest in the Kulturkampf, Denifle's last work didn't attract much attention.

Martin Spahn had a special position in the world of Catholic historians. He was the son of a leading deputy of the Center Party, and because of the recommendation by Lenz (a follower of Ranke's) he had become a *Privatdozent* and then finally an *Ordinarius* at the hotbed at Strassburg, all when he was still quite young. He was also helped by the personal intercession of Wilhelm II. This had called forth a lot of protest; Mommsen spewed forth the most violent objections. Since that time Spahn continually created a stir, first when he was a Center deputy in the Reichstag in spite of the protests of a number of party members, later as a deputy of the German Nationalist Party, and finally as a Nazi.

The church historians who were members of Catholic theological faculties were even more interesting, although for a different reason. They were in a complicated situation. On the one hand they were priests and therefore bound by the teachings of the church, and on the other hand they had life-tenure as officials of the state. In the latter capacity they could not be fired; in general, the state had no great interest in their theological conformity, and so they enjoyed an immeasurably greater independence than their colleagues in the seminaries. They were limited only to the extent that the predominantly Catholic Center Party intervened, and this tended to happen when Rome censored a particular man or at least let him feel its displeasure, as it had with certain writers who are now dead. Around the year 1910 (the period with which we are concerned), this displeasure was felt particularly by three men, Reusch, Ehrhardt, and Franz Xaver Kraus. Because Kraus is of importance in this narrative, I shall characterize him briefly. He was one of the leaders of the so-called Reform Catholic Movement. He favored a purely religious Catholicism rather than a politically oriented or, as we said before the war, an Ultramontanist Catholicism. He was critical of the hostile attitude which the church had taken in regard to the newer scientific positions in various fields. Thus he was embroiled in constant conflict.

In our present context, however, non-Catholic historical science is more important than its counterpart outlined above. Ancient history had long since parted company with classical philology. Nevertheless, the chief exponents had received a classical, philological training. In addition to its school concerned primarily with textual criticism, which included Gottfried Hermann and which found its chief representatives in men like August Immanuel Bekker, Lachmann, Lehrs, and Friedrich Ritschl, the research on antiquity was directed primarily to a realistic historical interest as demonstrated by Niebuhr and Boeckh. Thus it came about that a research interest in ancient religious history was established. In this connection we should think of the Romantics as an offshoot of this branch of interest in ancient history. It began with the correspondence of Schelling and Creuzer, continued with Karl Otfried Müller, and finally ended with Bachofen. This latter looked for traces of a matriarchal past in oriental and ancient societies; he thought that all societies had passed through such a matriarchal form, which he tended to glorify. Because Mommsen, a pronounced rationalist, thought that such a view was absolute nonsense, we didn't discuss it for a long time. This view was resurrected by Klages, Schuler, and Bernoulli and was taken up by some of the members of the George circle.

Another group to be discussed here was quite different. This group played a part in the classical period of the comparative history of religion. This is not the place to discuss manifestations of their research interest in oriental and Christian phenomena. Their work on Roman and Greek antiquity must be mentioned as the basis of later studies. The chief representatives of this group include Deubner, Albrecht Dieterich, Erwin Rohde, Eduard Schwartz, Usener, and Willamowitz-Moellendorf. Their investigations took them far into the area of ethnology, and they did research on the Dionysian, Eleusinian, and Orphic mystic cults, as well as on the Mithraic cults.

Of the people mentioned above, Erwin Rohde and Albrecht Dieterich are, because of their work in Heidelberg, the links between the older group and the circle that concerns us here. The historians of antiquity had been either exposed to or involved in these various interests. This gave them a breadth of information that could scarcely be found among the younger men.

The school of the aforementioned Niebuhr was firmly pushed to the background by the appearance of Mommsen. He was simultaneously a numismatist, an epigraphist, and a political historian. He had begun by studying Roman law, and he was much respected by scholars in this area. In Heidelberg his views were represented by some well-known names, such as the contentious Thibaut, then by Karlova and Immanuel Bekker, and, at the latter period of Weber's time there, by Endemann and Gradewitz. A universality similar to Mommsen's in the area of Roman studies was manifested by Eduard Meyer in Greek studies. In addition, Meyer included the history of Egypt, Mesopotamia, Persia, and in general the entire Near East, including its cultures, in his research and publications. Almost everybody liked his work; and yet when he was compelled to discuss his methods, there was a difference of opinion in which Weber was involved. Exactly the same thing happened to Rostovtzeff who, because of Czarism, had fled to Germany and later to the United States. Even so, his relationship with Weber continued. Finally, it must be mentioned that the field of ancient history also had representatives who thought that in essence change took place because of the will and the actions of particular individuals. This view was represented by Domaszewski, who worked in Heidelberg for a long time. His most important work was thus entitled not *History of the Roman Empire,* but *History of the Roman Emperors (Geschichte der römischen Kaiser,).* But this position had stronger representation outside the circles of ancient history, although this was not so true of the non-Catholic historians of the Middle Ages. In this area, the after-effects of the Romantic movement lasted a long time, but on the other hand, because of the Romantic inclination to study ancient folk customs and their manifestations, special fields of study evolved. They finally excluded the Romantic elements and in fact killed Romanticism. Thus the Grimm brothers created Germanic philology; Johann Caspar Zeuss developed Celtic; Dietz, Romance; Miklosich, Slavic; and Karl Otfried, Etruscan. In addition, Ranke's students, such as

Dümmler, Hirsch, and Waitz among others, published a German yearbook. Anemüller, Falk, Hegel (the son of the philosopher). Henselmann, Lacomblet, Lappenberg, Mack, and Dietrich Schäfer became famous when they edited, bit by bit, ancient records, documentary summaries, and city chronicles of bishoprics, monasteries, and municipalities. Schäfer is important with respect to Weber's disputes. Georg von Below (who was mentioned in connection with Sombart) along with several of his students worked on the history of social and economic phenomena, as did others.

Ranke's followers were incomparably more influential in modern history than in ancient or medieval history. Although their master had been dead for two decades, they dominated history in the universities. That meant that history was interpreted primarily as the history of the state and above all as the history of foreign relations. Ranke's treatment had been more or less like this. When he discussed literature, for example, he had written only short chapters called, "A Glimpse of Literature," or "View of Literature," or "Trends in Literature." Titles like these occur in the sixth chapter of the twelfth volume and the third chapter of the eighteenth volume of his work on French history, as well as in the sixth chapter of the fourth volume and the twelfth chapter of the fifteenth volume of his work on English history, with similar treatment in other works. Those of Ranke's followers who are of interest to us in this context include Max Lenz and his student, Felix Rachfahl, and Hermann Oncken; Hans Delbrück is somewhat apart. Delbrück belonged to an old urban family from east of the Elbe. It had already produced men such as these: the free-trader and supporter of the Customs Union who admired and supported Bismarck until he sided with the Center Party and favored a protective tariff; a fermentation chemist, a comparative linguist, and an archeologist. Delbrück himself was primarily interested in military history, particularly strategy; in political affairs he was a hard fighter and was not at all inclined to turn the left cheek if someone hit him on the right, but nevertheless he was a "fearless knight above reproach." He was often a controversial figure as, for example, when he spoke out against Prussian policy with regard to the Poles. This was quite remarkable if one remembers that the man had been the tutor of the Hohenzollern Prince Waldemar, who died quite young, as well as a deputy in the Reichstag and the Prussian *Landtag* for the *freikonservative Partei.*

There were other exceptions. This can be explained in part by the overlap of the Ranke school with the school favoring the Prussian-provincial-Protestant point of view. Johann Gustav Droysen, who had been trained as an archeologist, was the founder of this latter school. He had written a history of Prussian politics in many volumes *(Geschichte der preussischen Politik)*. In this work he defended, among others, the thesis that for a long time Prussian politics had consciously been nationalistically German. Ranke had spoken out against his coming to Berlin, and when he came anyway, Ranke remained reserved toward this colleague who was close to his own field. Erdmannsdörfer, Hausser, Sybel, and most pronounced among them, Heinrich von Treitschke, as well as the previously mentioned Dietrich Schäfer (although somewhat later and only to a certain degree), all belonged to this Prussian-provincial-Protestant group. Schäfer was primarily a medievalist and wrote a history of the German people *(Weltgeschichte des Deutschen Volkes)* in a style more or less like that used by Treitschke; during the First World War he became an ally of von Tirpitz and one of the leading representatives of the *Vaterlandspartei*, which put out propaganda supporting the notion that territorial enlargement was the goal of the war.

These Prussian-Protestant historians named above had anti-Catholic and anti-Austrian views, in strong contrast to Ranke's followers; in addition they flaunted their political passions, a display quite different from Ranke's regal coolness. Finally, Erich Marcks, Veit Valentin, Friedrich Meinecke, and Adalbert Wahl must be mentioned here. Marcks was one of the most extreme in his emphasis on artistic elements in the depiction of historical personalities, and his biography of Bismarck received wide attention. Possibly his student, Veit Valentin, went even further in this direction. He combined elements from the work of Treitschke with elements from Schopenhauer and Nietzsche. Later on he went in an entirely different direction and became a well-known pacifist.

The latter certainly wasn't true of Meinecke. We spoke of him briefly in connection with Driesch. He has been assigned to very divergent schools. In his book on Boyen, his treatment of the subject was similar to that used by Erich Marcks in his works on Wilhelm I and Bismarck; that is, he emphasized the importance of an intuitive understanding of personality. He was not just a historian of monarchs, battles, and generals but became a historian of ideas.

Therefore, many persons thought of him as a daring pioneer. And one should not forget that for many years he was the editor of the *Historische Zeitschrift,* whose title page listed the names of Max Lenz and Hans Delbrück as co-editors. Both of these men followed the tradition of Ranke and Treitschke, and they could not have thought Meinecke so different from them. In addition, Meinecke's book on international citizenship and the nation state was followed by another on the subject of the doctrine of *raison d'état (Die Lehre von der Staatsraison).* This was a discussion of the famous theory that ethics for the state was quite another matter than ethics for a private individual. In addition to Machiavelli, Meinecke treated Bodin, Campanella, Rohan, Naudé, and Pufendorf, as well as authors who were less well known at that time, for example, Botero, Boccalini, and Courtilz de Sandras, among others. The critical point was that Meinecke insisted that it was impossible for nation states to avoid a Machiavellian type of relationship with each other.

Adalbert Wahl didn't care much for Lenz, and when we were going for a walk one time when I visited him in Hamburg in 1908, he told me that Lenz was "a professor of liberal tendencies." Wahl himself was unbelievably conservative, and in this spirit he wrote a history of France in the period before the revolution *(Vorgeschichte der französischen Revolution).* He called Rousseau a "sick genius," tried to whitewash Louis XV, pictured the French Court nobility as though they were members of the Farmers' Association (Bund der Landwirte), and complained that because of his conservative outlook he wasn't appropriately advanced at Prussian universities.

The social, constitutional, and economic historians were relatively independent of those who followed Ranke and Treitschke. The Schmoller school should be mentioned first. We already spoke of Schmoller in connection with social welfare politics. At the same time, he was a historian, and indeed was the real founder of the so-called "second historical school of political economists." The first had been represented by Roscher, Hildebrand, and Knies, all of whom likewise played a role in Weber's life. Because of Schmoller's dual role as a social historian and as a person involved in German social welfare politics, his followers were divided into two groups: on the one hand there were practical economists and social welfare politicians in teaching and in governmental offices, and on the other hand there were economic and social historians holding chairs in economics and history in the universities. Among these latter were Naudé who died young, Kauske in Königsberg, and Otto Hintze. Hintze was the best known; he conducted a seminar on constitutional history at Berlin, he was co-editor of a journal on the history of Brandenburg and Prussia *(Zeitschrift für brandenburgischpreussische Geschichte)*, and he published a number of special articles on constitutional history which were later collected and edited. Later on he moved beyond administrative history to the threshold of administrative sociology.

More or less independent of Schmoller's school was another distinct group who could be subsumed under the title of social historians. This included several Austrians; among these Gottl (who later called himself Gottl-Ottlilienfeld) was important. At the previously mentioned Historical Congress in Heidelberg, he gave a lecture on the limits of history. As one could expect from the subject, the lecture was quite abstract. At that time I was just a rosy-cheeked freshman. However, the philosophy of history was already my most absorbing interest. All the same I have to admit I had some difficulty in following the train of thought. It was some consolation that I wasn't the only one. A history professor told Friedrich Mensel (who was killed in the First World War), who later repeated it to me, "Everything Gottl said is just plain nonsense." Another went even further and said, "I came into the hall, I saw a man speaking, but it was absolutely impossible to make any sense of his remarks." In Heidelberg itself, however, they felt differently, and years later his remarks were not forgotten and were still discussed. It is not necessary to tell the reader who was responsible for this.

The agrarian historians were relatively independent of the Schmoller school. There were not too many of them. Georg Hanssen and August Meitzen might be mentioned. Meitzen, in addition to his activities as a teacher and as director of the Office of Statistics in Berlin, had published a comprehensive account of the history of migration, settlement, and agriculture in Europe. At the time he was the first specialist in that field, for Maurer, along with others who could have been called Meitzen's predecessors, was still deeply immersed in Romanticism.

The school of historical jurisprudence was also rooted in Romanticism, and this school, following Gierke, was influential until the turn of the century. Gierke thought the fact that the German territorial states had adopted Roman law at the end of the Middle Ages and had thereby abandoned a specifically German type of law was not only unnecessary but even tragic. With this in mind he wrote his "System of German Civil Law," and finally, using an enormous mass of historical material, he wrote the history of Germanic corporate law *(Das deutsche Genossenschaftsrecht)*. He traced this history from the founder of the school of glossologists, Irnerius, through the glossologists and post-glossologists, through the theories of Baldus and others who combined Roman and canon law, to the eighteenth century and its natural law. He conceded to the Calvinist Althusius an important position in the development of natural law. All of these matters were important in Heidelberg, particularly in the circles with which we are concerned.

In contrast to Gierke, Lamprecht was not influenced by the Romantic tradition, but by economic history, which he interpreted in a positivistic sense. He classified history systematically, and he elaborated a schema of stages which, he thought, could be demonstrated in spiritual as well as socioeconomic life. Along these lines he wrote a multi-volumed German history *(Deutsche Geschichte)*. He was an academic success in spite of the fact that Ranke's followers scorned him and Delbrück called part of what Lamprecht did mere"humbug"; relatively early he had become a full professor and Institute director at the University of Leipzig.

Things didn't go this way for Breysig. He had begun as a member of the Schmoller school, and had edited Prussian state documents and was a specialist in economic history; but then he went to work on the construction of a system based on a series of stages. Thus within the Schmoller school, then outside it, he was considered an outsider in the world of historians. Consequently, for a long time he was just an *Extraordinarius* in Berlin.

Gothein could have met the same fate. He had begun as a historian, but, because he looked at history from the viewpoint of economics and civilization as a whole, he had little chance to become a history professor and he accepted a call as an economist. Even this was not without difficulties, only from another direction. In Berlin, Adolf Wagner was dominant as well as Schmoller. When lecturing, Wagner would often use the phrase, "My honored colleagues, and opponent Schmoller ..." Although Wagner agreed with Schmoller on the necessity of emphasizing social welfare politics, he also emphasized the importance of theory (which wasn't often done by the Schmoller school) and he thought economic history of little value. Even in the lecture halls he would remark that he could scarcely accept Gothein as an economist. Because he had a phenomenal memory and stupendous knowledge, Wagner was able to give lectures on the history of culture as well as on economics. And this man who was neither a history professor nor a Catholic could write papers on the Catholic Counter-Reformation with the deepest understanding; evidence of this is the classic biography of Ignatius Loyola, the founder of the Jesuit Order.

To a certain extent Wagner thought himself the successor of Jakob Burckhardt. It is risky to try to characterize this detached and isolated Swiss historian. At most, one can call him a pessimistic individualist. To him culture was a world in which an independent personality could develop—in this view Burckhardt was somewhat like the liberal optimists. He believed that culture, as understood in this sense, could really exist—and in this respect he differed from Schopenhauer. On the other hand, the few epochs of true culture were separated from each other by long periods of time during which such culture did not exist—and in this respect he was unlike the liberal progressives who, since the days of their extremist Condorcet, had believed in uninterrupted progress. Burckhardt thought such periods of culture had existed in Athens and in the days of the Italian Renaissance. He expected nothing of the sort in the near future. On the contrary, he saw the emergence of mass society in the image of the United States or the imperialist state. Even more characteristic than his often-repeated remark, "The wife of the German professor is a perversity of nature," were three other observations: "Culture blooms only in small nations," and the sarcastic remark he made when he was offered Ranke's chair in history at Berlin, "I'm too stupid for the nation of Herr von Bismarck," that is, the unified imperialistic state. The statement that is perhaps most revealing of him is, "Power is absolute evil."

Position on Historical Schools

The echo of these words was heard in Heidelberg. This will be demonstrated in the context of a discussion of Weber's position with regard to the various historical schools and historians. We shall dis-

cuss this on the basis of our numerous conversations and the remarks he made to me. I shall do this in the same order in which I
described the various schools in the preceding pages. In so doing, I
shall be able to present Weber's position in its purity and unity without having to interrupt constantly in order to discuss less essential
matters.

Weber's judgment of the work of socialist historians is so much a
part of his total outlook toward socialism that a special discussion
here would be superfluous, considering the remarks that have already been quoted. It might be mentioned, however, that Hans
Delbrück tried to make use of and to spread Weber's Calvinist-capitalist theory as a type of anti-Marxist idealism; Weber protested and
told me, "I really must object to this; I am much more materialistic
than Delbrück thinks." Naturally the confusing terms "idealistic"
and"materialistic"are being used here as a kind of theoretical shorthand. I might add that this remark was made just as I was going out
the door.

Weber didn't like Catholic historical writing. This was a consequence of his basic principles. The advocate of an ethic of autonomy
that went even further than Kant's ethic could not approve an authoritarian church, particularly in the discipline of history. He maintained inexorably that history was an empirical science, particularly
with respect to its value neutrality and independence from extra-
scientific authority. He was acquainted with Catholicism through
intensive study, through personal discussions with his Romantically
inclined relatives who were sympathetic with it, as well as through
personal contact with Catholic historians and philosophers in
Freiburg, before he had come to Heidelberg.

In Freiburg he had had the opportunity to become acquainted with
the ideas and activities of Franz Xaver Kraus. One time we were speaking of the desperate battles of the non-Scholastic Catholics. Weber
related two incidents concerning Kraus. Once, when one of his works
had again been banned by Rome, Kraus ordered that it be reduced to
pulp, all with a regal and disdainful gesture. Weber also spoke of Kraus
in connection with a story told about an American student. The first
part of this anecdote (which is all that concerns us here) goes, briefly,
like this: A young man had received a stipend from his local Methodist church to study abroad. The only condition was that he was to take
a course in theology each semester. After he came to know Max

Weber, the student was extremely impressed with him. He therefore decided to study in Freiburg. Weber pointed out a major difficulty; the theology faculty in Freiburg was Catholic. The American only shrugged his shoulders and said in broken German, "Oh, that doesn't matter. Where I come from they're so dumb that they won't know the difference." The young man then took a course from Franz Xaver Kraus and reported back to Weber, "He complains much more about the popes than we do at home." In the long run, however, studying in Freiburg was not particularly beneficial to the young man.

The second part of the story is relevant to Weber's position with regard to diverse orientations in Protestant theology, and we shall take it up at the proper time. Weber also liked a story, which he told with a grin, about a meeting with another Catholic historian; aside from the fact that Max Weber repeated it, the story is so good that it deserves to be remembered. In shortened form it goes like this: At an international historical congress in Rome, a group of Germans were sitting together at a cafe during a break between sessions, and among them were Max Weber, Harnack, a Catholic historian, and the Dominican priest Heinrich Denifle, whom we have already mentioned. The door opened and in came the Catholic historian's wife, who stormed up to her husband and exclaimed, "Did you forget that His Eminence, the Cardinal . . . has invited us to his mass with a sacramental blessing? It's high time; come on now." Not without showing some embarrassment, the husband obeyed and went along with his wife. Those who remained smiled but did not speak for a few seconds. But Harnack was a man of the world who did not easily lose his composure. He turned graciously to the Dominican priest and said, "If you also have religious duties to fulfill, I hope you won't let us detain you." In just as friendly a fashion and with a straight face, the priest replied, "Very kind of you I'm sure, but you see, I don't have to be religious; that's the advantage of celibacy."

A Catholic historian whom Weber didn't like very much was Martin Spahn. He came once to Heidelberg to a meeting concerning the relations of journalists and historians and particularly history and the press. I went to one of the open meetings and told Weber about it. He replied at once, "I can explain Spahn's behavior only on the assumption that he wants to be in good standing with the Catholic press," after which he dropped the matter.

The history of antiquity is certainly one of the cornerstones and points of departure for Weber's scholarly work. First of all, he was everything but an opponent to humanistic education, and he often mentioned that unbiased natural scientists reported that students who had a humanistic education at the secondary level were much more accustomed to logical thinking and scientific observation than others. Now, although Weber had not extended his studies of the sociology of religion into antiquity, his knowledge of that period was nevertheless apparent. This does not mean, however, that he agreed with Bachofen's position. It is true that in his later lectures in Munich Weber discussed matriarchal societies; he never denied that such societies had actually existed. But he denied the assertion that such societies represented a stage through which all peoples had to pass. This was in accordance with Weber's basic opposition to a more or less mechanistic parallelism. Yet I do not remember having heard the names of Bachofen, Bernoulli, Klages, and Schuler at that time. They were not generally well known until after the First World War, when it became fashionable to look at myths. I didn't even hear them mentioned in conversations with Salz and Gundolf, who were friends of Stefan George, whose circle had included Klages and Schuler for a time.

In contrast, Weber's relations with the comparative historians of ancient religion were much more positive. He admired Usener and this point of view was pervasive in the Heidelberg group connected with "Eranos," which we mentioned in connection with Windelband. But Weber was most firmly linked to Mommsen. This went back to his days in the home of his parents. To be sure, the author of the Roman history had joined the *freisinnige Partei,* which was firmly opposed to Bismarck, while Weber's father remained a National Liberal following Bennigsen and therefore supported Bismarck. In spite of this, the relationship between the two families continued. And when Max had grown up and had qualified as a university lecturer, Mommsen was said to have tried to get him a chair in ancient history or Roman law. Indeed, Weber was qualified in both commercial and Roman law. As he said, he had had some interesting experiences with regard to Roman law.

In the first place, Gierke had been annoyed when Weber had qualified. We have already mentioned Gierke's Germanistic position, and he was displeased with Weber's combination of commercial law (the domain of the Germanists) with Roman law. But Weber combined them anyway, and in his first semester as a *Privatdozent* he announced a lecture on Roman law. At that time, whoever had just been qualified to teach would have to realize that, as a man unknown to the students, he would have a very small class in the first course he taught, and this was the case here. Among the few people present was a young man still wet behind the ears. He didn't seem to know anything about the special things that were being discussed and felt quite out of place. Naturally Max Weber realized this and asked him, "This isn't at all what you expected?" The embarrassed young man mumbled something like, "Well, I guess so." Then Weber continued, "As a beginner, I have a certain interest in keeping at least a few people on my class list; therefore I should like to keep your name on it. But since you aren't getting what you wanted, naturally you don't have to pay for it." And he handed the young man, who was so astonished he couldn't say a word, a shiny, ten mark piece, the amount of money he would have to pay to attend the two-hour course.

But even when Weber had long been established as an *Ordinarius* in economics at Heidelberg, Roman law was the cause, although only indirectly, of his being put in an uncomfortable situation. The chair in economics at Heidelberg at that time was, as at other universities, in the law faculty, and in that prewar period one invited one's colleagues to very formal dinners with several courses and various wines. Such a dinner was given by the senior *Ordinarius* of the law faculty, Immanuel Bekker, who was at that time one of the most famous authorities on Roman law. In 1886, the 500th anniversary of the founding of the university. He had been made *rector magnificus* and was thereafter addressed as "Excellency." In addition, he was an expert on women and wine, married when he was eighty, bought 500 bottles of French claret, and said that he was going to let them age for five years. Max Weber related all this with great pleasure. Weber, too, received an invitation from Bekker soon after the move from Freiburg to Heidelberg; he declined because his seminar was on the same night. A few days later, his friend Jellinek slapped him on the shoulder and said, "I fixed things up, but don't do it again; don't decline an invitation with such a weak excuse. Once and for all, the obligation to teach is never an excuse."

Jellinek knew some amazing stories about his Roman law colleague, Gradenwitz, who was a Jewish anti-Semite. When asked why he had not married, Gradenwitz would reply earnestly, "How can I, when I belong to an inferior race?" For the same reason he declined the title "privy councillor," which was offered him when he came to Heidelberg. Weber had deep sympathy for the tragedy of this unfortunate man. Naturally Weber's relation to the history of Roman law did not always involve such piquant incidents. On the contrary, his works particularly on agrarian history showed his familiarity with and his constant study of the material. Thus he took great interest in the work of Conrad who had come back to Heidelberg and occupied himself with the history of Roman law in the Middle Ages. Weber said of Conrad, "If I had more time, I would try to meet with him more often." To Weber, the history of Roman law was part of the total history of antiquity, particularly of the countries of the eastern Mediterranean and Asia Minor. Study of the latter area is, of course, related to his position on religion and theology and will be discussed at an appropriate time.

Eduard Meyer's research on the Old Testament also belongs in this context. Meyer's book on methodology appeared important enough to Weber to become the subject of a special article. This work is widely known and is easily available in Winckelmann's new edition and in English translation. Weber never said anything about Meyer's methodology in my presence, however. But he had unlimited admiration for Meyer's scholarship in ancient history and particularly ancient oriental history, even though he might criticize him regarding certain details. On the other hand, he was very reserved toward his intellectually narrow colleague, von Domaszewsky: "The man just doesn't know how he feels about me; one time he admires me and another time he feels a deadly hatred for me." The hatred was probably a result of Weber's political views, because von Domaszewsky was a pronounced anti-democrat.

We didn't talk as much about the Middle Ages as about antiquity. Not that Weber wasn't interested; after all, as a historian of law he had begun with the Middle Ages. At this time, however, the greater part of his research was in other areas. Nevertheless, I can still remember three remarks which show clearly how important medieval studies were to him. We were speaking once of the families in the region east of the Elbe, such as Limburg-Stirum, and of other families just as influential. I asked about the origin of their wealth and social position, and he said that some of these noble families had originally been vassals of the Teutonic Order. He went into some detail on this and then commented that the history of this order had long since needed some new research. He thought this was even more true of the Normans with regard to their settlement and establishment of a state in Sicily. In these two instances I was more the curious student; on the other hand, because of our common interest in the sociology of religion, we met on equal ground when we discussed the genesis of the European, particularly the French and English, established churches. It is now necessary to recall my studies then of Gallicanism and Jansenism.

Weber praised the work of Haller on these subjects. Haller had presented a new theory for the first time at the Heidelberg Historical Congress I already mentioned: The Gallican declaration of freedom was simply an imitation of what had already happened in England. He presented this thesis later, in greater detail and with the introduction of new material, in a comprehensive work on the papacy and church reform *(Papsttum und Kirchenreform)*. There had already been a number of investigations of this subject, although they had stemmed from other areas of interest, for example, the works of Fincke, Rietzler, Scholz, Wenk, and others. I was familiar with the works of these men as well as with their sources. Using this knowledge, I observed that, even in the days of Boniface VIII and Philip the Fair, the French had unambiguously insisted on an established church and needed at most only to borrow the English formulation. But Weber maintained, "It is nevertheless a very profound book." He also liked Haller as a person. As a young professor, Haller had encountered difficulties with the university administration and had had the courage to resign his position. As one can imagine, Weber felt in him a kindred spirit and he tried, although in vain, to get another position for the man.

Whenever one examines in detail the origin of the state church, one is at the beginning of modern occidental history. Because Weber had a strong interest in modern historical research, the subject had an important place in our conversations. Weber certainly didn't identify with Ranke and, at least in my presence, he didn't often speak of him. Yet I can see the following scene floating clearly before my eyes: on a summer evening while walking in the garden of the old house with Marianne, Arthur Salz started to talk about Ranke and said some words to the effect that Ranke's work would still stand when all this "Schmollerism" had disappeared. Frau Weber gave her unconditional approval to this remark, and she explained, in the spirit of her absent husband, that Ranke's sovereign objectivity was quite admirable. Not everyone completely agreed with this notion of Weber's, even in the circle of his friends and those who shared his outlook. Georg Jellinek, for example, although so close to Weber in so many ways, noted the unacceptable role that diplomats played in Ranke's conception of history, and said sarcastically, "According to Ranke, history is made by impeccable gentlemen after dinner, over their cigars." At that time I was, as I have continued to be, rather anti-Rankian in my position, and I repeated Jellinek's remark; but Marianne and Salz didn't concur. Another time I emphasized the value of the lectures and seminars given by members of the Schmoller school such as Otto Lintze, of whom we will speak again. Weber only replied, "One learns more from other people," namely, from Ranke's followers.

With regard to individual members of the Ranke school, I can remember the following: Weber, with Lenz, was solidly opposed to Breysig, as the following incident demonstrates. At that time there was a journal called the *Future (Die Zukunft)*. It was edited by Maximilian Harden, a supporter of Bismarck's, but in sharp opposition to Wilhelm. In this journal, articles by and about outsiders of various origins were published. Breysig published three articles on systems of history. In these articles he asserted that the downfall of ancient civilization had been caused by too much individualism. Max Weber commented, "Lenz and I wonder why anyone would want to ruin his career in this way." He gave direct support to Lenz's student, Hermann Oncken, that he might be accepted into the Heidelberg Academy of Science, and he thought Oncken's book on Lassalle was "of real value for us," that is, for economists.

Weber's sympathy for Oncken was the cause of his criticizing me quite sharply. On the whole, he wasn't very pleased with me at this time, and he had good reason for this. After receiving my Ph.D., I had asked for an extension of time for the publication of my dissertation. I wanted to reorganize it and add some things. Because I kept thinking of things to add, it looked as though I would never be finished. It was finally published under the title, *Die Staatsund*

Soziallehren der französischen Jansenisten im 17. Jahrhundert ("Political and Social Ideas of the French Jansenists in the Seventeenth Century"). Naturally, I no longer agree with many of the things I said there, and I don't like the style at all. But the point is that I kept dragging my feet. If the faculty and my parents hadn't had so much patience, God knows what would have happened. The continual delay was annoying to Jellinek, Troeltsch, and Weber, particularly because Jellinek had recommended that I be formally qualified to lecture. Max Weber said to me categorically, "I really don't see how we can speak of your formal qualification when you haven't published a single line." At that time I was also going a bit too often to the Café Heberlein, and Weber told the social welfare politician, Maria Bernays (who repeated it to me), "If he [Honigsheim] gets the reputation of a bohemian, he's finished." My formal qualification, urged by Jellinek, was delayed more than ever, and then, because the World War intervened, didn't take place at that time. Twice Weber told me very bluntly how he felt about it, and twice he said right to *my* face, "You will never finish."

Something else made Weber extremely angry. My dissertation was classified under the rubric "history" and Oncken was the faculty advisor. I really should have consulted him more often, but I didn't do it because I was embarrassed. Weber didn't like this, and shortly after the first World War he said with vexation to Helmuth Plessner (whom we have already mentioned as one of the younger philosophers and who visited him in Munich), "Why didn't Honigsheim go to Oncken? He doesn't bite." Plessner reported this to me in Cologne in 1920.

Weber also praised the work of Felix Rachfahl (who was a follower of Ranke's and a student of Lenz's) on the House of Orange in the Netherlands. This, of course, doesn't say much about his position with regard to Rankianism. For Rachfahl, at the instigation of his master, Max Lenz, was one of the first who sharply attacked the so-called Calvinism-capitalism theory. Thus even the reader who doesn't already know it can anticipate Weber's reactions from what we have already said: Weber's exemplary nobility forced him in this, as also in analogous situations, to praise those who attacked him. And finally there was Weber's relationship with Hans Delbrück. Neither one was inclined to turn the other cheek if someone hit him first. The temperaments of both were similarly structured and both were in bloody earnest about their work. Thus they were forced to cross swords in the public arena in the fight over Sombart's being called to a chair.

Another remark of Weber's will complete the picture. I have already noted Weber's protest against Delbrück's exploiting the so-called Calvinism-capitalism theory as, in a sense, an idealistic conception of history. Weber had said, "I am much more materialistic than Delbriick thinks." Naturally the point at issue is this rather shorthand designation for the otherwise confusing terms "historical idealism" and "historical materialism." Weber didn't go into any more detail in this conversation, which took place just as I was leaving. But this frequent antagonism did not prevent Weber from emphasizing the value of Delbrück's works on military history. Later on, there were times when Weber and Delbrück were in agreement, particularly in their criticism and opposition to the Treaty of Versailles, although Delbrück was much further to the right.

With regard to Weber and Treitschke, in retrospect I can remember only a few characteristic remarks on the entire group of Prussian Protestant authors and their followers. The importance of Droysen's *Historik* with respect to Weber's thinking on history has been mentioned elsewhere and I can remember no particular remarks on this. I remember only one remark concerning Treitschke. I emphasized the danger of publishing a book based only on lecture notes. Weber agreed with me, and added, "It was no service to Treitschke when they posthumously published his *Politik*, which was based on his lecture notes." I had a certain obligation to Dietrich Schäfer. For his seminar I had written a paper called "Der Limes Sorabicus." It was written as a correction of a special point in Meitzen's book on migration, settlement, and agriculture. Schäfer had taken the trouble to have it published, although I was only in my fifth semester. On the whole, however, I differed from Schäfer's ideas on history and politics. I emphasized this when I spoke to Weber about Schäfer's "World History of the German People." Without actually endorsing the book in this way, I observed that Oncken recommended it for intensive study. Weber admired Oncken indeed, as we saw, but he regretted this recommendation very much and observed that at most the book was good only for cramming, "like the Weber-Baldamus." This latter was a widely used textbook for students. Naturally I had no reason to contradict him. Schäfer had also sent a letter to the ministry at Baden-Baden and sharply expressed his opposition to an appointment for Simmel at Heidelberg. In this same letter he had come out against sociology as such, and ended with the words, "In my opinion sociology must still struggle for a position as a scientific discipline. To see society as the primary determinant of social life rather than the church or the state is, in my view, a dangerous error."

Whether or not Max Weber was familiar with this statement, which has now been published, is not quite certain; in any event he, who with Gothein and Jellinek had worked so hard for Simmel's appointment, knew that Schäfer had opposed it, and his feelings were bitter.

Much greater excitement than all this was aroused by the appearance of the first volume of Erich Marcks' biography of Bismarck. Marcks, with his unfamiliarity with regard to questions of methodology and the philosophy of history, was certainly not Weber's man in all respects. But in the presence of a number of friends, Weber didn't hesitate a minute in saying, "He has the grasp of a historian." In this judgment he differed from his brother Alfred. In a discussion following a lecture Gothein had made to a large audience on this book, Alfred said, "Marcks has prepared Bismarck as a Christmas offering to the German Virgin." Weber had never met Veit Valentin, the best-known student of Erich Marcks'. In Meinecke, Weber perceived a nature similar to his own, and he valued him highly. Of Adalbert Wahl, however, Weber said quite frankly to Emil Lask and me, "I don't particularly like people who act like martyrs because of their conservative views."

Naturally this did not hinder him from thanking Wahl, in his replies to the critics of the Protestant-capitalism theory, for a valuable hint about the Reformed and Lutheran patrician families in the Hanseatic cities. We spoke much more often, however, of the Schmoller school. We have already spoken of their position with regard to social welfare politics. Weber also had some misgivings concerning the historical research of the Schmoller school. Three aspects were of importance to him: first, Schmoller himself had been somewhat influenced by August Comte's notion of three successive stages. As we have already noted, Weber didn't like systems of historical philosophy, which, in his opinion, could not be made legitimate either by a sound epistomology or by reference to actual source material. Secondly, Schmoller was not only the head of a school but a sort of university pope. And last but not least, there was the glorification of the Hohenzollerns in the historical works of the school. Because of his stringently ascetic position regarding the individual sciences, Weber heartily disliked value judgments. Therefore he could not approve the adulation of the Hohenzollerns. Lack of objectivity is a mild expression for what Weber said about Schmoller and his school. Remember the words cited in reference to Ranke's followers, "One learns more from other people," that is, not Schmoller's students, but Ranke's.

Of social historians outside the Schmoller school, Weber had great respect for the Austrian, Gottl-Ottlilienfeld. Six years after that Historical Congress, Weber and I spoke of the lecture that Gottl-Ottlilienfeld had given there. I reported what Mensel had told me, and Weber repeated the sarcastic observation we have already quoted. Hesitantly I mentioned that the lecture might really have been nonsense. Weber interrupted me at once and said, "It was everything but nonsense." Weber had undivided admiration for Meitzen even though he knew that many aspects of his agrarian economic research were no longer tenable, particularly with regard to his theory of Celtic settlement. When he once became angry in my presence because someone had criticized him as a student of Schmoller's, he said with humility and pride, "Meitzen was my teacher," and he was right. His work on the agrarian history of antiquity with which he was preoccupied in his earlier academic years shows the influence of Meitzen.

He could also, as he had done on other occasions, have mentioned Goldschmidt as one of his teachers. Weber had taken his doctorate in law under Goldschmidt, had delved deeply into legal science, and was well acquainted with the history of law. Of the legal historians in Berlin who were greatly upset at Weber's combination of disciplines for qualification as a lecturer, Gierke was foremost; this simon-pure Germanist couldn't bear the fact that Weber qualified in and taught both Roman law and commercial law. I remember another incident in regard to the relations of Weber and Gierke, which were sometimes friendly, sometimes antagonistic. Gierke had stressed the importance of Althusius in the history of natural law; Jellinek protested this and asserted two things in this context: Althusius actually thought more in terms of estates, and furthermore he had exerted almost no influence and had long been forgotten by those who worked in the tradition of the natural law. Weber accepted Jellinek's opinion, which was, of course, quite contrary to Gierke's view. Weber was fascinated by the history of natural law to which he ascribed considerable historical influence. At the time, I was preparing the lecture that I gave at one of the previously mentioned meetings at Baden-Baden. Weber had shown great interest in this as in my other studies in the area of natural law, a matter to which we shall later return.

If Weber's judgment on the historical aspect of the Schmoller school seemed occasionally unfriendly, it was harmless compared with the way in which he gave Lamprecht and Breysig a dressing down. This requires some comment because it has given rise to a certain misunderstanding. Both of these men, but especially Breysig, were ridiculed, and obstacles were placed in their way. I can still see how Eduard Meyer, sitting in his study in Berlin-Grosslichterfelde, showed me the recently published first volume of Breysig's work on prehistoric peoples *(Die Völker ewiger Urzeit)*, flipped over various pages, and made sarcastic comments on some of the statements. One might suppose that our battler for justice would come to the rescue of these fugitives. The situation here, however, was indeed typical of those in which Weber found himself. He had to make an autonomous choice between two obligations: in this instance, between protection of the persecuted and the rigorous demands of intellectual integrity. He chose the latter, for two reasons: he missed an epistemological substructure, an empirical foundation and conceptual clarity, which he thought absolutely necessary in the sort of work these men had undertaken. In addition, he believed that his conscience, which was so fixed upon the requirements of justice, could be clear in this instance. It is again characteristic of this man that the consideration of justice played a decisive role in his decision. He knew that my sympathies, up to the point of contrary evidence, normally lay with those who were not well known, and he respected my position. Also, I had not used the words "justice" and "injustice" themselves. In spite of this, he said to me, "Breysig cannot complain about injustice; early in his career he became an *Extraordinarius* in Berlin and that is the same as being an *Ordinarius* at another university." This was followed by the episode I recounted when discussing Weber's relations with Ranke's followers regarding the opinions of Weber and Lenz about Breysig's articles in *Die Zukunft.*

In this disagreement with Breysig, Weber was not actually condemning the history of culture as such. This was clearly demonstrated by his efforts to bring Gothein to Heidelberg. Gothein was supposed to lecture on both the history of culture and economics. The official in charge of appointments asked doubtfully whether Gothein would really be able to handle all this diverse material in his lectures. Weber calmed him with the assurance, "He can teach many other things as well."

If there were a historian of whom Weber spoke only with obvious awe, this was Jakob Burckhardt. Here he found it unnecessary to speak much about it. He contented himself with repeating the words of his friend Jellinek, who, when a professor for a short time at Basel, had dared to speak to the great isolate: "One felt as though one stood before one of the giants of this earth."

Ethnology and Sociology

Ethnology and pre-history had at that time relatively little point of contact with the historical sciences (this latter phrase is used in its older meaning, which is incorrect if one thinks of history as a systematic science). There were no chairs of ethnology or prehistory at any of the universities. One of the roots of German ethnology developed from Herbart's school of philosophy. This came about in part by applying various elements of Herbart's psychology to human groups in a configuration of ethno-psychology. Theodor Waitz, Lazarus, and Steinthal were the chief representatives; Adolf Bastian, the tireless world traveler, had combined the ideas of these men with elements of English evolutionism, and thus a system was created. It went like this: each group collectively conceives of a number of so-called "elementary ideas," which follow each other in determined sequence and are manifested in special culture forms and values. There is correspondingly a parallel in the development of cultural levels. In spite of this, however, there are differences between groups that are on the same level of development. They can be explained by the existence of geographical divergence.

All of these ideas appeared in a plethora of books written for the most part as notes on Bastian's travels. There wasn't much system to the presentation: there were parenthetical remarks that lasted for pages, and even the simplest exposition would be interrupted by these side remarks. As a result, Bastian's influence was confined to just a few persons. Those who became well known included von Luschan, who began his career as Dörpfeld's archaeological assistant in South Greece and then turned to research on the mixing of the natives of the Near East with African Negroes. Another was von den Steinen, who sought out the Xingú in central Brazil and visited Indians who still lived in a pre-Colombian culture. Others were Seler, Preuss, and Ehrenreich, who were among those few Germans concerned with ancient Indian high cultures. At the same time there was another kind of ethnology which scarcely found expression in the universities. It was either socialist, following Friedrich Engels, or leftist-bourgeois, and it manifested itself in groups of free thinkers, the Monist League, and organizations of similar orientation. Both types were inclined to naturalism and evolutionism—in this respect not unrelated to Bastian. Müller-Lyer was one of the most popular authors in this line of thought.

The situation was analogous with regard to the so-called ethnological science of law; here one might mention Post, who wrote on African jurisprudence, and Josef Kohler. This story was told about Kohler in my circle when I was a student at Berlin: "Each day he produces a poem, each month, an article, and each year, a book." Jellinek, who wasn't stingy with malicious remarks, wrote a nasty poem about him and said to me, in reference to the luxuriant, free-standing growth of hair on the head of his victim, "When I see Kohler's hair, I'm annoyed with God because he made me only a man and not a louse." It was also said that Kohler labored so hard and so long over the legal arrangements of the Aztecs and other non-occidental peoples that such arrangements could finally be fitted into his own categories.

Another school of ethnology quite different from those we have mentioned was the group that had its roots in the Romantic movement. Vollgraff had given this group an extremely pessimistic character. It followed the Romantic notion that the change to a technological and mass civilization was a sign of decline. This notion was not influential, and went almost unnoticed until it experienced a resurrection in connection with Spengler. In the meantime, however, objections were raised from a number of sides to the dominant doctrine of a parallel evolutionism. In the case of Bastian and his followers, the element of a migration of cultural values was present, but this element played a minor role in comparison with the notion of parallel development. Nevertheless, there were some who followed the theory of cultural migration: Eduard Hahn maintained this with respect to plough culture, Ratzel with certain bow and arrow cultures, Anckermann with respect to several Central African culture traits, which were said to be found in layers, and Graebner, who discovered a similar situation in Melanesia. With the help of Koppers, a student of American cultures, Wilhelm Schmidt elaborated a system. According to them, a number of cultures had originated in Asia and had then been carried to all the continents. A whole school was founded on this system, which was also widely accepted in South America but was almost completely rejected in the United States.

Max Weber had no direct relationship to ethnology. He was not close to the intellectual line of descent that ran from Kant through Herbart, Drobisch, and Bobrik to Friedrich Albert Lange, and hence he was equally distant from the branch that began with Herbart, was continued with Theodor Waitz, Lazarus, and Steinthal, and ended with Bastian. I can really find no reason to believe that Weber had any close contact with any ethnologist. Why should he? Those circles with whom Weber felt a kinship in terms of a general philosophy were far removed from ethnology. It was true that the founder of the neo-Kantian movement, Friedrich Albert Lange (whose character structure was not unlike Weber's) had used ethnological material in his battle against economic and naturalistic materialism. He had both studied and cited Steinthal, Lazarus, and Bastian. However, the physiological-psychological element that had played a role in Lange's argument disappeared from neo-Kantianism, and along with it the ethnology, which in the case of Lange had become almost a kind of natural science. Windelband, once Lange's successor in Zurich, had remarked in his Heidelberg lectures that the destruction of the ancient Inca culture" by a handful of Spanish adventurers" was a crime against mankind. This really means something if one remembers that Windelband, of all the people discussed here, was the most strongly rooted in ancient occidental culture. This was the only time he made a remark of this type, however; the Hindus played no role in his works on the history of philosophy. And as for Jellinek and his school, Jellinek only shrugged his shoulders at Post's attempt to depict African jurisprudence. Troeltsch didn't go quite so far, but for him the research on Asiatic cultures was at most only a means of obtaining comparative material to make possible a more exact knowledge of occidental culture. In comparison with these, Max Weber's position, particularly in his later days, was quite different.

On his American trip he had become interested not only, as we reported, in Negroes (in line with his interest in the protection of the oppressed) but also in American Indians. He never published on these subjects. This follows naturally from his rigorous sense of obligation to avoid writing about anything with which he was not completely familiar. However, Asiatic peoples, as is generally known, played an increasing part in his outlook on the sociology of religion; the Hindus were traced back to the days when they had no written language; totemism played a role as did the problem of matriarchal law in his lectures on economic history, published posthumously. In all of this he remained true to his basic position. He avoided constructs that seemed impermissible to him. He had not studied Bastian. When I asked him about it, he replied, "No one can read this," a judgment in which he certainly didn't stand alone. In questioning him on other authors, I discovered that he respected von den Steinen's book on the Xingú. Von den Steinen had avoided the broad generalizations of which his mentor, Bastian, was so fond. Weber also liked Hahn's book on domesticated plants and animals, although with some reservation, because Hahn rejected the old theory of three inevitable stages of evolution, which maintained that culture developed from hunting to cattle raising to farming, of an automatic necessity, and with the three stages quite independent of each other. Father Schmidt and the problem he raised were overlooked except for a single reference, in connection with totemism, which was not especially important. In general, there wasn't much discussion of peoples who had no written language. This might be for a reason other than Weber's own interests. At that time I was not so interested in ethnological questions as I had been previously at Berlin, nor as much as I was later on.

The reader who has followed these memoirs thus far has probably asked more than once when we are finally going to discuss sociology. After all, Max Weber is known as a sociologist the world over, and not least in the United States. But this is the situation: although in Heidelberg at that time many things were considered from the standpoint of sociology, the science of society as such did not appear in the college catalogue. Johannes Scherrer had indeed given some lectures in sociology, and Max Weber was twice involved in affairs having to do with this lecturer. Because of this, Scherrer has a place in this text. Scherrer was personally a man who was worthy of the greatest respect. His grandchildren had been orphaned at an early age and he provided for them like a father. In 1886, the 500th anniversary of the founding of the university, he had received, after a long wait, the non-civil service title of *Extraordinarius*. One could just as well have called him an eternal *Privatdozent*. Because his classes were small he earned very little. Unfortunately he was known only to a few people. Thus the philosopher of law, Radbruch, once asked me directly, "Is this man really alive? Isn't he a phantom?" Scherrer was thus the object of many funny stories. They said that once when the semester had ended, Scherrer had got only as far as the apes in his history lectures—because he had started with a discussion of the primeval nebula. At the Heidelberg Historians' Congress in 1903 which we mentioned earlier, Scherrer had entered the discussion that took place after Gottl's lecture. As soon as Scherrer had the floor but before he had uttered one syllable, von Below said in his cynical way, "Aha, it's Scherrer," and the chairman simply cut Scherrer off after a very short time. This wasn't very nice and certainly wasn't proper parliamentary procedure. During a meal several years later, Windelband reported that he had never heard "such twaddle" as Scherrer's remarks at that time. As I noted above, Weber was twice involved in incidents concerning Scherrer. This is his report: the university was at one time concerned with Scherrer's personal life. Because the poor devil didn't earn very much and, as noted, had to provide for his family, he rented furnished rooms to students and offered the noon-day meal in order to keep his own head above water. Scherrer was anything but a calculating businessman and he was soon headed for bankruptcy. Now there were among the faculty a number of people who thought that a professor was no ordinary mortal but a kind of deity. German public opinion at that time—in this respect very different from opinion in North America—supported this view and was indeed probably responsible for such a notion. And so a number of people thought that it was beneath the dignity of a man who bore the title of university professor to go bankrupt, and they even raised the question as to whether or not he should be removed from the list of teachers. However, mercy prevailed over justice and things didn't go this far. As one can imagine, Weber was very happy about this.

The other incident, as Weber told it, concerned the publication of a work by Scherrer. At the time, when a manuscript was sent to them with the request that it be published, some publishers would ask one or more persons whom they thought knowledgeable and objective whether the work should be published or not. The adequacy of this measure is the subject of some dispute. For my part, even in the United States, I have politely declined passing judgment when the decision is not made known to the object of the judgment and is, therefore, *de facto,* not subject to control and ultimately unanswerable. In this matter, as in so many others, Weber thought and acted differently than I. He told me that he had complied with the wishes of a particular publisher and had written something like this: in view of the attractive title of Scherrer's work, there is little risk in publishing it; this was followed by a purely mental reservation that the work was really nothing but nonsense.

Although Scherrer's preoccupation with sociology certainly created no stir in Heidelberg, Gothein's impact was greater. Although he was primarily a historian, he broke through the barrier that had kept sociology out of the universities up to this time and announced a series of lectures on the subject. Max Weber was probably happier than anyone else about this. Weber came even more directly into Gothein's sphere of interest in the matter of founding a sociological society. I have already referred to this in the anniversary issue published for the fiftieth anniversary of René König's periodical, the *Kölner Zeitschrift.* To recount this in detail would be superfluous, but I shall recall one incident that makes manifest in a particularly expressive way the deep-rooted conflict of conscience that tore at Weber's innermost being. Besides Weber and those of like mind (who, in this case, included Sombart), there were other people interested in the establishment of an association. These people had different intellectual positions and, to compound the difficulties, this difference lay at just that point which, as one can easily imagine, was of central importance to Weber—the meaning of value judgment. The best known spokesman for this other group was Rudolf

Goldscheid. He was a progressive evolutionist and he thought, as did others of that persuasion, that his inspiring belief in progress could be given a scientific foundation. This notion was based on the implicit conviction that it was possible to evaluate unequivocally the diverse cultural phenomena and cultural levels. Weber found this idea untenable. On the other hand, Weber knew, and he told Goldscheid freely, that most of the persons who favored such an association tended to be progressive evolutionists. From a democratic standpoint, Goldscheid's position ought to take precedence. Thus Weber was forced to choose between two obligations: on the one hand, integrity of scientific practice, and on the other, respect for the convictions of people who thought differently, and who constituted the majority. The decision was made even more difficult because of another consideration: he was well aware of the sincerity and selflessness of Rudolf Goldscheid, who, as a private scholar, was above any suspicion of acting for the sake of personal gain. Many years later Marianne confirmed this to me in the presence of other witnesses in Cologne, and added that Max had suffered greatly because he felt obliged to hurt such a good man. From my own experience I can confirm the fact that Goldscheid was a most decent sort of person. I had worked with him for years at pacifist enterprises, particularly at international peace congresses, to our mutual enrichment. Weber decided to give precedence to the principle of value neutrality, a condition that would be the *sine qua non* of his cooperation. At the next meeting, this condition was respected by only one of the speakers; therefore Weber indicated that he very likely would not work with them. He was certainly within his rights. Further discussion in the Sociological Society was cut short by Weber's unexpected death.

Other protagonists and other sorts of problems appeared and commanded undivided attention. A few might be mentioned: von Wiese and his *Beziehungslehre,* Father Wilhelm Schmidt and his cultural-historical school of ethnology, and Oppenheimer and his explanation of critical phenomena and changes through the nature of the relationship of man to land. This story was embedded in a rational utopia of the reign of justice. Like the teaching of Karl Marx, it was a secularization of the demands of the Old Testament prophets. This was not unlike the ideas of Max Weber. Weber didn't object too much if one set that part of his work which was relevant outside the

plane of the special sciences in parallel with the role of the Old
Testament prophets. Occasionally those of us who were younger
discussed Oppenheimer, but I don't remember that Weber ever said
anything about him.

Economic and Political Sciences

As we turn from sociology to the discipline of economics, it is
necessary to warn the reader of a possible misunderstanding when
Weber is called a "political economist" (*Nationalökonom*). This was
the customary title in German universities at that time, but it is mis-
leading, and fortunately the present designation is simply "economist." Weber was an economist, but he was competent in other
disciplines as well. This is demonstrated by the fact that Mommsen
considered him a possible candidate for a chair in ancient history or
Roman law. That Weber was called to Freiburg as an economist was
to a certain degree accidental and was perhaps not altogether fortunate, for he was required, in addition to holding seminars and
other duties, to give lectures for three large courses: "general political economy" (sometimes called "theoretical"), "special economics"
(sometimes called "applied"), and "finance." These were taught at
all universities and represented the backbone of the discipline of
economics. But this meant that Max Weber, who was trained in
Roman and commercial law, hastily had to prepare himself in areas
that he did not know in detail, even though he was not completely
unfamiliar with them. In this connection there is no doubt that he
overworked in Freiburg and thus prepared the way for his later illness. Nevertheless, he never felt that he was only an economist, at
least in his later years.

A remark by Weber's wife expresses this characteristically. During the First World War, because I had not previously served my
term, because I was unable to participate in active service, and
because, being half-French, I spoke French fluently, I was an interpreter with the rank of corporal in the civilian prison camp,
Sennelager, near Paderborn. During my leave I went to Heidelberg;
Weber wasn't there, but Marianne was. She reported that her
husband felt much better than he had before, and we discussed
whether or not he ought to teach again. She said he was not able to
do so and would like to teach sociology and a value-free political

and without being prompted by a question on my part, she added, "His development has taken him far beyond purely economic matters." Thus in my presence there wasn't much conversation on economic matters and on political economy as a science.

The situation with regard to political economy in Germany at that time was quite clear and I have already touched on it in the detailed discussion of trends in economic history. Schmoller dominated the field with his combination of economics, history, and academic socialism. Adolf Wagner, whom we have already mentioned twice, represented academic socialism, but his position was ahistorical, and he was much more interested in theory. In the Schmoller school, theory had only a limited role. This produced the consequence that one might expect: when Schmoller died, the school fell apart. His two-volume book on the foundations of political economy (*Grundriss der allgemeinen Volkswirtschaftslehre*) had been one of the most widely sold textbooks in political economics up to that time, but in a little while one could buy it as an antiquarian piece for a few pennies. People suddenly realized that theorists were really necessary; one looked around for some and discovered that they could most easily be found in Austria. Here Menger, Böhm-Bawerk, Philippowich, and later Kerschagl and many others established the theory of marginal utility, but apparently quite independently of its first discoverer, the unfortunate Gossen, who had long since been forgotten. Schumpeter was thought to be one of its most characteristic, albeit most independent, representatives and was regarded as one of the keenest economic thinkers of the time. From Vienna he was invited to go to Bonn, and then to Harvard in the United States; this latter took place before Hitler came to power and forced many persons to emigrate. But this lies outside narrow focus of interest of this sketch.

In the span of time under discussion, the theory of marginal utility was not the subject of conversation, at least in my presence, in the house on the Ziegelhäuser Landstrasse, although the theory certainly played an essential role in Max Weber's thinking. This is documented by his polemic against Brentano and his thesis that the "fundamental psycho-physical law" was the basis of the theory of marginal utility, and that this latter was only "the application of a special case." However, the so-called Ehrenberg case played a much greater part in our conversation. Ehrenberg was an economist from Rostock and the editor of the periodical *Thünenarchiv*, which he had founded. At that time all the dominant trends in political economy conformed in their emphasis on the importance of welfare policies. In contrast, Ehrenberg emphasized the importance of the question of profitability. It seemed to him that this concept was endangered by comprehensive social welfare policies. This constituted an attack upon a position that Max Weber, in spite of certain reservations, thought worthy of defense. Yet this would not have upset Weber had it not been for something else that happened. He heard that an industrial association had been pleased by Ehrenberg's remarks and this group had offered the University of Leipzig the means to establish a research institute on the condition that Ehrenberg be made the director. This was too much for Weber; at the meeting of the *Verein für Sozialpolitik* he brought the matter to public attention, and the plans then fell through. But the affair had an unhappy after-effect. Hans Ehrenberg has been mentioned twice in these pages, once in connection with an incident in Baden-Baden. He was the nephew of the person attacked on that occasion. I knew him very well and he dared to speak freely to me, and so he told me, "All of us [that is, members of the Ehrenberg family] suffered because of it." It is scarcely necessary to add what the reader will have already concluded: Weber never allowed his argument with the uncle to affect his relations with the nephew.

In any discussion of the younger economists in the Weber circle, one must not for a minute forget Weber's insistence on one particular principle: he would not take part in the examination of his own students when they attempted to be qualified as lecturers. Thereby he may have, in fact he did, injure a few young people. For they then had to go elsewhere for the examination. These other professors would perhaps wonder why the student's own major advisor would not approve him as a lecturer, and they would therefore regard these young men with some skepticism. Weber was aware of this result, and often talked to me about it. Again he was forced to choose between two obligations: on the one hand, the well-being of his own students and, on the other hand, an obligation that seemed more essential; it seemed to him that to insist on the licensing of his own students was a misuse of the power position of an *Ordinarius* (which doubtless existed), who, in this roundabout way, would propagate his own views through the teaching of his disciples. To this unimaginably humble man this seemed to be an ethically impermissible form of the use of influence. The consequence was that one found a number of economists both in Heidelberg and even in Weber's own circle who were not his pupils.

Let us look at them. One might argue that a number of them have been forgotten and one should, so to speak, let sleeping dogs lie. Although some of them may not be particularly interesting, still they are of importance because Weber's relations with them were of significance. When Weber came to Heidelberg from Freiburg, he found Leser and Kindermann there as *Extraordinarien*. They had attained this rank under Weber's predecessors. In theory, that is, according to the prevailing rules of the university, a man who was not an *Ordinarius* still had the right to teach anything relevant to his field of competence; in practice, it was possible for an *ordentliche* professor to create all sorts of difficulties. As one can imagine, Weber did not do this. He told both of them, as he reported to me later, "You are free to lecture as you will." He did this in spite of the fact that he had no great respect for either one of them. Kindermann took advantage of this opportunity, but Leser confined himself to the history of economic theory. In this area Leser edited some older publications and published some new things of his own.

I was particularly interested in the field. At the time I liked to work with the history of social and political ideas (as I did in my lectures) and naturally that made close contact with economic theory unavoidable. In addition, I was just as stubborn then as now and felt that I had to take the part of men who were unimportant, who had suffered set-backs, and whose careers were without success. I therefore attempted to put in a good word for these two with Weber. But love's labor was lost. Naturally Weber took my remarks seriously, but he replied with respect to Leser, "The stuff he has published is obviously trivial," and with regard to Kindermann, "He believes that he has a mission to fulfill, but one needs only to read his work on political economy and art (*Volkswirtschaft und Kunst*) to know enough about him." On another occasion Weber reported that Kindermann represented one of the few cases where he, Weber, had gotten rid of someone, namely by recommending him to the Academy of Agricultural Economics in Hohenheim.

At another time, however, when Weber was faced with the question of obtaining a suitable economist at Heidelberg, the situation was much more difficult. It was at the time that he resigned his chair, and the administration, as we already mentioned, didn't want to name Sombart as the successor. They finally decided in favor of Karl Rathgen. Some people just winked and made wise remarks: "That's because he's Schmoller's son-in-law." But he was more than that. In particular, he had been in Japan for years and had published some popular pieces, as well as some strictly scientific works on the political economy of Japan, especially on the continuous adaptation to modern occidental methods. I had been in his house myself and had also attended his lectures on practical economics and financial science; last but not least, I had attended his seminars and I was grateful to him. I expressed myself in this sense to the Webers. But Weber commented, "In the long run, he gets on one's nerves with his proper behavior and his way of never getting out of line." Rathgen was always correct and cautious and didn't want to offend anyone. I mentioned to the Webers that as students we had hardly been able to keep from smiling when we saw Rathgen pull his lecture notes out of his side pocket. They were encased in a much-used, almost dirty, blue envelope. Weber looked at Marianne, who smiled back at him, and he replied, "Well, thank God; at least there's one occasion when Rathgen wasn't so everlastingly correct."

I never met the young Heidelberg social scientists Schachner and Jaffée because both had already accepted appointments elsewhere. I do not remember that their names were mentioned, at least in my presence, in the house on the Ziegelhäuser Landstrasse. Jellinek, whose judgment on men and scientists often agreed with Weber's, spoke of Schachner with great respect. He was one of the first of those few European economists who had traveled extensively in Australia. His interest, unlike that of Baldwin Spencer who did systematic research on the natives, was concentrated on the white men's Australia for which he prophesied a great economic and cultural future. I don't remember ever having met Edgar Salin at the Webers' house. Unfortunately I had only a fleeting acquaintance with him. Weber didn't care to have Hermann Levy at the Sunday afternoon gatherings. He felt the same way about Bloch, although this was not because he didn't respect Bloch as a scholar. Weber once told me quite bluntly, "His social behavior is so naïve that many people would stop coming to my house if they knew they would meet Bloch here." But this opinion did not prevent Weber, as in the case of Adalbert Wahl, from gratefully citing Bloch in his so-called Calvinism-capitalism work.

Another person the Webers didn't care for was Rudolf Biach. He had done a lot of work on the history of mercantilism, and had a personal relationship with Henri Bergson, the most-discussed French philosopher at that time. Biach did not lecture in Heidelberg. Before the First World War, many of the younger Ph.D.s, if they had enough money, lived in German university towns even though they had not formally qualified as lecturers. Biach was doing just this. He came often to the Webers' house. Later on during the war he was a British prisoner-of-war in India for quite a long time. Marianne told me later that they didn't care much for him because of his inner coldness and unkindness. In any event, as in so many cases, the relationship was terminated as a result of the war. The relationship with Emil Lederer and Arthur Salz was quite different. With regard to Lederer, this is demonstrated by a remark Weber made. I told him that Lederer and I had struck up a friendship during vacation; Weber exclaimed with pleasure, "I'm really very glad." Weber knew him as a result of a long period of close cooperation in editing the *Archiv für Sozialwissenschaften*. Weber was one of the founders and editors. Lederer had to write regular reports on important events in the sociopolitical area, as well as reviews of books and articles in that field. Weber explained the situation to me in this way: According to the original intention, Lederer should be writing nothing more than informative accounts. "However, Lederer goes to so much trouble that he is actually producing strictly scientific articles." Max Weber's position on this was ambivalent: on the one hand he respected and admired Lederer's willingness to work and the high standard of his output; on the other hand, he almost regretted that his young colleague spent so much time on this sort of thing. He felt morally responsible for the precarious situation of the Lederer couple. "They are both living on what they earn with their pens." In addition, the possibility of moving the editorial offices of the *Archiv* from Heidelberg to the location of the publisher (to the Siebeck [Mohr] offices in Tübingen) was another threat. A great many Heidelberg writers were published at this latter location, among them Jellinek and Troeltsch. Now Lederer's post in Heidelberg was not permanent; he was an unsalaried *Extraordinarius*. He would have to give this up, which he presumably would not want to do. Max Weber said sadly, "I don't know what I ought to do. "When I interjected that both the Lederers had a great deal of courage, he agreed and expressed his own admiration for them.

We have already met Salz as an admirer of Ranke. Nevertheless, to use one of Weber's occasional expressions, he was also "something more." With regard to that point which was of such central importance to Weber, that is, the theory of value neutrality, Salz showed an uncompromising independence. This always impressed Weber. In some respects, the two men were quite alike. In a way that was really worthy of Max Weber, Salz aided the persecuted at the end of the First World War, not without putting himself in severe danger. In those Heidelberg days, he was also distinguished by his friendship with Stefan George and Friedrich Gundolf. Gundolf was the link between George, who at that time lived only within his restricted circle, and the outside world, in particular, the Weber household. We will take this up again when we discuss Weber's position with regard to art and artistic genre.

To complete the picture of Weber as a sociologist and economist and to eliminate misunderstanding, it is necessary to remember that one does him an injustice if one calls him an opponent of psychology as such; it is just as wrong to conclude that he neglected statistics because he emphasized history so strongly. At least three characteristic remarks demonstrate this. The first was his speech to the first meeting of German sociologists in Frankfurt in 1910. The second was a conversation with the psychiatrist Gruhle when I was present. Gruhle was concerned with the fate of prostitutes and asked Max Weber whether he ought to take a course in statistics. Weber replied, "I myself have never taught it, but...." I cannot remember the rest of his words, but I do know that he expressed himself positively with regard to statistics as such. He gave undeniable support to statistics in a conversation with Gothein which I overheard. They were talking about the newly founded Academy of Science in Baden. Weber was very angry. He thought that they were simply throwing money away to support natural science research that could be conducted in the existing, well-endowed laboratories. Sociological research, on the other hand, needed a great statistical apparatus which it did not have and which it could not yet finance. He felt that the Academy should support this sort of research.

Jurisprudence

To complete the entire picture, I must add a few lines on his relation to jurisprudence and jurists insofar as this was not discussed in connection with the discipline of history. Weber himself had begun with the study of jurisprudence but thought that the value of knowledge in this area would be limited. This was the tie that bound him to Jellinek. This man who was officially a professor of civil law had made four characteristic remarks on this subject, some orally, some in print. Thus, "Philosophy was my first love; I have made a marriage of convenience with jurisprudence;" further, "It is too bad that Kant didn't write a fourth critique, namely, the critique of the juristic power of judgment;" in addition, "The jurist who is aware of his limitations remains in the empirical world where the life of the law unfolds and where action, not theory, is sovereign;" and finally, "The categories with whose help one can understand various social phenomena are not those of the law."

All this reveals a style of thought that could not possibly be strange to Max Weber. And thus they were friends in the fullest meaning of the word, in spite of, or better, because of, the fact that they were different in certain ways. Jellinek was not inclined to be very radical; his writing, even when he expressed the most abstract ideas, had a pleasing style. He had grown up in Vienna and that is the city where—as I put it one time—even drunken cab drivers curse each other in melodies reminiscent of Schubert. But Jellinek and Weber also had many interests in common. In fact, Jellinek had been the first person to show the socio-historical importance of Calvinism, particularly in North America. This was in 1891, and it constituted a point of departure for Weber's research. In addition, both men had a pronounced interest in the history of natural law. I myself had given several papers on it in Jellinek's seminar. My studies of Gallicanism and Jansenism had also touched on natural law. At the previously described meeting in Baden-Baden, I had lectured specifically on "The Role of Natural Law in Occidental Culture," which I repeated forty-five years later as a guest lecturer in Heidelberg. Weber wanted me to tell him about this lecture, and he commented that I would have been able to talk for two weeks without exhausting the subject. In any event, this interest constituted one of the many ties between Jellinek and Weber.

Above all Weber admired Jellinek's "unique style" of dealing with public law; by this he meant that Jellinek went far beyond a purely juristic treatment and treated the subject sociologically. Jellinek, as he told me, considered Weber his superior. This really means something, coming as it does from a man who had high regard for his other contemporaries, he also admired persons like Adalbert Merx, Erwin Rohde, Jakob Burckhardt, Friedrich Dernburg, and Adolf Hausrath, among others. On the other hand, he was also capable of being sparing with his praise, and he could make very sharp remarks as we saw in the case of his sarcastic observations on Josef Kohler. Weber was one of the first, outside Jellinek's immediate family, to visit Jellinek after he had suffered a heart attack. Weber spoke about this soon after the visit and observed that although it appeared that Jellinek would recover completely, "We will naturally have to wait to see how his next book turns out." Jellinek was working on the second volume of his work on the law of the modern state *(Das Recht des modernen Staates)*. He wanted the first volume, with the subtitle "general theory of the state," to be followed by a second with the subtitle "special theory of the state." He was not able to finish the work. One evening Jellinek was reading from Goethe's *West-östlicher Divan* to his wife; at that moment he suffered a second heart attack, collapsed, and said, "This is the end. Farewell."Thus his death was beautiful and without pain.

The fragments of the second volume, which he left unfinished, were assembled and published by his son, Walter Jellinek, in a volume of selected writings and lectures *(Ausgewählte Schriften und Reden)*. The first (and in fact the only) volume treating general political theory was later re-titled *Allgemeine Staatslehre*. Although Weber admired Jellinek's way of dealing with public law, he was not pleased with the way other professors treated public law. Until just a short time before this, the other chair in public law at Heidelberg had been occupied by Georg Meyer. He was highly regarded by the Weber circle and, along with Jellinek and the young Max Weber, he had been a pronounced National Liberal and was the first to develop the well-known formula for the new German state: "The sovereignty of Germany is exclusively based on the collectivity of the federalized states. The individual German states still exist as states, but they are no longer sovereign; there can be non-sovereign states. The old theory that sovereignty is the essential characteristic of an individual state must be abandoned in view of the complicated structure of the federal state."

For a number of years it was customary to see Georg Jellinek and Georg Meyer taking a walk before lunch from the university to the old castle. Although Jellinek was aware of the greater universality of his own intellect, he never let Georg Meyer know this. Frau Jellinek told me later, "My husband (who was so much more than a jurist) could, if necessary, be a jurist among jurists." Now Georg Meyer had written a textbook on German constitutional law; the book was well received and in many respects contained some original views. Gerhard Anschütz was Meyer's successor after his relatively early death. Anschütz had had a meteoric rise, and he brought out a revised edition of Meyer's work. Max Weber had followed all of this and he observed to me, "The new edition is quite a decent accomplishment, but it is not enough to rest on one's laurels."

Along with Jellinek and Anschütz, Schönborn, a younger man, also taught public law at Heidelberg. He was a student of Jellinek's, belonged to his circle, and was strongly interested in history. All of this made him a suitable friend for the Webers, but I don't remember meeting him there or hearing any discussion about him. But this could be due to mere chance. The not quite friendly judgment of Anschütz was mere child's play compared to the judgments on three other persons who taught public law and whom Weber really didn't like, namely, Arthur von Kirchenheim, Ferdinand von Martitz, and Konrad Bornhak.

Von Kirchenheim had taught at Heidelberg for a long time, from 1881 as a *Privatdozent*, then from 1886 as an *Extraordinarius*. He claimed descent from an old family of army officers, but many of the students, because they suspected that he was trying to conceal his true origin, knew him by the nickname of "Synagogovich." To understand the following, one must remember that Weber, as an economist, was originally in the faculty of law, and so Kirchenheim, in a certain sense, was his colleague, a fact which, considering Weber's character, put him in a somewhat painful position. At that time there was a rule, as there was for other faculties, that a person who was not an *Ordinarius* could, if he wished teach the same course in the same semester as an *ordentliche* professor on the condition that he teach as many hours as the latter. This may have been of only theoretical significance in many faculties. The large required courses in physics and the official clinics in the faculty of medicine were often under contract to the *Ordinarien* who served as directors of institutes or clinics. The *Privatdozenten* and *Extraordinarien* gave only special courses, for the most part. In the law school, it was different in many respects. Most of the courses had to be taken by all of the students in order to prepare for the bar examination. The number of students interested in courses other than those required was always small in the law school. Therefore in most semesters the same courses would be offered at the same time by several teachers. This was the practical purpose of the rule previously mentioned. Although von Kirchenheim was aware of the rule, he ignored it. The faculty politely requested that he not do that. As that didn't help, they took energetic action against him. To a certain extent he became an outcast. Nevertheless, Max Weber continued to greet him first, because von Kirchenheim was the elder of the two. Finally there came a moment when by chance Max Weber did not greet him quite soon enough, and von Kirchenheim went by without speaking." Since then I don't greet him any more," Weber told me, and probably von Kirchenheim is the only person who enjoyed this doubtful distinction.

Weber's antipathy toward von Martitz was for another reason. I had attended some of his classes in Berlin, and I reported to Weber that, among other things, von Martitz taught the history of social and political theory. Jellinek's course on this subject was internationally famous; I was particularly interested in the subject myself. When Weber heard that von Martitz was also teaching the course, he just smiled and stroked his beard and repeated what he sometimes said on such occasions: "He must be propounding a lot of beautiful nonsense." He also knew some other unedifying stories about the man. When he and von Martitz had worked for the Administrative Court, his chief had declared with despair that the man was "just plain lazy."

Of all those in public law, the man Weber disliked the most was Konrad Bornhak. He had Gneist to thank for the fact that he passed his qualifying examinations at Berlin, as Weber said, and Gneist's support really meant something. For next to von Mohl, Gneist was the most famous proponent of the notion of the constitutional state. Apart from his general significance, he was especially important in Heidelberg. Here we must remember Jellinek's early fate. He was an *Extraordinarius* in public law and had just published his famous book on the theory of federalism and was giving lectures on international law. A somewhat anti-Semitic administration told him to desist; despite the fact that he was head of a family and had no private means, he had the courage to resign his position and to requalify for lecturing at Berlin. Gneist was the man who made this possible. Just as Weber admired Jellinek for the courage he had shown, he respected Gneist for the help he had given Jellinek and for other reasons as well. What he could not excuse was the fact that Gneist had helped Bornhak to qualify as a lecturer.

Bornhak was a rather astonishing figure even in Wilhelm's Germany. His political conservatism surpassed anything I have mentioned thus far. He equated the ruler with the state, and he believed that only the word "subject" was adequate to describe the people living in the state; he explained that the civil servants had no contractual right to any compensation and ought to receive only token pay; he described the chambers of the Prussian diet as organs of the King (therefore "royal Prussian deputies," as Jellinek sarcastically called them), and in principle he denied the claims of public law. In spite of this extreme conservatism, his success as a lecturer was limited. Weber, looking rather pleased, told an amusing story. At that time there was a professor of Christian archaeology in Berlin by the name of Nikolaus Müller. As Weber started to describe him, I interrupted: "I see what you mean; I know a pious old maid who is a friend of his and told me about him." Weber added at once, "Yes indeed, he was a pious old maid himself." And he continued, "One morning Müller was sitting there in his Institute for Christian Archaeology, but it was so terribly hot that he took his book and settled himself in a nearby auditorium that was cooler; the auditorium was empty so obviously a lecture wasn't being given there. He had scarcely seated himself when a man came running in, got up on the podium, and began to give a lecture on constitutional law. Müller thought that the man was probably crazy, and he remembered the rule for dealing with the mentally ill: do not, under any circumstances, disturb or irritate them. He therefore interrupted his reading and listened patiently for an hour until the bell rang and the speaker disappeared. Only later did he learn that the man whom he had supposed to be mentally ill was none other than Professor Bornhak. He had scheduled his lecture for that hour and had been so happy that finally someone had come in to hear him. "I imparted to Weber that I had heard that Bornhak had meanwhile received recognition to the extent of being invited to lecture on constitutional law at the War Academy. Weber commented, "If that's the case, it's only because of his conservative outlook."

Of other legal disciplines, criminology was not far from Weber's interests. Criminology transcends various spheres and is ultimately not too far from philosophy. Problems of the alternatives of free will and determinism, of heredity and environment, of individual and social rights play an essential role, closely bound to the problem of value. One can imagine that these and analogous questions must have interested Max Weber, who fought for the rights of the individual as opposed to the demands of institutions and their bureaucratic representatives. He particularly hated the typical representative of the state who opposed the unfortunate individual in the judicial process. Thus he spoke out, not only in private conversations, but in the presence of many people, against the Prussian public prosecutor. His comments were unambiguous and sharp with regard to these men who condemned as many poor devils as possible for the sake of their own careers. I had no reason to contradict him; I had learned to know a prosecutor of the worst sort when, at a dinner held by an association of which I was a member, he announced his basic opposition to the jury trial; and he told how, after an acquittal, he informed the court: "I want no second acquittal."

Ever since the Italian, Beccaria, had opposed torture in the eighteenth century and Voltaire had urged before a wide audience that punishment be humanized, there had been constant discussion of criminology. Theories emerged and disappeared again. I might mention a few of the most important: the theory of atonement, supported by the Hegelians. The criminal act was thought to be the antithesis of the law (therefore a negation of the thesis); the punishment was the negation of the antithesis (therefore a negation of this negation); therefore, in the Hegelian sense, the punishment was the synthesis. Another example is the theory of improvement. It stemmed mostly from the notion of natural law, and like it, involved an optimistic position: man was good and perfection possible, and therefore the most important or even the only purpose of punishment was the reformation of the delinquent. One of its most important basic principles was derived from the philosophy of

Friedrich Christian Krause. This man not only was one of the most original of Schelling's students during his third period, but among all German Romantics was the one who represented the strongest combination of pre-Kantian and Romantic-transcendental elements. A continuous line of influence extended from Krause to Jellinek through Krause's students, Ahrens in Leipzig and Schliephake in Heidelberg.

The arguments over these theories and their derivatives are now part of the past. In the meantime the Italian, Lombroso, had appeared with an anthropological theory of crime. He postulated a theory of the "born criminal" in which skull structure and other anatomical features played a decisive role. At first he had many students and enjoyed great popularity, but he soon had many opponents. Among these opponents, the founders and adherents of sociological theory attracted attention. They attempted to explain the criminal and his behavior through analysis of the social milieu. Liszt, a distant relative of the composer, was one of the pioneers. There was also a tradition in criminology in Heidelberg, and Mittermaier became a world famous name. Roder, a direct student of Krause's, represented the theory of improvement, battled against the theory of retaliation, and favored imprisonment in individual cells. Like most of Krause's students, he never became an *Ordinarius*, and he was able to attract a large number of students only to his courses on penology.

In Max Weber's time, criminal law and procedure were represented primarily by Karl von Lilienthal. He was certainly not so significant a figure as Liszt, who was the real leader of the new movement in criminology, but he was close to Liszt, and together they edited the journal that was the vehicle of the movement. After the death of Georg Meyer, he was, next to Max Weber, Jellinek's closest friend. Weber told me that he was glad, especially after Jellinek had his first heart attack, that Lilienthal was such a good friend of Jellinek's, and that he himself also considered Lilienthal one of his own friends. There was also Gustav Radbruch, then an *Extraordinarius* in this field. He combined the subject of penal law with civil procedures—not a particularly happy combination. This hampered his advancement. His political views hindered him even more. He supported the *freisinnige Partei*, spent a lot of time with Russian students, and spoke at the same Russian student meeting where Weber presented the speech I already mentioned. He identified two categories of law students: students of order and students of freedom, and he emphasized unambiguously that he was on the side of the latter. In his lectures on the philosophy of law, he documented the fact that he was a pronounced opponent of any group metaphysic. Later he became a socialist and was finally the renowned minister of justice. Both Webers respected him very much; Max even called him an *anima candida.*

Weber and the Arts

Poetry, music, and the plastic arts certainly did not play the same role in Weber's life as those areas we have discussed in detail: politics, philosophy, history, sociology, and economics. In spite of this, the picture of Weber would be incomplete without a discussion of his attitude toward the arts. Several aspects of his inner conflict with regard to the potentialities embedded in his personality were mirrored in his choice or rejection of particular artists and kinds or styles of art. To the extent that this was expressed in conversation, I shall discuss it here. If we disregard fleeting remarks, we can give our attention to the following: Ibsen, the Yiddish theatre, the French boulevard theatre, Parisian novels, Conrad Ferdinand Meyer, Dostoevsky, Tolstoy, and, last but not least, Stefan George and his circle. If one uses a common literary slogan, one can say, with all due reservation, that Weber belonged to the Ibsen generation. Naturally this label doesn't describe the whole man, but it does clear a path to comprehension.

Indeed, in those days before George was famous, the controversial figures of various foreigners had great effect in Germany. One might mention the names of Dostoevsky, Tolstoy, Strindberg, Björnson, and Ibsen. At that time Weber was not so deeply involved in the new literary and theatrical movements in Berlin as his sociological colleague von Wiese, who was about fourteen years younger; in spite of von Wiese's different epistemological basis, both men shared an interest in contemporary issues: a non-metaphysical basis for the individual sciences, and a respect for the autonomous decision on the part of the individual. In addition, Weber wasn't in Berlin very long. Nevertheless Ibsen meant something to him. Ibsen acquitted of any guilt the individual who had the courage to flout convention, and Weber was attracted to this notion. Weber made this quite clear in a discussion of *Rosmersholm*. In arguments with Lukács, the names of contemporary German realists such as Hauptmann, Sudermann, and Wedekind occurred more than once.

Because of sociological interest (and, in this case, also because of his eagerness to do justice to such matters), he visited the Yiddish theatre in New York, as well as the boulevard theatre in Paris. This was the basis of a rather droll story. I was visiting with both of them and gave them some pointers for their coming trip to Paris. We started speaking of the modern theatre. Someone mentioned the words, "Théâtre Antoine." At one time this had meant something in the history of literature, but that time had long since passed. Weber made a negative motion with his hand and said, "In the Théâtre Antoine they show only plays dealing with adultery. That isn't particularly interesting." Marianne replied innocently, "That depends." Max looked at her and smiled rather roguishly and said, "Well! Just listen to that; it sounds a bit suspicious," whereupon all three of us laughed. This incident had a certain piquancy, however, because at that time I went at least once a week to the house on the Ziegelhäuser Landstrasse. In the eyes of the women students at Heidelberg, I was apparently something like the young man Schiller described in "Gang nach dem Eisenhammer": "A faithful knight was Fridolin," or as some of them said, "Frau Weber's brown-locked little page." This was repeated in the fusty little town in which my parents lived, and it aroused a mighty chattering among the women there, particularly because Marianne Weber was one of those fearful beings who was concerned with the status of women. Naturally Max Weber got a hearty laugh out of all this.

When Weber returned from Paris, he had a lot to say about the world of theatre there, particularly about its comparatively low level. Among other things, he had seen *Papa,* a piece that was much performed. It had been written by De Flers and De Caillavet, who produced a new comedy every year. In this, their most recent comedy, the plot (as in so many plays by these authors and others who wrote in this genre) concerned the well-known psychological situation where an individual had to choose between two others, a man between two women, or, as in this case, a woman between two men. In this play the girl had to choose between the naive owner of a country estate and his natural father, who was a good-for-nothing

Parisian playboy who boasted about all his mistresses in typical French fashion. But this and the luxury in which he lived were decisive, and the girl chooses him rather than the son. The whole thing is characteristic of the tourist's notion of Paris, but it certainly was not typical of the French middle class, which was the most philistine to be found anywhere.

It was unlucky that Weber happened to see that particular play. I had to admit to Weber that I had not only seen the piece, I had also read it, and, to make matters even worse, I actually owned a copy. At that time all the new plays performed in the private theatres of Paris (with the exception of a few produced in the Sarah Bernhardt Theatre) were published in the *Illustration Théâtrale*. This was a supplement to the widely circulated magazine, *L'illustration*. My mother subscribed to the latter and thus she received the supplement regularly. This is how I happened to have a copy of this trashy comedy (which I still have). When I told all this to Weber, he could only exclaim, "This, too, for God's sake!"

Weber had a strong interest in the early French realists, Balzac and Flaubert, particularly in Flaubert's *Madame Bovary*, which he discussed in some detail with Lukács. He didn't think much of the later French society novels; he thought they had little artistic value even though they did provide a sociological mirror of the lives and values of certain segments of French society. He wanted me to tell him about the novels of Gabrielle Martel de Janville. She was descended from the old nobility, and wrote under the pseudonym "Gyp"; she wrote about those circles she knew best and often handled the material in dialogue form. The plots were concerned with the activities of the French nobility. Doing nothing at all, they lived on their incomes in Paris or on their estates in the provinces, in fashionable sea resorts or on the Riviera. The milieu always seemed to include a governess who took care of the small children, and the unavoidable abbé who gave private instruction to the older children. It was not fashionable to send the offspring of the old families to the public schools; they might meet children who had not been so careful in their choice of parents. In addition, the schools were an innovation of the accursed Republic that was so anti-Catholic. For naturally an aristocrat is a monarchist, reads the *Gaulois* as a daily paper, and is strongly Catholic. This latter does not hinder him from committing adultery. At the other pole one finds the Republic itself, industry, bankers—and Jews. The attempt of Jews to gain access to Parisian high society was the subject of one of Gyp's novels. As I said, Max Weber wanted me to tell him about the plots, which he found characteristic of a certain type of society. For example, an old aristocrat was explaining how his nephew had acquired one of the greatest fortunes in France because he had inherited wealth on a number of sides. The aristocrat added, *"Je parle naturellement des fortunes bonnêtement acquis et non pas des fortunes industrielles et financiéres."* Here we have a clear contrast of fortunes acquired "in an honest way," in this context, of course, by pre-capitalistic methods, and industrial or financial fortunes acquired as the result of capitalistic activity. Weber found this an important source of a continuing pre-capitalistic mentality.

When Weber returned from Paris, he was also disappointed in the Comédie Française, the official home of the traditionalist performance of the works of Corneille, Racine, Molière, and Marivaux. Among other things, he saw a performance of Victor Hugo's *Hernani* here. "They played it realistically." Naturally this made him think that this historical drama with its hollow pathos had been made to appear comical. This does not mean that Weber had no appreciation of historical plays, poems, or novels. Just as the historical paintings commissioned by royalty, such as those of Camphausen, Gehrts, Piloty, and so forth, had become less popular, so time had been unkind to the historical ballads, epics, and novels of Baumbach, Eckstein, Wildenbruch, Julius Wolf, and others. Indeed the life of these works was prolonged only because secondary school teachers had to know them in order to pass the state examination qualifying them to teach German and history in the upper levels of the secondary schools, and in turn they would require their students to read such books.

Naturally we didn't talk much about this sort of literature, but Weber did like Conrad Ferdinand Meyer. Weber liked Meyer's ability to understand the world of the past and to portray the tragic aspects of the use of power, to capture in a microcosm the confrontation of historical forces, as for example in the meeting of Hutten and Loyola in the collection of poems on Hutten's last days *(Huttens letzte Tage)*. He did not particularly like the verse form, but decided to re-read it when I offered to lend him a copy. This produced an amusing result. After a time I asked him if I could have my book back again. He was astonished but rather embarrassed.

"Good heavens! I put it back among my books. I had quite forgotten that it was yours and not mine." But he could also be charmed by passages which were not microcosmic replicas of world conflict; thus he liked the figure of the little Leubelfinger in *Gustav Adolfs Page,* and upon occasion one or the other of the three of us would read aloud from the poetry of Conrad Ferdinand Meyer if no one else were present.

For years Weber's illness had prevented his taking part in the world of the theatre. He was happy in those years in which he was able to do so occasionally. He spoke of a performance of the *Wallenstein* trilogy he had seen in the Hoftheater in Mannheim—at that time the right place to go for those in Heidelberg who loved the theatre. But all of this was of comparatively little importance in contrast with two other subjects which we discussed: Russian works, especially those of Dostoevsky and Tolstoy, and Stefan George.

In order to outline Weber's position with regard to George accurately, and to avoid misunderstanding and error, we must clarify three matters. First, what was the relation of George and his activities to contemporary trends? Even before the war, from more than one quarter there had been a trend away from the bourgeois way of life, city culture, instrumental rationality, quantification, scientific specialization, and everything else then considered abhorrent phenomena. The previously mentioned Lukács and Bloch, Ehrenberg, and Rosenzweig were part of this trend. This neo-Romanticism, if one may call it that, was connected to the older Romanticism by means of many, if concealed, little streams of influence; we can cite only examples: Schopenhauer, Nietzsche, and later Schelling, Constantin Franz, the Rembrandt Germans, and the Youth Movement. As was the case with all other German movements above the level of the purely ordinary, neo-Romanticism in its various forms was also represented in Heidelberg; and like those in the various Russian groups, its adherents knew on whose door they should knock: Max Weber's door.

Second, what was George's relation to the professors and the professional world? One may almost ascribe a symbolic meaning to one fact: outside his own circle, Stefan George saw almost no one, least of all the university professors. On the other hand, one could mention Gundolf and Simmel. Before Gundolf became a *Dozent,* however, he was already a privileged disciple. Gundolf was everything but a typical German university professor (to say nothing of his American colleague), who is so fond of hearing himself speak at faculty and committee meetings. This is demonstrated by the fact that Gundolf kept his distance from everything that resembled the faculty, the examinations, and the like. Neither was Simmel a typical professor; this helps to account, along with the other reasons I gave, for his late advancement.

Third, it is necessary that I say a few words about my own position with regard to George. I can serve as a source of information only within certain limits. I neither knew George personally nor was I present when he talked with Weber. It is probably unnecessary to say that I was never a member of the George circle or even close to it, as others were, nor did anyone connected with that circle attempt to introduce us. This was for good reason. My entire life, particularly my thirteen years' work in adult education in Cologne, proves that I am anything but the esoteric type who wants to participate in the cult of a master, aside from the fact that many individual aspects of this group made my participation quite impossible. Its attitude was pro-Catholic, and then there was its admiration of Ranke and the glorification of Napoleon by Gundolf.

When Gundolf arranged the meeting of George and Weber, I was not there. In addition to all this, I must add that a certain degree of intimacy was presupposed, and at the time I was only a young fellow " who had not published a single line," as Weber let me feel clearly more than once. However, Weber told me about it soon after, and he mentioned George's extraordinary personal simplicity. But Weber remained true to his own ideas. He felt obliged to work in the world for the world, and, at most, he could only tolerate George's esoteric spiritual aristocracy. The cult of authority in the George circle could elicit only an unconditional nay-saying on his part. He told me this shortly after meeting George. His remarks in abbreviated form, were something like this: "I quoted one of George's remarks to Gundolf, and I said to him, 'You must concede that this is simply wrong.' But, true to form, Gundolf answered, 'No, I can't concede that; for if George were to be mistaken in this matter, it would mean that he is not infallible.'" Naturally this was all this anti-authoritarian man had to hear.

Weber talked about George and his circle in a similar way in several conversations with Lukács to which I have already referred and which took place in my presence. Still Weber thought that particular attention should be given to the fact that George attracted so many gifted younger people. He therefore followed the literature on George and thereby discovered that Dora Busch, the daughter of his friend Jellinek and the wife of the previously mentioned psychiatrist Busch, had written the most perceptive article that existed on George.

Much more significant for the discussions in the Weber house was the fact that Tolstoy and Dostoevsky were, so to speak, actually present. Several factors converged to produce this effect. First of all, as I already noted, there were many Russian students in Heidelberg; but more important than their actual number was their intensity, for example, in the seminars of Jellinek and Windelband. Among them were such personalities as Feodor Stepun who later became very famous, and, among other things, through his book first introduced Soloviev to the German public. In addition, Nikolai von Bubnoff taught in Heidelberg; he was already mentioned and came often to the Weber house. His field covered mysticism in general, but particularly the Russian Greek Orthodox philosophers. Ehrenberg once remarked that, without a strong dose of Greek Orthodox Christianity, the Western world would be deficient in something. And one must not forget that, according to Lukács, Russian religiosity and literature had an important place. When Bloch spoke of the religio-collectivist realm of justice, for whose coming he had hopes, he could just as well have used the formula: "A life in the spirit of Dostoevsky."

Naturally none of this is mere chance and several of the names we have mentioned show how the matter is to be explained. The discontent with the West in general, and with Germany and its established Protestant church in particular, caused the Romantics to look back to the past; but it also caused Romantics and anti-Romantics to look to other countries. And thus these people I have mentioned had at least one thing in common with Max Weber. In addition, one should not forget that the notion of the autonomous individual was one of Weber's deepest convictions. The question is nothing less than the decision as to whether one ought to follow a radical ethic without regard to the consequences, an ethic stated in its purest form in the Sermon on the Mount; or whether one ought to follow an ethic of responsibility, in which case one can be no saint but, for the sake of responsibility, must exert power and thus become a sinner, like the man who becomes a politician from a sense of duty.

It was therefore unavoidable that Max Weber would be preoccupied with Dostoevsky. I don't remember a single Sunday conversation in which the name of Dostoevsky did not occur. Perhaps even more pressing, even inflaming, was the necessity of coming to grips with Tolstoy. Indeed after his own day on the road to Damascus, in the period during which he was preoccupied with the ethic of the Sermon on the Mount, Tolstoy had favored acting according to this radical ethic with no concessions. He didn't act entirely in accordance with his own postulate, however; he continued to live on his estate, and explained this in his drama *The Light that Shines in the Darkness.* Here he had the hero, in this case, himself, announce, "It is my lot to be ridiculed by other people because I do not live according to my own teachings." Weber thought this was inconsistent and said so. During the war he wrote an article on the two ethics *(Zwei Moralen).* Although this is of significance with regard to Weber's thinking, the article is little known. In this article he said that Tolstoy had attempted to realize his ideal only in the last brief period of his life, when he actually left his estate and his family and lived as a wandering beggar. Only the man who lives as Tolstoy did in his last weeks can invoke the Sermon on the Mount and proclaim the merits of pacifism and disarmament. One might interrupt to say that this was written during the war and is to be explained by the situation at that time. On the other hand I must emphasize that before the war Weber told me that some day he would have to take a stand on Tolstoy.

Gundolf represented Weber's confrontation with literary history as an independent discipline. Gundolf was officially qualified to teach literary history and then was made a professor of the same subject. We have already noted his importance to Weber. On the other hand, Weber was skeptical, even scornful, of those who babbled about esthetics, particularly if such talk were garnished with patriotism. Thus he parodied their methods when, in order to endear the Queen in Hebbel's *Gyges und sein Ring* to the hearts of the audience, he compared her to Bismarck's wife. Likewise he laughed when he saw literary history degenerate into petty philology, as for example when I told him of the existence of the *Revue des Etudes Rabelaisiennes,* which I had discovered in the course of my studies on Gallicanism and Jansenism.

The plastic arts were not discussed very often, but this was not true of the art historians. Weber made fun of Henry Thode, but so did a number of others; in Heidelberg at that time Thode was a figure of fun to everyone except his students, the so-called Thode Bohème. Although Thode had had a respectable beginning, he fell into the habit of glorifying his favorite artists in his courses. His phraseology was even more extravagant in his public lectures. Consequently people would attend his lectures just to be amused. In a similar way Thode raved about Giotto, Mantegna, and Correggio, among others, in his works. His writing on these painters was quite suited to the best-selling Knackfuss collection of monographs on various artists in which it was indeed published. It is hardly necessary to add that the Weber circle didn't discuss Thode at any length, although they were quite interested in the history of art. This is demonstrated by their positive attitude with regard to Thode's successor, Karl Neumann, who was highly esteemed. For years Neumann was only a *Privatdozent* and then a mere irregular *Extraordinarius* in Heidelberg until he was finally called to Göttingen. Neumann's sphere of interest was broad, and in this respect he showed a similarity to Jakob Burckhardt. At the meeting of the Heidelberg Historical Congress which I mentioned several times before, he gave a lecture on Byzantine and Renaissance culture. I can still hear how several of the younger historians talked about the lecture and agreed that it was no wonder that Neumann had remained an eternal *Privatdozent* for such a long time: he was unable to choose between history and art history. I was given a warning glance on this occasion because I had allowed my broader interests to become all too obvious.

A proper member of the Thode school who in walking seemed to transfer his body weight to his generously developed backside, and whom we called "the kangaroo" for that reason, told me that there were no two ways about it: history and art history had nothing whatsoever to do with each other. The art historians at that time had the same limited horizons as the political historians. A few art historians, however, were of a different mind: Strzygowski, for example, was attracting attention because of his theory on the influence of Byzantine culture and art on the West, and for a brief period he was thought to be a possible successor to Thode. This did not come about, and Neumann was called back to Heidelberg from Göttingen, this time as an *Ordinarius*. I do not know what Weber did behind the scenes to make this possible. In any event, Weber regarded Neumann as a friend; Weber had met him in Italy and was happy to see him again. Soon after, Weber said in a manner that was half understanding but half regretful, "He has become much more sober."

Although the plastic arts were not discussed in great detail, one cannot say the same about music. For Weber, music was almost a necessity of life, and he regarded with favor someone who was musically inclined, he valued this quality in his colleague, the botanist Klebs. In a different context, we were once discussing the Orientalist Bezold, who was also known as an Assyriologist. I had met him only once, in a large group, but I said that students had told me that he was very dry. Weber interrupted with the words, "Don't say that; he is the kind of musician who sometimes has to interrupt his playing because he is overcome with emotion." Weber also complained to me that, because of his illness, he was cut off from the world of music. At times he had Mina Tobler play for him. The second volume of his *Gesammelte Aufsätze zur Religionssoziologie* is dedicated to her. When he began to recover his health, the first thing he did was to attend concerts again.

On his travels he attended a performance of *Die Meistersinger* in Munich. When he went to Paris in 1910, I had to prepare a kind of musical itinerary, and, beginning in 1912, he postponed the Sunday afternoon gatherings for an hour on several occasions, so that he could hear the chamber music concerts that took place at that time.

Of course, the question of Weber's taste in music is much more crucial than these external matters. An old proverb that I have modified slightly appears true: if you tell me what music you like best, I will tell you who you are. When Weber was a student and a *Dozent* in Berlin, he enjoyed the classical period of German chamber music; he liked to speak of the Joachim Quartet. The Quartet was then composed of different persons than later; instead of Halir, De Ahna played the second violin. Weber was not disposed to admire only the great man, who was, in effect, a prima-donna; he was just as interested in the second violin, De Ahna, whom he respected very much. The Klingler Quartet moved him greatly. In this quartet the two Klingler brothers, one the first violin and the other the viola, were firmly in the tradition of Joachim, both with respect to technique and the content of the programs. Beethoven and Brahms dominated the program as was the case with the Vienna Rosé Quartet. At a later time they played some of the moderns, such as Reger. But at that time the moderns were played very seldom. In any event, Weber found the chamber music of Beethoven and Brahms quite adequate.

This should not be taken to mean that he didn't like other types of music; quite the contrary. Liszt meant a great deal to him, and he was extraordinarily pleased when Mina Tobler played Liszt's music. When Weber went to Paris, as I said, I made him a sort of musical itinerary. I told him about the two most important symphonic presentations of the time, the Concerts Colonne and the Concerts Lamoureux. When I added that the latter was accustomed to playing, in addition to the more classical works, the compositions of the Impressionists, as well as Liszt, he interrupted and said, "That alone is sufficient reason for going there." I myself admired Liszt's compositions for the piano, as well as his technique of orchestration. It stems from Berlioz, who was a real revolutionary in his technique of combining instruments. On the other hand, I was rather skeptical with regard to the programmatic music composed by Liszt and Berlioz as well as by Richard Strauss in his second period. Max Weber knew that. Now he was always fond of provoking opposition. And so, in my presence, he praised Liszt extravagantly and looked at me; I replied, "You know indeed how skeptical I am about Liszt's symphonic music." He answered, "That's just why I said what I did." Newer composers such as Schönberg began to attract attention and were occasionally played in Mannheim, but so far as I can remember these people were not mentioned at the Webers' in my presence.

Wagner, in accordance with the contemporary *Zeitgeist,* was discussed at length. If one wants to understand Weber's position with regard to Wagner, one must keep in mind the time when Weber grew up, as well as the role played by Wagner and ascribed to him by his followers. It is necessary to add a few words in order to explain the apparent contradiction in Weber's attitude. The War of 1870-71 had produced a feeling of exaltation like few other wars because it had meant the definitive step toward the unification of Germany. But with regard to the artistic expression of this state of mind, matters were quite different. For example, after the Seven Years' War and the Wars of Liberation (1813-15), which, in part, concerned the people of Middle and East Germany, the literature that was produced was of considerable significance. But the artistic response which followed the War of 1870-71 involved pathetic painters of battle scenes, like Camphausen, and comedies such as *Der Veilchenfresser* (He Who Gobbles Violets) and *Krieg im Frieden* (War in Peacetime). The plots tended to revolve around the Prussian officer, far from the front lines, who twirls his mustache and is sure to get the girl. One must view Wagner's popularity in the context of this national character, but the man himself must be viewed differently. In Wagner's personality there were elements of a post-Romantic, socialist anti-capitalism; Bakunin had fought along with Wagner in the Dresden Revolution; and in addition there were even elements of Schopenhauer and Buddhism. Why then did he use the Nordic Edda myth as the subject of the *Nibelungen* tetralogy? Because he thought that here, as nowhere else, he could find a pessimistic but simultaneously heroic Weltanschauung.

But the generation that grew up and lived under the influence of the events of 1870 saw in them primarily the patriotic, Germanic myth. And then Gobineau and Houston Stewart Chamberlain, a Frenchman and an Englishman, came to Bayreuth, and both proclaimed the supremacy of the Germans. Last but not least, there was Cosima, Wagner's second wife. She let the world believe, as Nietzsche's sister had done, that the whole idea was hers. She took an interest in the public appearance of anti-Semites, such as Zimmermann, the author of the book on the joy of sorrow *(Die Wonne des Leides)*, and even managed to find an understanding word for Ahlwardt. This "Rector of all Germans," as he was sarcastically called, behaved in such a way that even the leading anti-Semitic party, the so-called *Deutschsozialen* would have absolutely nothing to do with him.

This detour through the contemporary Wagner domain is necessary if one is to have a real understanding of Weber's position on Wagner and Wagnerism. Indeed he met Wagnerism in all its vulgarity *(Kitschigkeit)* right outside his door. Henry Thode, whom we have already mentioned in connection with the history of art, was one of the most pronounced Wagnerians. His wife was legally the daughter of the famous conductor Bülow, who had helped to make Wagner's work popular. But everyone knew that in fact she was

Wagner's daughter. Therefore Thode was in the innermost circle at Bayreuth. Extravagant as he was in his courses, he outdid himself in his public lectures on Wagner—in the presence of the fashionable ladies of Heidelberg in their pompous outfits.

The story about the beginning of his lecture was told to me by Jellinek, not by Max Weber himself. We have already learned to know Jellinek as a charmingly malicious storyteller. Because the story was told in the Weber circle, and because Max Weber liked to tell stories of this sort, it is only a coincidence that I didn't hear the story from him. In any event, the story is too good to be forgotten, and so I shall tell it briefly: Thode began his lecture on Wagner with the words, "Darkness covered the earth, the heavens were merciful, the heavens opened, the dove of the Holy Ghost descended, and the Mystery of Bethlehem was born. And then darkness again covered the earth, the heavens were merciful, the heavens opened, the dove of the Holy Ghost descended, and the Mystery of Bayreuth was born."

Nevertheless, Wagnerism had not only a droll but also a serious aspect for Weber. We can consider one after another of Weber's reactions to Wagner's various works. As previously mentioned, when he started feeling better, one of his first visits to the theatre was to witness a performance of *Die Meistersinger* in Munich. The Wagner performances in Munich were held in just as high regard as the performances in Bayreuth, and some people even thought them superior. When Weber mentioned that he had been there, I asked, "Is that the cast in which Geiss sings the part of Beckmesser?" I regarded this role as one of the most difficult in all opera. The performer must sing with a polyrhythmic beat in such a way that it fits in with the singing of the whole chorus. In addition, because he is the representative of a dying world and is fighting for a lost cause, he must convey an impression of tragicomedy, not just comedy. His part at the end of the second and third acts is one of the few in history which is not only amusing but really comic. For the effect of the Italian opera buffo is not comic, but rather amusing. This is true of the melodies of the lightly draped muse in Millöker's *Bettelstudent*, Suppé's *Boccaccio*, Johann Strauss's *Fledermaus*, and countless other Viennese operettas. In answer to my question, Max Weber said only, "I no longer remember whether he was called Geiss, but he sang the part very well." Then he added, "Really, the important thing was to have Soomer as Hans Sachs." I then asked whether Soomer had been able to convey the humorous nuances intertwined in the character. But Weber said only, "Not too well; but he did convey the inner dignity."

He really liked *Tristan*, and he even asked me to learn the lament of King Mark at the end of the second act so that I could sing it of a Sunday afternoon. However, this never came about. On the other hand, his opinion of *Parsifal* was negative. I can still hear how he repeated, with agreement, the opinion of the botanist Klebs, whom Weber, as we said, thought very musical: "Any man who is born a eunuch should not be surprised if nothing happens to him." Naturally he had in mind the scene with the flower girl in Klingsor's garden at the end of the second act. He was not one hundred percent in favor of the *Nibelungenring*. Once I talked with him and Gundolf about the possibility of a metaphysical tragedy (as I understood it, based on my knowledge of metaphysics at that time), and I said that I expected such a creation from one of my friends, who then went in a different direction. I pointed to analogous works of art in the past, and mentioned the *Nibelungenring* in this context. Weber cut me short, and said, "I know, I know. Alberich is supposed to represent capitalism," and he shrugged his shoulders.

On the other hand he felt deep emotion on hearing Siegmund's conversation with Brunhilde, who forecasts death, in the second act of *Die Walküre*, as we know from Marianne's description at the end of her book. And thus we round out the picture; there were three things, with respect to Wagnerism that Weber hated: the tendency to elevate the unrealistic elements to a Weltanschauung—in Bayreuth almost to a religious cult; the nationalistic ballyhoo surrounding Wagner; and finally, as mentioned before, the Wagnerian paneroticism, which, as he told Gundolf and me, he hoped some day to oppose in writing. Nevertheless he was moved by Wagner, the poet of the tragic, and the notion that one's fate was inescapable, but one was nevertheless obliged to meet it with courage. And he did like the music as such. This is not surprising in a man who liked Liszt's type of orchestration.

Matters pertaining to the theory and history of music were often discussed. One can remember the previously mentioned argument with Ernst Bloch, particularly the sharp rejection of the position that musical norms could have a universal validity. Questions concerning a sociology of music came increasingly into the foreground. I can remember many of these quite clearly. In the spring of 1912, we were walking in Weber's garden one Sunday afternoon. He was having a lively discussion with a musicologist from abroad, and he designated two sets of problems as being well worth relevant scientific investigation. First, what reason is there for the fact that a particular instrumentalist chooses one particular instrument, oboe or bassoon, for example, and not another? The second, to what extent is the individual who plays an instrument for which few solos are written, for example, the trombone or the tuba, satisfied with his situation and to what extent does he regret having mastered such an instrument? We didn't find the answers to these questions on our brief walk; such answers could be found only as a result of careful study. Nevertheless, it is worthy of note that Weber was then preoccupied with such questions.

When he wanted to go to Paris, I called his attention to the Concerts Touche (not to be confused with the Concerts Rouge being given at that time in the south part of the city—this was no better than beer music). The Concerts Touche in the north part of the city had a certain charm. There was a small number of instrumentalists, often only a double string quartet, conducted by the notable first violinist, Dorson, and Touche himself as cellist, and only one wind instrument but not the trombone or tuba. Every evening they played classical music for which their number was sufficient, or, in the case of Haydn, just right. On the same evenings they would also play chamber music, particularly compositions arranged for string and wind instruments by Mozart, Beethoven, and others. One didn't often have the opportunity to hear such music. The entire performance had a slightly bohemian aura. Refreshments were served and were included in the price of the ticket. The artists mingled casually with the guests during the intermission.

Naturally the Webers went there. After their return, Marianne told me that I had really done something when I directed her husband there. It had been an effort to keep him from going there on every evening for which he did not have a previous engagement. He liked going there for two reasons: first, because of the opportunity of hearing compositions he had not heard before, an opportunity of which he always took systematic advantage whenever possible, and secondly, because he really liked the opportunity of conversing with the musicians and he made good use of it. In particular he made inquiries into the training, the examinations, the salaries, the retirement insurance, and like matters that had a bearing on his sociological interests.

Perhaps of greater significance is the fact that before me and a few friends he developed a theory of the factors that had a bearing on the form of instrumental music, particularly the suite, the sonata, and the symphony—a theory that is not contained in the manuscript on the sociology of music left at his death. Briefly, this was the theory: Christianity was the only one, among the scriptural religions, that had never had a cult of the dance. For Christianity abhorred the body. It was therefore necessary to have a music based primarily on melody rather than on rhythm, to an extent scarcely found anywhere else. To my mind, the theory is untenable, at least in this form. In the first place there are at least two examples of a Christian dance cult, in Seville and in the old Ethiopian Church, the Monophysite offshoot lost to the Imperial Roman Church. In addition, the ancient Persian Zarathustrian religion with its pronounced metaphysical dualism was just as inimical to the body as ancient Christianity had been, but there is no evidence of a parallel musical development. However that may be, this is not the place to inquire into the correctness of a Weberian theory.

Position on Religion

Weber's personal attitude toward religion has already been depicted in connection with his meeting Ernst Bloch and Hans Ehrenberg. However, the subject requires additional comment with regard to the situation at that time. As long as he was not a Catholic or a member of a theological faculty, the typical professor at that time in a west or south German university had no external relationship with the church. One knew that the church was closely connected with the Conservative Party, the Junkers, and the highest ranks of the officer corps, and one therefore rejected or ignored it. Even for the liberal circles in industry and trade, the church was at best a means to domesticate the masses, and this wasn't particularly successful because the majority of factory workers regarded the Protestant church as "the mouthpiece of reaction" and "the ideological face of capitalism." Finally, those circles that were labeled "liberal Protestant" and professed an interest in theology kept their distance from the church. The religious development of Max Weber is too well known to be repeated in detail. We shall discuss only the most important names.

Who then was important to Max Weber's religious existence? His mother, who was deeply religious but who responded emotionally, without giving much weight to theological argumentation and trends; his uncle Hausrath, the moderately liberal Heidelberg church historian who, because of his loyalty to the state of Baden, was not a strong supporter of Bismarck's Reich; and then his uncle, Hermann Baumgarten, the well-known historian of the Protestant Reformation, who was an increasingly severe critic of the governing ability and the mentality of Wilhelm; and, last but not least, his cousin, Otto Baumgarten, son of the above, who was later a professor of applied theology at Kiel, and who was also dissatisfied with the German situation and was a particularly sharp critic of Stoecker, Waldersee, and other "Christian anti-Semites" in the milieu of Wilhelm II. In addition one must mention that Weber felt obliged to concern himself with the historical criticism of the Old and New Testaments as well as with other historical sources. This produced a definitive rejection of Protestant orthodoxy.

But this meant, as we shall soon see, everything but a rejection of religion and God. With regard to his position on Catholicism, one thing is immediately understandable: this firm representative of an ethic of individual autonomy who opposed any group that would turn itself into a metaphysical entity was naturally an unconditional opponent of Catholicism. At that time, Bloch and Lukács had rapturous praise for Catholicism. However, Marianne said to me directly, "No, Catholicism is out of the question for us." Weber also disliked the Catholic "chaplainocracy." He was referring to the authority of chaplains in their capacity as local leaders of Catholic labor organizations. He was often in contact with them in the course of his investigations for the *Verein für Sozialpolitik*. They occasionally got on his nerves. For the most part they were sons of farmers, who with the help of scholarships had gone through the Gymnasium and then through the seminary; Weber found them somewhat lacking in good manners. And as little as he liked superfluous formality, this man whose manners were above reproach preferred to encounter good manners in other people. His lack of friendliness to Bloch and Levy was related to their behavior in this respect.

The picture produced by these remarks on Weber's position with regard to Catholicism would be one-sided if we failed to examine the other side of the coin. This man was almost like one possessed with regard to freedom of conscience and the rights of minorities. The Catholics, of course, were a minority. He was in the habit of using every opportunity to learn more about Catholicism. It follows that this man who had investigated Calvinism would be familiar with the opposite pole. Namely, with the Catholic Counter-Reformation. His closeness to his friend and colleague Gothein was useful in this respect. We have already met Gothein in our sketch of the economists; he was really unsurpassed as an authority in this field, particularly with regard to the Jesuits' theoretical and practical position with respect to the state, society, and economic affairs. Weber's interest in the history of music and in sociology impelled him in the same direction. He not only knew the Counter-Reformation, he actually loved many things about it. He had read Calderon intensively, and he liked many of his dramas, particularly the play whose title in translation is *The Mayor of Zalamea.* Weber usually called it *The Alcalde of Zalamea.*

It is also important that he had relatives whose outlook was basically Romantic. They were enthusiastic about Romanesque churches and Gothic cathedrals. Even more, they had an extensive sympathy for Catholicism, and the Webers were almost afraid that they might one day be converted. This had already happened in their family. He gave a detailed account of Schnitger, a lawyer in Detmold. He had been discontented with the state church and had first become a Baptist; but he felt something lacking there too, and so he came to the harbor of Catholicism.

On several occasions Weber wanted me to tell him about my Catholic upbringing. I told him everything I could remember, for example, about my mother's relatives in Roubaix and Tourcoing in the extreme northeast of France. They were textile manufacturers and merchants. Their situation as one of the few groups of firmly Catholic capitalists made one feel that this would be splendid comparative material, an unexpected outcome, to test the correctness of Weber's theory on the relation of ascetic Protestantism to the spirit of capitalism. I later investigated this myself and published the results.

I also spoke to Weber several times about my paternal ancestors, small farmers in the so-called *Bergische Land* east of Cologne. I told him about my great-uncle Hansen, who looked and acted like a character in one of the old stories by Johann Heinrich Voss; my uncle had a triple position as "organist, schoolmaster, and upright sexton," but in contrast to the "honest Tamm" in the poem by Voss, he was Catholic instead of Lutheran. His church was the only one in which I ever played the organ. Weber was even more interested in my paternal grandfather. In general this man was typical of a whole stratum. He knew classical philology and ancient history, as did most of the teachers in the secondary schools at that time. He had written two articles on the latter subject. They appeared as supplements to the prospectus of the *"Realschule* of the First Rank, with Latin instruction," in Düsseldorf. Later on this school developed into our city *Realgymnasium.* My grandfather was born in 1823. He therefore grew up at a time in which the situation of the Catholic Church was rather peculiar. Because of the establishment of the state church, the Enlightenment, the French Revolution, and the dissolution of the Holy Roman Empire in 1803, Catholicism had received apparently deadly wounds. In addition, a short time before this, in 1773, the Jesuit Order had been dissolved by Pope Clement XIV, acting under pressure from the Bourbon Court. It was re-established by Pope Pius VII in 1814—but this action did not have the approval of everyone in the secular clergy, the older orders and many Catholic laymen. My grandfather was one of the latter. He said bluntly, "I don't like them," meaning the Jesuits, and he also disliked indulgences. Most of his friends, retired schoolmasters and *petit bourgeoisie* who were church wardens, felt as he did.

What united them was their aversion to Prussia. This aversion was of relatively recent origin. The imprisonment of the pugnacious Archbishop of Cologne, Clemens von Droste-Vischering, provided the decisive impetus to the formation of Catholic action groups. Bismarck's Kulturkampf had done the rest. Thus in the seventies my grandfather battled none too gently on the Catholic side in the Kulturkampf. During school festivals he remained ostentatiously seated during the salute to the old Kaiser Wilhelm, and by this uncompromising action he forfeited his chance to become the director of the school. All of this interested Weber greatly; this was not surprising in view of the fact that he had a real aversion to Bismarck's

Kulturkampf, which denied freedom of conscience to the Catholic. Weber was also well acquainted with various internal trends in Catholicism, especially the German Catholic heirs of the Enlightenment, and the anti-Jesuit and Romantic trends. Thus he mentioned the efforts of the Theiner brothers in Silesia to do away with priestly celibacy, to restrict the cult of the Sacred Heart of Jesus, and to effect various other reforms of which the Jesuits would not approve. "That was really something," was Weber's comment on the efforts of the Theiner brothers. This undertaking befitted only the abortive movement of the anti-Roman, Catholic splinter church *(Deutschkatholizismus)*.

We didn't speak of the Old Catholics. This was another German schism from Catholicism, an army of officers, in this case of university intellectuals, without any troops. As in Baden, the home of the older liberalism, it had adherents in Heidelberg among the professors, but we didn't actually see much of it.

I told Weber about my visits to Cloister Hain at Düsseldorf. At that time it was the only Carthusian cloister in Germany. The Carthusians were the most contemplative of all orders. Indeed, one could almost say that, because each Carthusian father lived all by himself in a little house, they formed—however contradictory it might sound—a society of hermits. As a youth I had been extraordinarily impressed, and often in the evening before going to sleep I would wonder whether or not I ought to enter the order. Weber understood my feelings. He told me that he had once met and talked with a contemplative. Now of course Weber's whole life tended to be under the sign of the *vita activa*. But this man who favored entering the political arena told me, "Indeed, there is no ethical or any other sort of viewpoint which can justify the rejection or negation of the contemplative life. If someone chooses to enter the contemplative life—very well—one should not hinder him." This is an understanding attitude that goes far beyond that of many strict Catholics.

The mentality of the Carthusians was strikingly presented in an essay on the apostolic effectiveness of the reflective life *(Das beshauliche Leben, seine apostolische Wirksamkeit)*. It was written by a Carthusian, appeared anonymously, and was translated into German by the abbot of the previously mentioned Cloister Hain; he gave me a copy. I gave it to my grandfather to read; he returned it with the words, "I really don't think much of those monks who only pray. "Weber was just as interested when I told him about my life as an altar boy with the Franciscans, how my heart had pounded the first time I served, the high degree of excitement felt by all of us boys when we served, that is, assisted the priest, in our red or blue robes with rochets and the lace vestments used at that time. We felt this excitement especially at a sacramental mass, or a high mass when there would be three people conducting the service: the priestly celebrant, the deacon, and the subdeacon, or at a Holy Day when there would be four because a Franciscan father, appropriately vested, helped serve. It was a special distinction to assist the officiating priest when during the singing of the *Asperges me* he walked through the church and sprinkled the faithful with holy water. The altar boys had to walk beside the priest in order to hold his vestments and free his arms so that he could sprinkle the holy water. I told Weber all about this myself, as I had once told Jellinek, not without emotion at these beautiful memories of my early years. Max Weber did not regard my feelings as comic or superstitious but rather showed a complete understanding of the fact that an eight- or nine-year-old boy could be so stirred emotionally that he felt compelled to wonder whether or not he should be a Franciscan. Max inquired what I had been reading at the time. I told him that, among other things, when I was about fifteen, I read Jakob Burckhardt's *Die Kultur der Renaissance in Italien*. He replied, "I'm surprised that they didn't inquire into your choice of reading material." I answered that at the humanistic Gymnasium the Catholic religious instructor whom we called "the holy rocking-horse" because of his waddling walk had become rather comfortable and phlegmatic in the presence of the Lord, and like many German Catholic intellectuals at that time, he was not quite orthodox in a Roman or Jesuitical sense. He had become a bit careless in his remarks on the cult of the Sacred Heart. And so they kicked him upstairs to the post of capitular, to a post, that is, that had a lot of prestige but whose occupant could do little damage, a post, moreover, about whose occupant our religious instructor had made jokes when he thought none of his superiors was listening.

What I have said here is all that can be said about Weber's attitude toward Catholicism. The assertion that one also hears in America, that if Weber had lived longer he would have become a Catholic, is completely false. We would sometimes hear similar remarks in those days. Even Troeltsch was supposed to have declared on his deathbed that there was only one way to salvation, the Roman way. This is completely untrue. The same thing was said of Kierkegaard. He considered himself a Lutheran, but in fact his sharp criticism of the established church and his firm demands on the clergy made him a belated Anabaptist, and certainly he was not about to become a member of the Roman Catholic church, which in a measure unknown to any other Christian group is legalistically constructed and institutionalized. And with regard to Max Weber, his extreme emphasis on autonomy indicates an unambiguous opposition to a church whose members ascribed such importance to a heteronymous ethic.

Weber's interest in Protestant affairs was incomparably greater, because he was often strongly involved in them. He was quite familiar with all the important parties within the Evangelical Church and with all the major trends within Protestant theology. Groups on which he often commented included the Lutheran Missouri Synod in the United States, which he regarded as the most conservative group, denominational Lutheranism, the *Positive Union,* the various nuances of the theologically mediating groups, the Evangelical Union (a Centrist group), and liberal Protestant groups of various kinds. Hans Ehrenberg, who was already mentioned in connection with the revival of Hegelianism and the meetings at Baden-Baden, gave a lecture at one of those meetings on the change in the interpretation of the history of dogma within Protestant theology. Max Weber had not heard it himself; I told him about it shortly thereafter and he was not only interested but extremely pleased. He said, "That's really something," and commented that the lecture ought to be published.

Thus he grimly followed the internal history of the German Protestant Church. We have already noted his intense annoyance with the hollow pathos of the sermons of Wilhelm II. He was also annoyed at the new Prussian law on heresy and for a reason so typical of Max Weber that his observation on the subject should not be forgotten. The law provided for a disciplinary committee and a pension for a pastor who was dismissed because of his teachings. The influence of Wilhelm Kahl had helped bring this law into effect. Kahl was a professor of church law at Berlin, a leading member of the Evangelical Union (the *Mittelpartei),* and the co-author of its new program in 1905. In certain other respects, Weber regarded him highly. What he disliked most about him and his law on heresy was the fact that it made heresy almost too easy. If one is certain of getting a pension, one needs little courage to stand on alleged heretical convictions and to suffer for one's views. "No," he added in a manner characteristic of Max Weber, "one would only be making martyrs." Indeed he dared say this because, as we know, he had rejected the pension offered him, and he was really prepared at all times to bear unconditional witness to his convictions.

This was also true in regard to his position concerning particular theological areas. He was well acquainted with Protestant piety through his mother and other relatives but mostly through the stories his wife told about her childhood. She came from Lippe. The area had been influenced by the Pietism of the seventeenth and eighteenth centuries as well as by the religious revival of the nineteenth century. In addition, Marianne had spent the greater part of her youth in Lemgo. Three things characterize this city, and it is worth repeating them for the information they convey on the style of life there. Lemgo was the last city in Germany to have burned a witch, it was a city that, even during part of the twentieth century, had no railroad line, and where at about the turn of the century there had been a rather sticky affair involving anonymous letters.

Both of the Webers knew the story and could recount it in charming fashion. The daughter of one rich merchant married another rich merchant, but she was soon bored to death with her life of luxury. She therefore took to sending anonymous letters describing what had been said at a meeting about a third person, always the addressee; but the letter would be written in such a clever way that it could have been authored by any one of a number of people. This went on for years; friendships, business relationships, and even an engagement were broken off because of it. It ended with the discovery of a blotter that she had used; she was sentenced to prison because she had perjured herself in swearing that she knew nothing about the letters during a court case that had involved the letters. The story itself could have been written by Flaubert; the solution of the case through the discovery of the blotter could have been the work of the French amateur detective Rouletabille or the American Perry Mason. But it happened in Lemgo in Lippe around the turn of the century and characterizes the entire milieu.

Lippe is also of interest because of the confession professed there. In contrast to the nearby area of Paderborn, which remained Catholic, and the neighboring principality of Schaumburg, which was Lutheran, Lippe was one of the few German territories that went from Lutheranism to the Reformed faith. True Calvinists in the *Gereformeerde* and the *Herformete* churches in the Netherlands, as well as in the Christian Reformed and Dutch Reformed Churches in the United States, might not have regarded the Lippe Calvinists as the genuine article. For, in Lippe, the Calvinist faith was connected with an established, monarchical church. Yet this helps explain the penetration of Pietism in Lippe. In addition, only part of the province was Calvinist. The old commercial city of Lemgo remained Lutheran. This situation merits a closer examination with regard to the Weberian thesis. It will probably be shown that the Reformed faith in Lippe, aside from its monarchical character, is not too typical of Calvinism. But this will have to be proved by future investigations. Here one can say only that both confessions displayed a continuing antagonism to one another that extended even to their religious and confirmation instruction. This is seen particularly with regard to the difference in teaching regarding the Eucharist. Partaking of the sacrament in the communion service is just a symbol of the heavenly gift to the Calvinist; the concept of the Real Presence in the element has been discarded. For Luther and for Lutheranism in general, the concept of the Real Presence remains, and this means that the wine consumed at the communion service is identical with the real blood of Christ. This latter notion upset the catechist of the Reformed faith who was giving instruction to a group that included Marianne Weber and other young girls in Lemgo. His interpretation was, "The Lutherans pour our dear Lord down the drain." By this simple but tasteless comparison, he meant that the Lutherans were so shameless they poured the blood of Christ right down their throats.

In order to understand how funny the situation was, one must know something about the people of Lippe. On the grounds of my frequent residence among them, I have called them the "super-Westphalians," not just because of their notorious thick-headedness but because of their speech. They accent the gutteral sounds even more than the other inhabitants of Westphalia, and one can just imagine how the gutteral sounds in *"Herrgott"* and *"Gosse"* must sound. The Webers, some of whose ancestors came from the area not too far from Lemgo, could imitate them magnificently.

To understand Weber's position with regard to Protestant orthodoxy, it is incomparably more important to know something about the people who were members of the Heidelberg theological faculty. At that time, the Heidelberg theological faculty was quite "liberal." Working in such a spirit—to name only the most famous—were the Old Testament and Oriental scholar Adalbert Merx, the church historian von Schubert, who was the successor to Max Weber's uncle Hausrath, and the applied theologian Heinrich Bassermann. The latter was the son of a leading revolutionary of 1848 and a member of a family that had produced the long-time leader of the National Liberal Party in the age of Wilhelm as well as the famous violinist and violist who played chamber music. He was a typical figure in contemporary Heidelberg in that he did not confine himself to the actual subject matter of his field in any strict sense. He was just as likely to give lectures on general pedagogy and the history of pedagogy in addition to his lectures on applied theology. Ernst Troeltsch went even further in extending the limits of his field. Officially Troeltsch was a professor of systematic theology, but he gave lectures on the history of Protestant theology and similar historical themes.

On the other hand, the administration forced the faculty, contrary to its wishes, to accept a man whose views were rather fundamentalist. This was Ludwig Lemme. His viewpoint can best be characterized by the term "biblical Pietism." He published works conceived in this sense such as, for example, a book on the infallibility of Jesus. Officially he had been hired to teach the history of dogma, although he had published scarcely anything in this area. It was for this reason that I said the faculty was "forced" to accept him. It was said that he owed his post to the influence of the Grand Duchess of Baden. She interfered now and then in the affairs of the university. Lemme was therefore a good example of what we called a "penalty professor." They were appointed to the faculty by the ministry of education if they did not behave themselves, that is, were too liberal.

Siegfried Goebel and Eduard König were appointed by the Prussian administration to the theology faculty at Bonn for the same reason. One could find "penalty professors" outside the theological faculties, especially in the faculties of economics and public law. Understandably, Max Weber could not tolerate such men at all.

Coming back to Ludwig Lemme, in addition to his biblical Pietism, three things characterize him: he was a leading member of the Conservative Party. In addition, he defended a prince of one of the many Saxon houses that ruled in Thuringia who was leading the life of a good-for-nothing in Heidelberg. He looked as though he were a character out of *Simplizissimus,* a contemporary magazine that was often really witty and that often caricatured that type of figure in a really brilliant way. He was the subject of considerable ridicule and it was even whispered that he would be declared mentally incompetent. And finally, Lemme took a leading part in a bazaar that was officially held for some good cause, but that in reality only gave the fashionable ladies the opportunity they desired of showing off their new clothes and of presenting their daughters of marriageable age to the public. This use of religious good causes for trivial social purposes was painful to pious Protestant groups.

All of this and many other things along the same lines made many people in Heidelberg rather unsympathetic to Lemme, who was the object of jokes that were not always kind. For example, there was at the time an assessor by the name of Schwarz. He fancied himself in the role of a cynic and liked to "murder" the illusions of the younger students. Now at that time, as it is now and probably always will be, a number of idealistic young people came to the university, to study philosophy, to follow artistic interests, or perhaps even, with a silent determination, to become poets. If they fell into the clutches of Schwarz, he would try to part them from such "illusions," and he was not content until they buried their hopes and decided to study law with the purpose of becoming a lawyer or judge in some small town. In order to kill time, Schwarz would attend all kinds of lecture courses. As he himself said, he made his choice by the following standard: in the winter he would attend the lecture being held in the warmest room. According to Schwarz, this was usually the case with Lemme's lectures. We reported this to Windelband who took a knavish pleasure in the tale and declared, "I shall tell my colleagues that Lemme keeps his audience warm with hot air." Whether or not it is proper to pass judgment on one's colleagues in front of students may be left open in this context.

Weber would occasionally speak of Lemme, although I no longer remember the exact context. I attempted to point out that perhaps Lemme had accepted the call to Heidelberg for reasons of conscience, even though he knew the faculty was opposed to him. Max Weber answered unambiguously, "No, certainly not Lemme, who is one of the worst of these types." Weber put von Kirchenheim in the same category as Lemme. We already discussed von Kirchenheim along with the law faculty. He was a zealous member of the so-called *Kapellengemeinde,* which was a sort of *ecclesiola in ecclesia.* The movement stems from the beginning of the so-called Precisian movement in the Netherlands in the seventeenth century, and it involves a small group of people who believe that they themselves are particularly faithful, and who therefore keep their distance from the mass of average Christians and children of the world, whom they regard as the other members of the church; nevertheless such a group stays formally within the church. In brief, it is a form of Pietism within the church, and it is a continuation of the Pietism of North Germany through the eighteenth century and through the revival that occurred after the breakdown of the Napoleonic Empire. It is scarcely necessary to emphasize that Weber, as a sociologist of religion, was extremely interested in this, as indeed I was also. Whenever the opportunity presented itself, I associated with members of the smaller religious congregations and attended their worship services. Thus, I visited the Darbyites (the Plymouth Brethren), the *Evangelische Gemeinschaft,* and the Methodists, among others. I also visited the *Kapellengemeinde* in the company of Sigsbee whom we already met among Windelband's students. The preacher that day was an important guest from out of town. He said something like this: "If I knew that workingmen would go to heaven, then I would think over quite carefully whether I would want to go there, because the workingmen today aren't a bit satisfied with their lot and are always trying to better themselves." When I repeated this to Weber, it was like waving a *muleta* before him, as one can imagine. "This really ought to be published," he said; this was just at the time that he was meeting and working with various theologians at the Evangelical-Social Congress.

This Congress was the place where the sequel to the story of the American theology student took place, the story we mentioned in the discussion of Max Weber's relations to the Catholic historians.

We left the young man an inspired student of Franz Xaver Kraus. Weber told the rest of the story in more or less this way: "Soon after, the young man came running to me and said, 'A new election has taken place in my Methodist church at home, and another group is in the saddle. They have ordered me to send them a statement of my beliefs. Can you help me?' I could tell him only that in general I was more than ready to help, but asking that I write a Methodist statement of belief is really demanding a little too much of me. Seeing the puzzled look on the young man's face, I went on to say that I was going to go to the Evangelical-Social Congress in a few days and that he could come along—he might meet all sorts of theologians there and he could perhaps pick out one who seemed suitable to help him prepare a statement of faith." No sooner said than done and they went there; after some time the young man told me that von Soden had helped him. (I am referring here to Hermann Baron von Soden, a Berlin theology professor who was well known and much discussed because of his critical work on the text and history of the New Testament; he is a controversial figure even today. Moreover, he was the father of Hans von Soden who was perhaps even more famous than his father as one of the founders of the Confessing Church and the author of the Marburg opinion on the Aryan paragraphs.) The creed which the American student produced with the help of the elder von Soden, translated into English, contained the following relevant sentences: "Jesus was born in Palestine as a son of Joseph and Mary . . . ; that is a matter of fact. . . . Jesus is the son of God . . . ; that is a matter of faith." In this form it was sent to America. After a time the student came hurrying up to me and said, "They have excommunicated me." The rest of the story doesn't belong here (Schulze-Gävernitz, another well-known Freiburg economist, was the protagonist in the remainder).

One must accentuate the quiet scorn that Weber had for those theologians who took with the left hand what they had given with the right, that is, those who always argued, "on the one hand, . . . on the other." To Weber this seemed to be an impermissible transgression against the demands of intellectual integrity. Thus he was skeptical with regard to some of the middle-of-the-road theologians, with the exception of Ritschl. After all, he had constant opportunity to learn about this man. His friend Troeltsch not only had been Ritschl's personal student, but in his early writings had followed in Ritschl's footsteps before coming closer to the South German neo-Kantian notions. Ritschl's sharp disengagement from metaphysics as well as his starting point eased Weber's approach to Ritschl even though both men demarcated the individual spheres of cognition at different places. It seemed to Weber that the so-called liberal theologians preserved intellectual integrity relatively better than the others. We shall turn to this group now and discuss them to the extent that they are relevant to Weber's life.

Everything that has the remotest connection with the Enlightenment or with liberalism had not been accorded much importance in Europe for a long time and this is especially true of liberal Protestantism. At best, many people only shrug their shoulders. Whatever one may think about it, whether one regards it as meaningful or possible to build religion and religious life on it, one thing is certain: the works of many of those who criticize liberal Protestantism are still indebted to it. The comparative history of religion, and the sociology of religion that is based upon it, would be unthinkable without the spadework which the liberal scholars of the Old and New Testaments had undertaken: for example, the way in which they used the results of the work of Egyptologists and Assyriologists. It is essential to note in this connection that Max Weber emphasized the great importance of this literature, something he seldom did. By no means do I wish to tag Weber with the label "liberal Protestant." What I have said refers to only one aspect of his intellectual perspective. This man who always saw the dark aspects of life before him had nothing to do with the optimism and the evolutionary belief in progress of the typical liberal Protestant. In spite of this he not only took a great interest in liberal Protestant theologians, he went a step further and supported them.

The extent to which he was familiar with the literature on all the trends of study regarding the Old Testament is made clear in his preface to the second volume of his work on the sociology of religion. Naturally he placed a high value on such works that were based on scholarly research and that attempted to show the connection between ancient Hebrew and other Near Eastern cultures. He spoke highly of the Orientalist on the Heidelberg faculty, Adalbert Merx. He too was, as one expressed it then, a faculty-jumper. He had started as a *Privatdozent* in Old Testament theology; then he became a professor of oriental philology in the philosophy faculty at Tübingen, and later a professor of Old Testament theology at Heidelberg. He had mastered nine oriental languages and, in addition to his works on textual criticism, he had authored works of a universal historical character such as the history of mysticism. He was thought to be vain. The following humorous story was told about him: Question: "What is the difference between God and the Privy Councillor Merx?" Answer: "God knows everything but Privy Councillor Merx knows everything better." I repeated this to Max Weber but he insisted, "The man is really significant," and to my question, "Does he deal only with philological specialties or with larger matters?" he answered at once, "No, no, he really sees the larger relationships."

He was not so intensively preoccupied with the literature on the New Testament. Yet I can remember two incidents with regard to this. Once someone complained that there was too much material that was really necessary to read and there was unfortunately too little time. Marianne looked at her husband and said, "We absolutely have to read the new edition of the history of the period of the New Testament" (*Neutestamentalischen Zeitgeschichte*). She was referring to the famous work by uncle Hausrath, whom we already met. Secondly, Weber was familiar with the scholarly Christological controversies that were particularly lively at that time. A brief interpolation must be made here about the contemporary state of research on the life of Jesus.

The mythological theory advanced by David Friedrich Strauss had long been rejected, as had the radicalism of the brothers Bruno and Edgar Bauer. Both, when they were young men, had denied the historical existence of Jesus. On the other hand, there was widespread support for three theories that asserted the following: first, that there must be a sharp line of demarcation between the three synoptic gospels on the one hand, and that of the fourth Evangelist on the other, as Ferdinand Christian Bauer and his so-called Tübingen school had taught; second, both Matthew and Luke go back to Mark as an original source, as Lachmann and Wilde had emphasized; and finally, along with Mark as original source, there is another source, a thesis elaborated by Christian Hermann Weisse.

In connection with these studies, however, the picture of Jesus was not always, but relatively often, seen apart from its historical milieu, and the fact that this milieu had a Jewish background was sometimes forgotten. Now, however, the pendulum swung far in the opposite direction; the eschatological character of Jesus' appearance was emphasized, and the content of the studies was closely related to the Jewish apocalyptical movements and expectations of those days. Along with other works of lesser influence, the works of von Ghillany (written under the pseudonym of Richard von der Alm), Colani, Weiffenbach, Baldensperger, and particularly Albert Schweitzer were written under the influence of these ideas. All this took place, naturally, long before the excavations at Qumran produced some entirely different material on the strength of the eschatological movements in the early days of Christianity.

Max Weber was involved in all this to the extent that he was familiar with the works of the two Weisses (not identical with the previously mentioned Weisse), the father, Bernhard Weiss, who had long been a famous *Ordinarius* of the New Testament, and the son, Johannes Weiss, since 1908 an *ordentlicher* professor of the New Testament and therefore a colleague of Weber's. It is significant that, although the father and son taught the same subject, they did not agree with each other. With some reservation the father could be classed with the liberal group in the tradition of Weisse to the extent that he found Mark a useful source in the history of the appearance of Jesus. Likewise, with some reservation, the son could be classified in the tradition that stemmed from Ghillany and continued with Albert Schweitzer—a tradition that placed decisive weight on the eschatological elements with regard to Jesus.

As we know, Max Weber had been interested in all these questions since his days as a student, and his close relationship with his cousin, Baumgarten, and his uncle, Hausrath, helped to maintain his interest. Hausrath had become well known for his work on David Friedrich Strauss; this work had appeared only a few years before Weber became a student. Therefore Weber was familiar with the intellectual world of Bernhard Weiss, and he thought highly of it. He found the son less able as a critic and he regretted this. It scarcely needs to be emphasized that church history was directly in his field of interest. Every line he wrote is evidence of his knowledge in this area and for a long time his relation to his uncle Hausrath was very close. Hausrath died fairly soon after he received his pension. His death was quite an event in Heidelberg because Adalbert Merx (whom we have already met in connection with his studies of the

Old Testament and oriental philology) presented the eulogy by the open grave; right at the moment he was doing so, he suffered a seizure and fell dead on the spot. I shall never forget the shocked look on Jellinek's face as, dressed in a dark suit and a top hat, he came out of the churchyard, plunged up to me, and told me about it.

Now it was necessary to find a successor for the chair in church history. Many persons thought that Grützmacher, whom we mentioned once, was the obvious successor. This foundered because of the policy of promoting no one who was already at the university; it might establish an unsuitable precedent. And so Hans von Schubert was chosen. Weber was not completely satisfied with him. It is true that the new man used a critical historical approach; however, he also had literary success to his credit. On the other hand he had also worked in the *Rauhe Haus* in Hamburg. This had been founded by Wichern who was also the founder of the "Inner Mission." These happened to be affairs with which none other than Troeltsch was concerned in the days about which these lines are written on the milieu of Max Weber. Troeltsch was then working on the social teachings of the Christian church. His work appeared first in the *Archiv für Sozialwissenschaften,* and then as a series of articles. The endless succession of articles put Max Weber, as one of the editors, and the owner of the Mohr Publishing House (Paul Siebeck) in Tübingen in a quandary. Troeltsch maintained that a real social reform based on a fundamentalist German Lutheranism was impossible; at most one would have only a form of social welfare that was quite different from social reform. Max Weber found this train of thought quite adequate. But Hans von Schubert was quite opposed to social reform. Weber said to me directly, "He doesn't dare to support the workers because his wife forbids it."

It has long been known that Weber and Troeltsch's inclusion of religio-historical materials in their works on the sociology of religion brought them into conflict with several church historians; I shall tell only of a few incidents of which I was a witness. Hermann Oncken, the historian in the tradition of Ranke, once said to me, "It wasn't Jellinek in that little book of his on the origin of human and civil rights, but rather Max Weber, who is the father of the idea of the Calvinistic origin of the declaration of human rights in the constitutions of the individual American states" (this isn't true), and in the course of the conversation he went on to say "The Calvinism-capitalism theory is now definitely disproved." He had Rachfahl's critique in mind; this had been written at the suggestion of Max Lenz, who taught both Oncken and Rachfahl.

Soon after this critique had been published, Troeltsch, Weber, and I met in Weber's house. Weber originally didn't want to answer it, for the reasons he gave later in his public reply. He thought it uncivil of the editor to have called on Troeltsch who was only partly involved, instead of Weber himself, to defend the theory. But Troeltsch insisted, "You must answer." Weber replied hesitantly, "I could at most cite several English authors characteristic of that time, one of whom Hermann Levy called to my attention, and then the reader would have the alternative choice between believing those English ascetic Protestants or Rachfahl." "You can do that if you wish," Troeltsch replied, "but in any event you must answer." Weber did so, in the *Archiv*, and then sent me a reprint. He never spoke much about the problem later on; he probably was tired of it.

With regard to other special investigations of church history, he followed with interest my studies of Gallicanism and Jansenism. This picture of Max Weber in relation to the theological faculty and its trends would be incomplete if we did not touch on his relation to applied theology. This would seem to be rather far from his interests, but this is mere appearance. First of all there was his favorite cousin, Otto Baumgarten, whom he had known so well in his youth. Baumgarten had become a professor of applied theology. In addition, it was natural that a man who, like Weber, was constantly concerned about the development of Protestantism in Germany would also be interested in the academic field that constituted almost the only connection between the theoretical material to which the young theology student was exposed in his courses on the Old and New Testaments, dogma, church history, and the like, and the practical demands that arose when he later became a pastor. Thus it is no wonder that Weber directed his interest this way and that he did not confine himself solely to theoretical interests but could become quite outraged about practical matters.

The so-called Simons case gave him opportunity for this. Simons came from a family of the Reformed faith in Wupperthal. He was a pastor for a few years, then for a longer time he was a *Privatdozent* and unsalaried *Extraordinarius* of pastoral care at Bonn, the author of a number of publications for example on the establishment of the Calvinist faith in Jülich, Cleve, and Berg, and particularly on the so-called "Churches under the Cross," that is, the persecuted Reformed congregations of the 17th century; in addition he wrote about Tersteegen. (This latter was one of the most typical figures who appeared in the Reformed Pietistic movement in Wupperthal in the 18th century. His influence was felt on Pietism within the church as well as on various sects, as, for example, on the group incorrectly called "Darbyists"; they called themselves simply a "congregation." In America they are called "Plymouth Brethren.") After many years of service to the church and a long waiting period as *Privatdozent* and *Extraordinarius* at Bonn, he was finally called to Berlin as *Extraordinarius* with civil service status. This happened when Paul Kleinert was still alive. Kleinert was *Ordinarius* of applied theology, but, just as his one-time predecessor Schleiermacher had done, he combined applied theology with other disciplines and for a time served in the Brandenburg Consistory and in the upper councils of the Evangelical Church. At that time there was no legal obligation to retire upon reaching a certain age. Thus just as the young girl waits in doubt for the young man to ask for her hand, the younger *Dozenten* waited in desperation for a chair. In many cases, however, the hoped-for event just didn't take place. Among those who were waiting, the expression, "Full professors never resign and rarely die," was common. Thus it was with Paul Kleinert and so this is what they did: to assist him they called in the previously mentioned Eduard Simons, and although it was not expressed officially, nevertheless it was with the intention—in the words of contemporary university jargon—*cum spe succedendi,* that is, in the normal course of events with the expectation of succession if the person who held the office should die or retire. But when Kleinert actually retired, they did not promote Simons to *Ordinarius* as everyone had expected. Under pressure from the orthodox, they called Friedrich Mahling from Frankfurt.

Mahling was known for his activity in the Hamburg city mission, and also through his writings on the "Inner Mission" and its chief founder Heinrich Wichern. But he had never even been a *Privatdozent* at a university or even an instructor at a pastoral seminary. But without this, and in spite of the fact that it went contrary to German academic custom, he was called directly as an *Ordinarius* to Berlin. Because of the prestige enjoyed by the university in the capital city, this meant that he had been called to one of the most desirable positions in Germany. All interested people in Heidelberg, Max Weber among them, were enraged, not just because of the victory of othodoxy, but more because of two other aspects. First, this new act of interference on the part of the administration was a breech of academic freedom. In addition, there was this aspect of the incident: in this fashion, without further ado, they put a man who had never endured the heavy sacrifice of serving long years as a *Privatdozent* and unsalaried *Extraordinarius* in that kind of position.

This does not mean, however, that Max Weber had an especially high regard for Eduard Simons. Naturally he was quite familiar with his writing, because the Calvinism of the lower Rhineland as well as the Pietism in Wupperthal were in the problematical area of his (falsely) so-called Calvinism-capitalism theory. In addition, Weber was soon involved personally in this affair. The previously mentioned Bassermann, who up to this time had held the chair in applied theology at Heidelberg, died unexpectedly at the summer resort of Samaden. It was therefore necessary to find a successor and, among others, people thought of Eduard Simons. This is quite comprehensible in view of the Heidelberg mentality; he was a man of whom it was believed that an injustice had been done because of his point of view. I myself personally knew Simons quite well. He was the uncle of my life-long friend, Adolf Schill; in addition he was, as I had been, a former member of the Bonner circle, primarily a student philological organization that had been founded in 1854 by the students of the exegetical philologist, Ritschl. Jellinek knew of my acquaintance with Eduard Simons and asked me in confidence what I thought of him. I replied that it was my impression that he was a very good and decent sort of man, but on the other hand he was everything but a great scholar. This opinion was confirmed by others a few days later.

In Weber's house, Weber and Troeltsch were talking about Simons in my presence. Weber said, "He certainly isn't a great man." Troeltsch replied, "He doesn't take himself to be one." Simons received a bandage for his wound in 1911 when he was called to Marburg as an Ordinarius. In a smaller way, Simons represents what happened to Dreyfus on an incomparably greater scale: a case where a man becomes famous out of all proportion to anything he has done simply because public opinion holds that he has been treated unjustly.

Neither Simons nor Friedrich Niebergall—the *Privatdozent* there, soon to be an *Extraordinarius* of applied theology—was called to the chair at Heidelberg. Max Weber did not think it tragic that Niebergall failed to get the chair. There was an unwritten law among the faculty that no person who had qualified to teach there should be called as *Ordinarius*. Georg Grützmacher was not called for the same reason. He was an *Extraordinarius* of church history and the author of a well-known historical investigation of early monasticism; moreover he was the brother of a much better known Richard Grützmacher, a contemporary leader of the so-called "modern-positive" trend.

To come back to Niebergall, one finds that Weber did not quite like him for another reason. In a fashion similar to that of Ernst Bloch and Hermann Levy, Niebergall would have changed the form of the Sunday afternoon gatherings. Weber told me, "The man has an annoying habit. In the course of conversation someone may drop a catch-word with whose content Niebergall isn't quite familiar, Marxism, for example. Then he says, 'Can't you explain what that means?' Then I would have to interrupt the conversation, apologize to the other guests, and say, 'We shall have to speak about something else and make a detour.'" Now Max Weber had a sense of proper form in all life situations, as was illustrated previously by his remarks on the "chaplainocracy." He therefore found Bloch's prophetic manner, Levy's pompous tactlessness, and Niebergall's gaucherie quite tedious and good reason to keep such men away.

Bauer was finally called to Heidelberg. Weber was not especially pleased, and he said to me, "He really isn't much; he's a nice man and he looked at my apartment here." This was shortly before the Webers moved from another residence to the first floor of the old house on the Ziegelhäuser Landstrasse where his uncle Hausrath had previously lived.

Conclusion

Whoever reads the preceding pages without knowing anything else about Weber might almost believe that he was interested only in the intellectual and practical aspects of religion. That this is not so is known by everyone who is familiar with his swan song, "Science as a Vocation" *(Wissenschaft als Beruf)*. First, and importantly, he had a feeling for mysticism. He listened with interest when Nikolai von Bubnoff reported his studies in the area of mysticism; Bubnoff's lectures on the subject stemmed from these studies. But Weber could be pitiless when mysticism did not fulfill two qualifications: it could not enter the sphere of the special sciences, and it had to be genuine and not some artificial creation. In this latter case Weber could really become angry. In order to understand his wrath one must bear in mind a particular aspect of the situation at that time. The previously mentioned Ernst Bloch had said a number of things over which one could only shake his head, but at least in one thing he was right. This was when he asserted that the wife of every professor keeps a cup of tea ready in her salon every day at five in anticipation of the Messiah whom she expects to come straight to her. In those years, the Eugen Diederichs Publishing House was established in Jena. Without passing judgment on his initiative, his courage, and his other publications, I shall cite only the judgment of Otto Zirker: "Eugen Diederichs has made irrationalism suitable for the salon." This was indeed true. Printed on hand made paper, bound in pigskin and with gilt edges, various books by mystics appeared on the tables of ladies who talked themselves into believing that they had a religious experience while reading them. We know Max Weber's sharply sarcastic critique of such behavior from his article, "Science as a Vocation." From my own experience I can add two items. First, what I saw in Cologne with respect to the women following Scheler: they talked themselves into believing that they were attracted to his philosophy when in reality he had only excited them sexually. Second, above and beyond its importance in characterizing the contemporary situation, the following is significant for what it reveals of Max Weber's position: one of Weber's younger friends said in desperation, "It would serve Eugen Diederichs right to have his ears boxed continually." Max agreed without any reservations.

On the other hand, Weber's respect for real religiousness was all the greater. This comes out clearly in the letters he wrote as a young man and is so well known that one further word would be too much. This is not so with his own religious concerns. Before we go into this and turn away from his attitude toward particular religions, it is necessary to remind the reader briefly, in order to avoid error, that all we have been discussing took place before two changes had occurred. Max Weber was indeed closely acquainted with the literature on the history and the activities of the Quakers; he had also studied them on his trip to America. What he did not live to see was the revival of Quakerism in Germany. This didn't come about so much just because here and there a few Germans became members of Quaker fellowships, or because they formed associations of friends of Quakerism; it happened rather because the Quaker mentality and more or less related notions extended far into Catholic, Protestant, and Jewish, and socialistic youth groups.

All that has been discussed took place before people like Karl Barth, Rudolf Bultmann, Friedrich Gogarten, and the two Niebuhr brothers had made an appearance, at least as far as Heidelberg was concerned, and therefore the religious and theological issues and groupings had not yet been affected by the new ideas. A real woman doesn't talk about her love affairs, and there is likewise a modesty of soul. Max Weber had this quality to the highest degree. He seldom expressed his innermost feelings in his writing and conversation. Once, in *Wirtschaft und Gesellschaft,* he spoke of the greatness of the death of the hero, the sacrifice of life for a cause in the highest sense. Thus also in his swan song, "Science as a Vocation." Here he said directly, "Today only within the smallest human circles, from one man to another, and in pianissimo, is there a pulsation of something that corresponds to that prophetic storm which in earlier days swept like wildfire through the nations and welded the peoples together." Some of the things Max Weber said in these rare moments may go to the grave along with those who were privileged to hear them and be lost forever. A god granted me one of those rare moments.

We had been speaking, as we often did, of Driesch and his neo-vitalism, that is, his anti-mechanistic system. As we said, Max Weber was far from being convinced by what Driesch said and wrote. He commented, in the rather mocking manner that was often typical of him, on Driesch's rather forced proof of the existence of God. "In order to see Driesch's God, one has to take the trouble to be at exactly the right spot in order not to miss Him." Two closely related modes of expression appear in Max Weber, as they once did in Pascal. The one is apparently witty but is actually meant in deadly earnest, namely, *ridendo dicere vera.* The other is in grave earnest even in its form. So it was in this particular case. We are neither able nor allowed to probe more deeply. *Favete linguis.*

There was a man who took upon himself the fearful burden of living in two worlds, the *vita contemplativa* of the researcher and the *vita activa* of the politician who is obliged to choose according to the ethic of responsibility. This man was Max Weber. He is one of those very few who lived according to a word that had been spoken 400 years before. In that same moment in which he made the observation above, his face changed and he looked at me in deep earnest and added, "This should not be taken to mean that it is not very essential to me to stand in the right relationship to that Lord." He went so far and no further. Here we have a key to the understanding of the inner man. The imperative of his predecessor Kant has here taken the singular form of a religiously based autonomy, but an autonomy that obliges a man to follow not just his own conscience but to decide on a much deeper level either for all time or in each particular case which of two ethics he must heed: an absolute ethic that disregards the consequences, or the ethic of responsibility whose followers assume the burden of sin. There are words that perhaps no one but Max Weber had so much right to say, except the man who first said them: "Here I stand, I can do no other, so help me God."

6

Max Weber

Max Weber was born in Erfurt on April 21, 1864. He studied law, economics, history, and philosophy, particularly under August Meitzen and Levin Goldschmidt. His dissertation, "The History of Medieval Trading Companies in Southern Europe," was written under Goldschmidt. In 1892, he was qualified as a lecturer in Roman and commercial law in Berlin, and—for financial reasons—he practiced law. In 1893, he married Marianne Schnitger, who published his work and wrote a biography of him after his death. In 1894, he was called to Freiburg as an *Ordinarius* in economics, and in 1897, he was called to Heidelberg. His friendship with Georg Jellinek and Ernst Troeltsch dates from the Heidelberg period. In 1903, because of a severe nervous disturbance, he retired from active teaching for many years, but he remained the center of a circle of scholars. He also had lively relationships with Friedrich Naumann, Stefan George, and Friedrich Gundolf. At the beginning of the First World War, Weber immediately offered his services to the armed forces. As a captain in the reserve, he became military director of army hospitals in Heidelberg. As an expert, Weber accompanied the German delegation to Versailles. The attempt to send Weber to the Reichstag and to obtain a ministerial portfolio, if possible, as a candidate of the *Deutsche Demokratische Partei* failed. After he had become a professor in Vienna in 1918, he accepted a call to Lujo Brentano's chair in Munich; there he died of pneumonia on July 14, 1920.

Paul Honingsheim,"MaxWeber,"Handwörterbuch der Sozialwissenschaften,Vol. II (Stuttgart: Gustav Fischer, 1961), pp. 556-562.

Ethical Foundations

Weber's Weltanschauung was based on the conviction that it was impossible, objectively, rationally, and scientifically, to pass judgment on the value of a fact, theory, or mode of behavior; on the contrary, the individual must autonomously choose between alternatives. This is especially true of ethical decisions, wherein an ethic of absolute value is opposed to an ethic of responsibility. The former, most clearly represented by the Sermon on the Mount, disregards the consequences of decision and action; the "saint," acting according to this ethic, feels responsible only to his own conscience or to God. The latter ethic bases action upon responsibility to a group, such as the family, the state, the church, or the party; therefore, whoever decides and acts according to this ethic assumes the obligation, if occasion arises, of sacrificing his own integrity and—in a religious sense— thus becomes a sinner. This decision cannot be taken from the individual unless he subjects himself voluntarily to an authoritarian organization, for example, the church. Weber advised everyone who was not in a position to lead an autonomous life to return to the church. This emphasis on the sense of duty, ultimately Kantian in structure, is linked most intimately with the Protestant consciousness of calling, whether as a politician, a scientist, or—characteristically for Max Weber—as a commercial or industrial entrepreneur.

Scientific Methodology

In his methodology, Weber is linked to the train of ideas of Christoph Sigwart, Wilhelm Dilthey, Georg Jellinek, Wilhelm Windelband, and especially Heinrich Rickert. Weber classified the sciences as being of nomothetic or idiographic character. The natural sciences belong largely to the nomothetic sciences, which are concerned with the crystallization of regularities, while the idiographic sciences are concerned with knowledge of unique events. The historical disciplines (including the prehistoric and ethnological) belong to the idiographic sciences. Within the historical disciplines, one must deal with the pluralism of causal factors; the individual phenomenon to be investigated is to be analyzed in terms of all the "constituent components" coming into question. It is a mistake to believe, on the contrary, that a certain factor, such as, for example, the economic factor in the Marxist system, is always the most important, or even the only, determining factor.

The unique individual is one of the factors that determines the development *(Werden)* of a unique historical situation. The individual's decision in a given situation cannot be predicted with certainty, and hence it also cannot be taken into precise account. For this reason, future development cannot be predicted, at least not with the precision that many natural scientists claim to be able to attain within their sphere (incorrectly, according to Weber).

The historical sciences—along with statistics—have the task of preparing the material which can be used for interpretive sociology. In order to understand and interpret the "intended meaning" of the things men do and leave undone, a meaning also expressed in institutions, "ideal types" must be constructed. This term has nothing to do with assertions concerning, perchance, "the idea behind the appearance," or "the essence of historical reality," or with ideals. The essence of the ideal type is demonstrated, rather, in the way the process of its construction takes place: one or several aspects are stressed in a consciously "one-sided" way, and that which is common to an abundance of "diffusely extant" phenomena is comprehended as a "mental image *(Gedankengebilde),* in itself a consistent unity" corresponding to those consciously exaggerated aspects. Likewise, the ideal type is "ideal only in a purely logical sense"; in "conceptual purity" it cannot be found anywhere empirically, but rather exists only in the mind of the investigator. The ideal type, however, can give direction to the process of forming hypotheses, since it provides an ideal limitation by which reality can be measured and can make possible an unambiguous representation of reality. Included here are concrete ideas of a certain epoch, historical developments, as well as the "forms of continuous collective action." All of these can be subsumed in the ideal type.

Weber classified possible types of judgment as he had classified the sciences: cognitive judgments (existential judgments) are concerned with matters of fact and causality; value judgments judge conditions and modes of behavior according to their value from a religious, ethical, esthetic, or other point of view. Cognitive judgment can, to a certain extent, give man the means that are to be used to realize the intended goals with a greater or lesser degree of probability. (This is also important for the understanding of Weber's own mode of behavior in both spheres.)

Social and Economic History

Weber devoted about one-third of the time he gave to scientific work to social and economic history. He had already, in his Berlin juristic dissertation, placed the trading companies that he discussed in an economic and sociological context. As an agrarian historian, he included even prehistoric ethnological materials and then developed his main thesis: large landowners, with overseers and slaves, existed in unbroken continuity from Babylonia to the period of the Roman Empire. Within this period the economy was transformed from a type involving absentee ownership of large estates and a slave and money economy to an economy based on *latifundia* with resident landowners, serfs bound to the soil, and a natural economy. The Germanic invasions meant only a change in ownership. Moreover, the size and organization of the landed estates remained in unbroken continuity at least up to the period of the Carolingians.

In his investigation of the history of cities, Weber distinguishes the following: the oriental city, whose inhabitants were not differentiated from non-residents by the possession of special rights; the ancient city, inhabited by slaves, bondsmen, clients, and artisans, but without any organized craft guilds and characterized, among other ways, by opposition on the part of those who were "politically *declasse*"; and the medieval city with its own administration and jurisdiction. Social conflicts arose here between, on the one hand, entrepreneurs and craftsmen with their rational-bourgeois conduct of life, and, on the other hand, the land-owning "blue-bloods" (*Geschlechtern*) with an aristocratic style of life. Ancient and medieval cities were transformed in these conflicts from aristocratic to plebeian cities. This development allowed the medieval city to become one of the various factors in the genesis of modern capitalism—and for this reason, research on the city was dear to the heart of Max Weber.

Sociology

Weber thought of sociology as "an empirical science that interprets the meaning of social action, which is based on the subjectively meaningful intent of the actors. Sociology is therefore a science that attempts a causal explanation of the course and consequences of social action." In this sense, Max Weber analyzed the forms of legitimate authority, the sociology of political structures, law, economics, religion, and music, especially in *Wirtschaft und Gesellschaft.*

Forms of authority. Weber's three-part division of forms of authority and obedience is so well known that it is sufficient to sketch the forms briefly. In charismatic authority, a leader proclaims himself to be extraordinary and endowed with special qualities; other men become his followers, as, for example, men have followed the originators of religious or political movements. Traditional authority is based upon a handing down of the authority system, as it is, for example, in feudalism. Under rational authority, obedience occurs because those who command have attained their positions in legal ways. This bureaucratic principle with its impersonal rules is found not only—as it is sometimes mistakenly supposed—in the modern, so-called "constitutional state" that legitimizes itself by appealing to its "legality," but also in churches, parties, labor unions, trusts, and other large-scale organizations.

Political structures. Weber defined the state as a structure not the least of whose characterizing criteria is its claim to the continuous use of "physical force" as well as the exercise of power. In contrast to this, the nation is a structure in which the memory of "common political destinies of vitally decisive significance" possibly represents the most strongly cohesive element. On the other hand, a distinctive form of honor that links many men together on the basis of a shared quality is symptomatic of the status group (*Stand*). The class represents a group whose members have in common a "specifically causal component of their life chance," a component completely determined by economic interests. The party machine and party bureaucracy are characteristic of parties, especially the patronage party as Weber studied it in America and as he predicted it for the German Social Democracy.

Law. Weber understood law as a system that is effective because people orient their action to it. In addition, it is provided with an enforcement apparatus consisting of a staff of men. Moreover, law stands in a sociologically necessary relationship within a specific social structure in whose frame it is empirically effective. Weber was particularly interested in the factors and types of people that shape the law, as well as in the creation of law, especially natural law. Weber himself was not an adherent of natural law, but he felt that his own views had an inner relationship with it, and he regarded it as if it were revolutionary law. He thought natural law was also a protest against state intervention in the sphere of competition within the economic world. Here Weber's sociology of law makes contact with his sociology of economics.

Economy. Weber understood economic action *(Wirtschaften)* as the peaceful exercise of the power of control *(Verfügungsgewalt),* which in its intended meaning is oriented toward meeting the demand for goods and services *(Nutzleistungen).* His primary interest was in capitalism, which he dealt with in its relationship to the genesis of the modern state and the formation of state monopolies; in his opinion, monopolies originally promoted capitalism, but later on they hindered it. To Weber, the factory was—regardless of the prevailing economic order—a workshop with a division of labor and a type of work oriented to machinery. It is especially important for Weber that the outcome of competition, in spite of chance and fate, leads to the actual selection of those who have the necessary personal qualifications in greater measure than other qualities such as devotion to superiors or demagogic talents. This is said without implying the value judgment that the victors in the competitive battle are for that reason more valuable from an ethical or some other point of view.

Religion. Here the relationships of certain social strata to certain religious attitudes are discussed in detail, and a classification is made of forms of religious groups, types of leaders, and systems of theodicy. In addition, his investigation of the relationships between certain forms of Protestantism (Calvinism, Anabaptism) and the capitalistic mentality is significant. The theory itself goes like this: except for Anglicanism and Lutheranism, Protestantism teaches that the earth was indeed cursed by God after the fall of man, but, at the same time, the earth was given to God's elect to rule and to make use of. Therefore, one should remain in the world but ascetically restrain himself completely from sentiment and pleasure. Instead, one should work all the time and thereby earn more; but because one cannot spend his earnings, one therefore accumulates capital. Because God gave authority to His own at a time when power was no longer bestowed upon feudal ownership and ground-rent but rather upon capital ownership and interest, it was quite easy to draw the following conclusion: I have ascetically refrained from the enjoyment of life, worked systematically, accumulated capital, and have thereby won power over those whom God has condemned, such as Catholics, Anglicans, and Lutherans; is this not proof that I shall go to heaven as one of God's elect? This conclusion amounts to the religious legitimation of the bourgeois who perceives and manages his affairs in a capitalistic way. Weber asserted no more than this. Therefore, for Weber, ascetic Protestantism was not the original cause of capitalism, and the theory is not simply "Marx turned upside down."

Plastic arts, literature, and music. On figures such as Feodor Dostoevsky, Leo Tolstoy, Stefan George, and others with whom Weber was so intensively preoccupied, there are only occasional observations in a sociological context. On the other hand, in a small monograph, the process of rationalization in occidental music is related to the same process one finds within Western ecocomic and social life. Thus, these special questions can be fitted into one of Weber's chief problems.

The Politician

Several lines converge in Max Weber's politics: his father was a Reichstag deputy of the National Liberal Party and an adherent of Bismarck's; he was influenced along the lines of individualist, democratic, leftist-liberalism by those who, as Theodor Mommsen, frequented his father's house; and finally, he felt the effect of social welfare politics on the part of contemporary academic socialists, such as Gustav Schmoller, and of the *Verein für Sozialpolitik*. His political position was derived from all of these and from his feelings of rigorous obligation to his beloved Germany. His position led him from the National Liberal Party, which had originally offered him a seat in the Reichstag but which he declined, to Friedrich Naumann. It is difficult to separate his share in setting up the program for the *Nationalsoziale Verein* in 1896 from Naumann's. After this party foundered in 1903, Weber, along with most of the members, went over to the liberals and after the war to the *Deutsche Demokratische Partei*. Meanwhile he worked in the *Verein für Sozialpolitik* and presented his convictions in numerous newspaper articles, especially in the *Frankfurter Zeitung*. His political critique went back to Bismarck, whose monocratic authority he held responsible—in a deeper meaning—for the blind obedience to the "crowned dilettante," Wilhelm II, whom Weber, in spite of his monarchism, despised just as much as the era named for him. Weber saw the danger resulting from the dominance of the feudalists east of the Elbe who had long since

ceased to be an aristocracy but were rather an economic entre-
preneurial stratum. Their power was re-enforced artificially through
the Protestant state church, which formed a far-reaching connection between them and the Conservative Party. The ability to give
satisfaction in a duel, membership in student fraternities, and a lieu-
tenancy in the reserves all were ways of assimilating the bourgeoisie into outmoded forms of feudal life and intellectual predilections,
and they also provided a means whereby unsuitable people would
attain positions of leadership.

For this reason Weber demanded that large estates be transformed
and given to tenants who would be permitted to have them tilled
only by German farmworkers because of the danger of Polish influence in the German East. He further demanded the extension of
social welfare policies, although this should not consist primarily of
the socialization of industry and the formation of a new kind of
leadership, on democratic lines "from below," along with the su-
pervision of the civil service by parliamentary control commissions.
Weber nevertheless emphasized that he did not fail to appreciate
the "shadowy side of democracy." In particular, he did not legiti-
mize it, as often happens, by the optimistic argument concerning
natural law and the rights of man. During the war, he insisted on
Russia's guilt and Germany's non-guilt as well as on the necessity
of explaining that Germany did not seek any territorial expansion
in the west but rather a "circle of semi-independent Slavic states"
in the east. Finally after the World War, he advised guerrilla warfare
against the Poles should they occupy Danzig, and he fought successfully for the direct election by the people of the president of the
Reich, as well as for increased powers for his office.

Weber's Position in the Total Structure of Occidental Culture

Weber's methodology was based on a long line of continuous development. Kant separated the objects of knowledge of "pure reason" from those of other spheres of knowledge. Many little streams
of influence flowed unobserved from this point, parallel to the Romantic transcendental philosophy. Their point of convergence is
Friedrich Albert Lange; he stood simultaneously against materialism, transcendental philosophy, Marxism, laissez-faire liberalism and
the quantitative psychology of the Herbart school from whence he came.

He separated knowledge that could be obtained empirically from all knowledge that was supposedly non-empirical and whose substance he designated as "fiction." This is Windelband's point of departure (although he owed more to Hermann Lotze and Otto Liebmann); he divested himself, to be sure, of Lange's physiological-psychological elements and was much less agnostic than Lange. Windelband contrasted "history and natural science." Rickert continued this and worked out, among other things, the two paired opposites, "natural and cultural sciences, "as well as" cognitive and value judgment."

Max Weber then used these terms, although with modifications. Moreover, he connected these with the conception of the "ideal type" as it had been worked out by Christoph Sigwart and Dilthey, as well as with his own conceptions of "intended meaning" and "*Verstehen.*" Max Weber's most original contribution concerned the way in which all of these elements were connected as well as the way in which the function of the individual personality is limited by and connected to the regularity of the course of history, which, according to Weber, could be determined to a certain extent.

All of this met with approval in Germany, although with some qualification. Among the authors who were directly or indirectly influenced by Weber's statement of the problem and answers (although they then went their own ways), we might name Edgar Salin (although he shows a stronger connection to Alfred Weber), Arthur Salz (although he diverged from Weber particularly in regard to value judgment), Helmuth Plessner (although to a certain extent he was also connected to Max Scheler), Count Max zu Solms (his work modified by elements from the philosophy of Nicolai Hartmann), as well as Gottfried Eisermann in more recent times. In France the importance of Weber's theory of value neutrality was stressed especially by Raymond Aron; on the other hand, Georges Gurvitch thought that Weber's reduction of the "social fact" exclusively to meaning and action represented a danger of impoverishment.

In the United States of America, Weber's classification of science, his conception of history, and his theory of value judgment were accepted with more or less strong modifications by Weber's translators, Hans H. Gerth, C. Wright Mills, and Talcott Parsons. With regard to his theory of value judgment, however, Heinrich Jordan and Howard Jensen said that existence and value could not be isolated from each other. The German-American Howard Becker accepted the classification of science, the theory of value neutrality, and the concepts of causality and *Verstehen*, but he went beyond Weber. Becker thought that Weber used arbitrarily created word-formations in order to construct the ideal type. In contrast, Becker, from among the types coming into question, insisted upon the choice of the "constructed type," which could be used most meaningfully for the purpose of classification. Pitirim A. Sorokin raised objections on principle against the causal concept, which was related to the functionalistic conception of cause common at the turn of the century; thus he opposed the conception of the ideal type because, although Weber intended it as an auxiliary construction *(Hilfskonstruktion)* which was thought to be different from an adequate definition of the corresponding phenomenon, actually it was identical to an adequate definition; finally he opposed the pluralism of causal factors. According to Sorokin, one could indeed determine, by various kinds of analysis, that an effect was produced by the convergence of a number of factors, but one could not determine what role a single factor had played in this. Obviously this issue has not yet been resolved.

From the point of view of economic history, the introduction of ethnology signifies something new, and not just in Germany at that time (with the exception of the Darwinistic evolutionists). However, it was in the most blunt contrast to the position of Jellinek and Troeltsch, whose ideas were generally like Weber's. As an agrarian historian, Weber may indeed have had a forerunner in the occasional speculations by Paul von Roth concerning the Roman *lutifundiu,* but in the decisive conceptions he had priority over Mikhail I. Rostovtzeff (with whom he later had a personal relationship), as well as over Alfons Dopsch. The contrast of the three types of cities and the type of interrelationship between the medieval city and the genesis of capitalism are Weber's own work. It was widely accepted at that time. Since Henri Pirenne, the statement of the problem has shifted.

Weber's typologies and writing concerning the sociology of religion were widely accepted and amplified, especially in America. In the discussion of Calvinism, Weber had a predecessor in Jellinek. But Jellinek had only pointed out Calvinism's significance in the history of the rights of man. The economic aspect is Weber's work. The debate itself was carried on most strongly in Germany and America. Felix Rachfahl, the German disciple of Ranke's, rejected the thesis *a limine.* But contrariwise Herbert Schoeffler and his school in Cologne later investigated a number of English phenomena as to their origin in a Calvinistic-Anabaptist milieu. Werner Sombart, Pitirim A. Sorokin, Richard H. Tawney and Milton Yinger have asserted in opposition to Weber's thesis that the "Calvinistic mentality" existed long before Calvin; Tawney and Yinger added that the economic attitude of the early Calvinists had been medieval. Howard Becker, Marshall Knappen, and Sorokin objected further that Methodists and similar groups did not hold the doctrine of predestination, and yet they seemed to have the capitalistic mentality as depicted. Therefore the belief in predestination could not be of decisive significance (although this is not opposed to what Max Weber asserted). In a number of articles, Parsons defended the theory against these and other objections. The debate on this issue continues.

Evaluation

The contradictions that many critics have noted between the foundations of his Weltanschauung and the program of the politician, between the postulate of value neutrality and the hymn he raised to dying for the fatherland (even in his scientific work) can, to begin with this objection, be seen only as an exceptional case. On the contrary, in the overwhelming majority of cases, he remained true to his own demands. He remained true even though in scientific work he often dealt with the same objects as in his political controversies and even though, given his fighting spirit, objectivity signified only an endless enterprise against himself. Nevertheless, he could still experience the scholarly joy of successfully attaining a result in his historical research. As has been correctly noted, even a part of his purely scientific work stands *sub specie vitae activae*. Thereby he is as far as the stars from another "disenchanter," namely, Arthur Schopenhauer, to whom he is occasionally compared in America, not just because they both took Kant as their point of departure, but especially because of the gloominess of their views of the world. But concerning the alleged antagonism between the foundations of his Weltanschauung and the postulate of the politician, in reality he always decided and acted according to his own teaching and made use of the right he preached, the right to determine values autonomously and, especially, to choose between two ethics; he autonomously chose either the ethic of absolute value or the ethic of responsibility, depending upon the object in question. Thus he decided in favor of the ethic of responsibility when it was a matter of the economic recovery and the power of Germany, and he praised the American "businessman" as a model; he decided in favor of the absolute ethic when it was a matter, as he saw it, of German honor, and he advised guerrilla warfare in the Danzig question.

His conduct in private and academic life was analogous. Wherever he saw offenses against justice, as he understood it, he intervened without concession; he intervened when he did not have the remotest personal interest in the matter; he intervened even, or more exactly, more than ever, when it concerned a scholarly or political opponent.

Whatever else it may have involved, it was not simply a matter of a radical unwillingness to make concessions, but rather a matter of the feeling of obligation to make an inexorable choice in each situation and, if the occasion arose, to retreat not one step for the sake of one's own integrity or, inversely, to make compromises for the sake of the cause.

The obligation to decide is embedded in a kind of Dostoevskian underground, deeper than Friedrich Nietzsche's temporary alternative, "Pagan or Christian!" Nietzsche definitely answered, "Pagan," and added unambiguously, "Dionysus against Christ! " Therefore, away with Christ and Christendom! And Max Weber's answer shows greater depth than that of Neitzsche's predecessor, with regard to stating the question, and of Nietzsche's polar opposite, namely Soren Kierkegaard, with regard to the answer given. Kierkegaard definitely answered, "Christ," and thereby rejected occidental culture. Unlike Nietzsche, with whom he shared the belief in the role of the hero, Max Weber loved his fatherland; and in contrast to Kierkegaard, he affirmed occidental culture, including its politics and its special sciences. Thus he demanded an autonomous decision at each moment: "the radical absolute ethic or the ethic of responsibility!"

And thus one must make the inclusive judgment, even if one has to say "No" without concession to Weber as a postwar politician: he is one of the very few contemporary leaders who decided, wrote and acted in accord with the command of the autonomous conscience.

7

Max Weber as Sociologist: A Word in Commemoration

When Max Weber died, the obituaries described him sometimes as a pioneering thinker, other times as a political force. Some persons, however also remember him as an unbalanced, self-contradictory, charming figure, or at least refer to the abundance of interests, without apparent interconnection, that he harbored. And indeed, for the person who did not know him in depth, it must have been tempting to judge him in this way. Yet seldom has a man segmented himself in his external relations with the world as much as this one and on every occasion presented himself not as a whole, but as belonging to a certain sphere—as an empirical scientist in his writing, as an academic instructor at the professor's lectern, as a party member on the platform, and as *homo religiosus* in the most intimate circle. Nevertheless the question must arise whether behind all these compartments, behind these separated spheres for which almost the only analogy is to be found in Franciscan nominalism, a totality is not concealed, indeed whether such a totality can find adequate expression only in this way. Perhaps his development can give us a hint.

In the beginning he had planned to become a politician, but he was long hindered by illness from most activities of this sort; at first a scholar of legal and economic history, he became an economist, then an investigator of the relationships between religion and eco-

Paul Honigsheim,"Max Weber als Soziologe,"*Kölner Vierteljahrshefte für Sozialwissenschaften.* Vol. 1, No. I (1921), pp. 32-41.

nomic life, then a sociologist of religion, then simply a sociologist. Again in health, he stepped anew into political life and tended to drop the other pursuits, although he remained a sociologist. To be sure, he separated politics and sociology more sharply than ever. And yet one must ask: do both of these areas to which he remained faithful, and which he simultaneously pursued, belong together in his case? Did he feel that the external separation was necessary in order to work out his own ultimate oneness? In order to answer these questions to which the following lines are dedicated let us proceed with a brief glance at some of his particular sociological ideas.

Contributions to Sociology

The man who hitherto had been an economic historian and an active member of the *Verein für Sozialpolitik* first became known outside economic (and political) circles through his investigation of the connection between *The Protestant Ethic and the Spirit of Capitalism*.[1] It was not Weber who first re-discovered the Puritans and the troops of Cromwell; this was done by the gentle person Weber loved and admired, Georg Jellinek,[2] who had emphasized their significance as originators of the kind of individual political freedom later given impetus by the French Revolution and by liberalism. But it was through Max Weber's special investigation that the fundamental question was raised for the first time: to what extent does the religious attitude of people form one among the possible and various constituent components that give concrete shape to the economic life of a certain age, a certain race, and so on? This not only made a breach in an entirely new direction in Marxist economic historical materialism, but, because economic life as influenced by religion had, in turn, an effect on social strata, it provided the primary object of research to the sociology of religion and indicated a new direction for the future. However much he was, and remained, deeply committed to an individual science and empiricism, Max Weber documented through this work his membership in that whole culture complex that can be described as a reaction against the naturalistic and intellectualistic age—an age from which would emerge a form of neo-Romanticism that Weber would oppose more than once.

Interpretive Sociology. But before we turn to the concept characteristic of his entire theoretical and practical position, that of value neutrality, let us examine yet another of his areas of activity, interpretive sociology,[3] because this presents him in the same context of which we have been speaking.[4] His starting point is the possibility of understanding human behavior through interpretation *(Deutung)*. But he rejects mere interpretation as unsatisfactory because the presence of even a large measure of evidence does not release one from the necessity of control through the customary methods of causal imputation. Only when causal explanation occurs does "interpretation" become "intelligible explanation." It appeared to him that the largest measure of evidence existed for the interpretation of instrumental rationality, that is, behavior that is exclusively oriented toward "means considered adequate for ends that are subjectively perceived without ambiguity." Despite the great evidence of technically rational behavior, sociology is not concerned solely with rational interpretation but rather is just as concerned with instrumentally irrational attitudes, even though it attempts to interpret them first on the basis of rationally intelligible relationships of action. Sociology has to deal with action, that is, with meaningfully differentiated behavior toward objects, indeed, with action related to the behavior of others, action that is thereby co-determined and is explainable in terms of the relationship to the behavior of others. Hereby, sociology differentiates in terms of meaningful relationships which are not identical to any underlying psychic constellations, so that there are categories of interpretive sociology that do not belong in psychology, as, for example, "acquisitiveness," which can be conditioned by contradictory psychic elements. Accordingly, interpretive sociology is no part of psychology.

This approach was completely different from that of many other, particularly foreign, sociologists, who are likewise to be counted as part of the previously described naturalistic age of quantification to which we contrasted Weber. This same juxtaposition can be clearly recognized in other ways: if the writings on the Protestant ethic and the spirit of capitalism manifest the strongest possible emphasis on religious experience (therefore of the nonintellectual) in its world historical impact, we now encounter, apart from the separation from psychology, a clarification of the instrumentally irrational in its entire breadth; thereby, on both counts, we return to the intellectual realm that is characterized, other than by Max Weber himself, by a plethora of names from Bergson to Spengler, to mention two of the best known.

The Theory of Value Neutrality

Nothing of what Max Weber has done, said, and written has been discussed, commented on, misunderstood, and ridiculed as much as his theory of value neutrality in the social sciences. The theory finally turned up in parliamentary discussions, party meetings, and in the Berlin commission charged with investigating war guilt. For these reasons, as well as for the reason that it was, as we shall see, truly the most personal of his theories and can be understood only by understanding his character and life, we shall deal with it here in some detail. But at this point it seems advisable to exclude the impact of Weber's own psychological make-up on his theory, to leave it to a later paragraph, and, here, to give only a summarized presentation of the theory itself. In addition, I shall omit the often related pedagogical-organizational problem of value judgment in university teaching. To be sure, this appeared to Weber as a not unimportant consequence and brought him not a few enemies, but it does not belong in the framework of this article. Let us begin with the theory itself.[5]

Evaluations. Weber's approach to value judgments was related to Rickert's theory of the difference between evaluations and value relations, but Weber applied it independently to social science. Weber interpreted evaluations (in this context, exclusively practical evaluations of social facts) as social facts "that were in practice desirable or undesirable from an ethical or other cultural standpoint or for other reasons." The first requirement for the researcher is that he separate, as two completely different things, the substantiation of empirical facts (to which, naturally, value judgments by individual men or groups of men can belong) from his own practical evaluations, that is, those facts which he evaluates as good or bad (including those value judgments by individual men or groups of men). If, mindful of this imperative, one then investigates the value position of the people doing the evaluating, one attains an intelligible explanation in the sense used previously.

The importance of using this kind of scientific procedure is that it makes it possible to learn to know the ultimate motives of human action. In addition, it makes possible an analysis of both the opposing value positions of the individual men and groups of men doing the evaluating and, likewise, the value position of the investigator himself. Such preliminary work further makes it possible "to deduce the consequences for a value position which would follow from certain ultimate value axioms," if the value position alone is taken as the basis of the practical evaluation of reality. In addition, one can determine the actual consequences that would appear if the investigated value position were to dominate the practical behavior. This can be done by identifying the means that would have to be used and the "side-effects that are not directly desired"; thereby, the possibility or impossibility of accomplishing certain value demands can be demonstrated *rebus sic stanibus.*

Evolutionary Tendencies. To those conditions that determine whether the value postulate can be carried out or not belong those called "evolutionary tendencies," a rather unfortunate term that the social sciences have borrowed from the natural sciences. However, the knowledge of the evolutionary tendencies can disclose no standard for the value position but, on the contrary, can determine only which means may be used to realize given ends. One especially cannot conclude from the presence of certain kinds of evolutionary tendencies whether an attitude (or an act resulting from it) that takes these tendencies into consideration is to be evaluated more highly than one that does not and prefers, for example, the role of Don Quixote. Accordingly, on the basis of such investigations one cannot talk about the justification, the worth, or the worthlessness of the "pragmatic politician" who takes such "evolutionary tendencies" into consideration. And this is just as true in regard to so-called "progress" in the political, economic, and social arenas to the extent that by "progress" one doesn't mean only a "progression" in some kind of "evolutionary process examined in isolation"; in that case one can use the concept in a completely non-evaluative sense, and one can, for example, speak of "progressive differentiation" in the area of the irrational content of our psychic reactions in the last decades.

Technical Progress. One is justified in doing the same thing with regard to "technical progress." One must then identify the technology with "rational behavior" and thus say: if the proposition "measure X is the only means for attaining result Y" (which can be verified empirically) is purposively applied by men "known to have oriented their action to result Y," then their action is technically correct. If human behavior in this sense is increasingly correct, then it is appropriate to speak of "technical progress."

Economic Progress. Finally, it is also possible to speak of "economic progress"without value judgment, although only if one makes a considerable number of assumptions, of which the most important are: given needs, a given kind of economic order, and a given possibility of providing the means. Using these and other assumptions, "economic progress" would consist of an approximation to the optimum of satisfaction of needs. The concept of progress, therefore, can be based only upon techniques, that is, on the means for an unambiguous end. Finally, if what is normatively valid for us is made the object of sociological investigations, "as an object it loses its normative character in this context; it is treated as existent, not as valid." Thus, for example, when mathematics or the multiplication table (which are valid for us) becomes the object of sociological investigation (as in a statistical investigation of the incidence of calculating errors among members of various social classes or larger or smaller groups of men working in the same place), it is nothing but a "conventional maxim of practical behavior, valid in a circle of men and followed with greater or lesser precision." But the demand is also incumbent upon the researcher to detach himself from these, his own conventions, and to comprehend, through imaginative projection, a pattern of thought that appears to him as deviant and normatively "false" in terms of his own customs. Thus we are back to what we already said about interpretive sociology.

The Meaning of Science

Whoever would sum up the results of the preceding presentation would probably have to arrive at the opinion concerning Max Weber that in this instance we are dealing with a thinker who, with regard to the method and content of sociology, had adopted his own point of view and had analyzed many concepts to which others had given little attention. But we must also conclude that he was a man who ultimately has been only *unus ex multis*—a specialist who, as others also, set himself in opposition to the uncritical transfer of natural science concepts and laws to the humanistic and social disciplines, and who considered it his task to undertake pains-taking work in an individual discipline, in analogy to psychologists and natural science empiricists. And indeed in our day seldom has anyone described his character as that of a specialist so sharply as this man himself. His swan song, the Munich address, "Science as a Vocation," makes this particularly clear.[6] But this address did even more; it announced to those who did not already know it what so-ciology, i.e., what science, was to him and, above all, what it was not. For how could science mean "everything" or "the highest"—science, about whose worth or worthlessness, meaning or meaning-lessness nothing could be said with scientific means, science which was not in a position to lead men to nature, to God, or even to good fortune. And so, even as philosophy was to him primarily logic and therefore an object with which one should be concerned not for its own sake but for the purpose of sharpening his own wits, which one could then apply in other areas, and even as philosophy was also epistemology, a means of remaining aware of the limits of knowledge, thus also was an individual discipline not an end in itself but a means for a higher purpose independent of scientific knowledge. Science was a means, a possibility, namely, of control-ling a technical apparatus for the realization of goals that arose from an extra-scientific establishment of purposes which a god or de-mon had given human beings.

The core of his existence probably lies here: Max Weber suffered under science; with Simmel, he understood clearly that the struc-ture which we call "science" presents a parallel to the naturalistic-capitalistic form of life, and further, that in all the world there has never been anything analogous to it[7]; it was a form of the "God-distant" age in which we are condemned to live. He suffered under this age, but he endured it, and he admonished others to do the same. He opposed those who believed they could escape by a bold leap into the future, and for this as well as for other reasons he turned against socialism. But he hated the neo-Romantic who, he claimed, lacked the courage to live in such an epoch, a man who convinced himself that he still had the naïveté or the religiosity of the primitive or the medieval man, a man who tumbled about in the ecstasy of mystical vision, or found his way back to the collec-tive culture of the old church. Weber forgave the latter if he were willing to sacrifice the intellect; Weber disowned such a man if he presented scientific and philosophical reasons for his step. For however much Weber suffered from living in a "God-distant" age, he did not suffer from its agnosticism. In contrast to his older friend Jellinek—who from his neo-Kantianism longed to return to mysticism and metaphysics, to Schelling and Hegel—Weber breathed a sigh of relief as soon as someone once again demonstrated the limits of knowledge, the impossibility of making objective, valid value judgments.

From these value judgments it was only a step to a hierarchy of values, to the sanctification and rank ordering of associations and institutions, namely, of the state, the church, the party, the university, and the school, among others. But then, in case of conflict between one of these and one or more individuals, a norm of practical behavior would have been given for the individual. To hinder the recognition of such a norm appeared to him as one of the most essential tasks. He demanded instead that men strive for the goals given them by their god or demon. In any event, his demon suggested to him that in this not exclusively meaningful world there is an eternal battle between two powers: the kingdom of light, namely, of those who fight, not for a state of perfection which may come earlier or later, but for the sake of storming against that other world, the kingdom of darkness, namely, those organizations and institutions that pretend to be more than they are, that in their would-be role as metaphysical realities, as emanations, as realizations of the Divine Spirit, or as whatever the political metaphysicians, Hegelians, or canon lawyers of revealed religion call their institutions, seek to hinder the individual in his free development, or even to suppress him. Indeed this world view and its transposition into action, thanks to its ultimate dualistic metaphysical core, brought Weber close to medieval heretics, the Hussite heroes, and Cromwell's Saints. With its emphasis on continuous movement, this world view did not bring him close to the Marxist eschatologists and revisionist relativists, but rather into the vicinity of the anarchists and, above all, the Bergsonian syndicalists. On one hand, this world view made him opposed to concessions, but, on the other hand, it did not make him a utopian.

Conclusion

Troeltsch called Max Weber a politician[8]; we have seen that he was something more. In fact, he was a pragmatic politician, but this was based upon asceticism. Even as the Puritans and Pietists, whom he resurrected, forced themselves to the non-euphoric life of daily work and economic gain, thus for the sake of intellectual discipline he demanded logical and epistemological study; thus he demanded above all the sober work in the individual sciences for the sake of control of the technical apparatus, control that is necessary for the realization of goals that stem from an extra-scientific source. To Weber, one of the highest of these goals was, as described, the battle for the sake of the battle and the transformation of men from the instruments of those institutions, from functionaries of those metaphysical entities, into fighters against making an instrument of man—in a word, into "human heroes." Science ought to present the weapons for this purpose: epistemology should deny the value claims of those who represent institutions and show that it is scientifically impossible to pass value judgments and establish a hierarchy of values; sociology should show the plainly relativistic character of organizations and demonstrate that any one organization is only one form among many and can never claim a value superiority on scientific grounds. And thus *from epistemological agnosticism and sociological relativism, Weber built a platform of negativity* upon which the human hero ought now to become active—but not just for the sake of empty activism. He ought to be unrestrained by any metaphysic of the state and other untenable ideas, but not, however, by sociology. He ought not to be a utopian but rather a pragmatic politician.

For that purpose sociology ought to be of assistance. Not that sociology should preach about the goals of human evolution or of one's own activities, but rather sociology could say: if you want this form of organization, then, under given conditions, you must choose such and such means; further, when you use these means under given economic, foreign policy, or other conditions, then, in addition to the sociological consequences that you want, such and such side-effects of a sociological nature occur (for example, the evolution or decline of certain religious organizations).

If one is aware of these two meanings that sociology had for Max Weber, the negative meaning that charges organizations with having a purely relativistic character, as well as the positive meaning, which offers the human hero the weapons for battle, then the apparent contradictions that we saw in him are resolved. Moreover, one grasps that this man battled from a position of dualistic meta-physics precisely because he was not a utopian but was rather a pragmatic politician and, because of his asceticism, had to embrace a godless science that could give him an answer to none of the ultimate questions. He had to become a sociologist in order to realize his highest goals.

Notes

1. *Archiv für Sozialwissenschaften,* Vols. 20 and 21 (1904 and 1905). Reprinted in *Gesammelte Aufsätze zur Religionssoziologie,* Vol. 1 (Tübingen: J. C. B. Mohr, 1920).
2. Georg Jellinek, *Die Erklärung der Menschen- und Bürgerrechte* (Leipzig: Duncker & Humblot, 1895).
3. See especially the article, "Über einige Kategorien der verstehenden Soziologie,"*Logos.* Vol.4 (1913), pp. 253-255.
4. As the publishing firm, J.C.B. Mohr, in Tübingen, advises, his comprehensive sociological work should appear in the next few months under the title of *Wirtschaft und Gesellschaft,* as Part III of the *Grundriss der Sozialökonomik.* [Note: The date of publication was 1922.]
5. See especially his article, "Der Sinn der Wertfreiheit der soziologischen und ökonomischen Wissenschaften,"*Logos,* Vol. 7 (1917-18), pp. 40-42.
6. Max Weber,"Wissenschaft als Beruf,"Lecture No. 1, *Proceedings of the Freideutschen Bund* (Munich and Leipzig: Duncker & Humblot, 1919).
7. See especially his introduction in *Gesammelte Aufsätze zur Religionssoziologie, op. cit.,* pp. 1-3.
8. A memorial to Weber in the *Frankfurter Zeitung.*

8

Max Weber in American Intellectual Life

The United States represents one of the most crass examples of the assimilation of immigrant masses to a certain type, in this case, to Anglo-American bourgeois Protestantism. Except for specialists in areas such as music, where this type was unproductive, even the lone intellectual who arrived later had to adapt his special knowledge and methods to this general pattern. As the social sciences had already developed in a particular direction, European elements were incorporated only with hesitation, as, for example, the ideas of Simmel, Sombart, Tönnies, Troeltsch, von Wiese, and Max Weber. This essay is concerned with the partial acceptance of the ideas of Max Weber. But influence presupposes—despite all hypotheses of unidirectional diffusion—the presence of factors that facilitate its reception: a predisposition toward or a feeling of a certain inadequacy, for example. Accordingly, as a preliminary, let us list some American characteristics that are relevant to understanding the positive or negative attitude toward Max Weber, and ignore for the moment those authors who play roles as protagonists in the process of infiltration.

The American Sociological Milieu

American sociologists[1] had at least three basic convictions in common, namely, the concept of society, on which, because of the ab-

Paul Honigsheim, "Max Weber in Amerikanischen Geistesleben," *Kölner Zeitschrift für Soziologie*, Vol. 3, No.4 (1950-51), pp. 408-419.

sence of the Romantic tradition, organicists and holistic meta-physicians scarcely exerted any influence; further, the belief in the possibility and justifiability of the practical effect of sociology; and finally, the belief in the desirability of supra-national organization. On the other hand, at least the following four subjects were de-bated: the limitation of Darwinism, by Ellwood and Hayes versus the radical Darwinism of Sumner and Keller, admirers of Spencer; then, social welfare politics, characteristically represented by Small and Ellwood, students of Wagner and Schmoller, in contrast to tra-ditional American laissez-faire; third, the theory that the origin of the state was primarily through power, a conception of Ward's re-lated to that of Gumplowicz, the antithesis of Hayes' theory of a more peaceful development; and, last but not least, a historically based social science, significantly represented by the previously men-tioned Small and Ellwood, who had studied in Berlin, as opposed to the quantifying, statistical sociology, which imitated natural science and was dominant for a time.

Moreover, there was a wealth of studies and systems, social-psy-chological, criminological, socio-geographical, demographic, and ecological (somewhat related to the German theory concerning the location of industry), which cannot be considered here. The devel-opment of ethnology proceeded in a fashion similar to that of the history of sociology. First, the parallel evolutionism of Morgan and his followers appeared, then the historical school (among whose representatives Boas, Kroeber, and Lowie were of German-speak-ing origin) with its interest in migrations and historical process, and finally, in contrast to these, the non-historical, functionalist school. Likewise the economists and jurists were oriented less to history and social welfare than in Germany—where the linkage of both areas of interest was for years characteristic of the two disciplines—as were the philosophers (even when they were not outspoken prag-matists) and even the theologians. American churches, with the exception of outsiders like the Calvinists from the Netherlands, German and Finnish Lutherans, Mennonites, and other "sectar-ians," often were largely social clubs that laid little stress on dogma and were not particularly well-acquainted with their own past his-tory. What was lacking was that typical German cross-connection of the theological, juridical, social science, and philosophy faculties as represented precisely by Max Weber. Why then, in spite of this, is there at least a partial interest in Weber? In order to answer this question, we shall look first at those of Weber's characteristic features that have proved relevant for the incorporation of his ideas and shall put aside for the moment any attempt to explain why these specific characteristics rather than others are being considered.

The Weberian Influence in America

Weber, as a political man,[2] became known through the portrayals of Brann, Falk, Salomon, and Gerth and Mills, the two latter having also translated some of his significant work. They stressed his opposition to the Kaiser Wilhelm (which distinguished Weber from the majority of his German university colleagues), as well as his views on social welfare legislation and his positive interest in the institutions of the United States; they also discussed his particular conception of democracy. Because the fate of the Occident had been to develop capitalism, the power of leaders, imperialism, bureaucracy, and rationality would continue to exist even in the face of democracy and nationalism; and rationality, after all, was the essence of occidental culture, science, and philosophy.

Influence on Philosophy

Weber's work as a philosopher, particularly in epistemology and ethics,[3] raised at least nine issues in the United States:

1. *The theory of value judgment.* This concept was accepted, although with peripheral modifications, by the translators Talcott Parsons and Gerth and Mills, as well as by the well-known historian of theories, Howard Becker; it was rejected by Jordan and Jensen on the grounds that existence and value could not be isolated from one other, and therefore the description and the establishment of norms could not be isolated.
2. *The theory of value relations.* According to this theory, historical phenomena can be made the objects of historical research when such phenomena stand in a continuous and comparable relationship to actual facts that, in turn, have some relationship to some of our values. Apparently only Howard Becker and Shils

(who indeed worked in England but whose translation of Weber was published in America and who therefore belongs here) thought this theory worthy of note. Shils, especially, saw the possibility that the theory would clarify the process of selection of the object of research, particularly in view of the far-reaching separation of sociological theory and individual research practice.

3. *The concept of causality.* Abel in particular described and accepted this. Criticism came only from one side. After the seizure of power by the Bolsheviks, Sorokin escaped from Russia to the United States and there taught and published his metaphysically transcendent system; he rejected the neo-Kantian conception of causality as belonging essentially to the functionalist idea of causality of the turn of the century.

4. *The ideal type.* It was accepted by Abel, Barnes, Becker, Manasse, Salomon, and Parsons (by the latter with the rejection of several special applications), as well as by Fischoff, although he pointed out the danger of underestimating the time coefficient. On the other hand, Sorokin, from his anti-nominalistic position, indicated that the adequate definition of a mathematical or social phenomenon would necessarily coincide with the ideal type. Accordingly, Sorokin thought that the Weberian construction of the ideal type was intrinsically wrong because it was meant to be an auxiliary construction to be understood as something different from the adequate definition of the corresponding phenomenon.

5. *The pluralism of causal factors,* i.e., the interpretation of a particular historical phenomenon through the analysis of its special constituent components. Regarding this, Fischoff and, even more emphatically, Sorokin, insisted that one might indeed determine that an effect had been produced by the convergence of a number of factors, without, however, learning what role an individual factor might have played.

6. *The method of* Verstehen *in sociology,* i.e., the suspension of one's own conception of rationality while hypothetically accepting the concept of rationality of the group one wants to analyze, at least during the period of investigation. Abel and Howard Becker in particular emphasized the indispensability of this part of the process of cognition.

7. *The philosophy of history.* From this, the contraposition of nomothetic and idiographic disciplines was essentially adopted by

Becker, Davis, Gerth, Manasse, Mills, and Salomon; meanwhile similarities were pointed out: with Marxism, on the one hand, by Parsons, Gerth, and Mills because Weber, in defiance of the idealistic historians, also stressed the indispensable function of the economic factor; and, on the other hand, with pragmatism, particularly by Manasse, Gerth, and Mills, because of the pluralistic rejection of a dominant central factor.

8. *The separation of sociology and psychology.* Despite a general agreement with this position, Parsons finds the complete elimination of psychology impermissible.

9. *Ethics.* Weber gave a new twist to the Kantian categorical imperative. He emphasized the tragic obligation to choose between the antagonistic demands of the Christianity of the Sermon on the Mount and the demands of the modern state and said that, whatever it might be, the decision would be essentially imperfect. Becker, Manasse, and Salomon understood this idea, although they did not accept it. But Jordan pointed out that such a formalist ethic, in contrast to an ethic based on substantive values, was philosophically just as untenable as the previously mentioned theory of value judgment. Finally, Gerth and Mills saw the emotional basis of Weber's neo-Kantianism in his sense of duty to the nation rather than in religious conviction, which here appeared to them as rationalized and secularized; additional evidence for this was the sociological treatment of religion and its integration into the total pattern of social and economic historical investigation.

Influence on Social and Economic Thought

Weber's investigations of social and economic history[4] have in America influenced only Roman agrarian history and the discussion of the genesis of capitalism. With regard to the former, Weber began with the ideas of Mommsen, Seebohm, and Paul von Roth as well as the ideas of the papyrologists Mitteis and Wilcken. The basic developments that he either elaborated for the first time or, had they been asserted hypothetically elsewhere, empirically supported are these eight: (1) upward social mobility of the plebeians as a result of their integration into the Hoplite army; (2) the interest of the plebeians in the conquest of non-Roman lands; (3) increasing consideration of the plebeians in the distribution of the *ager publicus;* (4) the unimportance of provincial grain deliveries to the capital city in the total process of the genesis of the *latifundia;* (5) the life of the slaves under military discipline on the *latifundia,* investigated by consulting the Latin writings in the field of agronomy as a source; (6) movement, in later Roman times, from coastal cities to inland *latifundia,* proved by evidence and analysis in contrast to the corresponding and rather vague assertions by Seebohm; (7) the development of *coloni,* in late Roman times, from the former free tenants who voluntarily chose dependence in order to avoid the load of taxes; (8) uninterrupted continuity of the late-Roman *latifundia* with their natural economy to the early medieval, Christian-Germanic type of land ownership, a theory that was based upon sources and analyses, in contrast to Roth's unproved hypothesis.

The best-known American agrarian historian, Gras, but also Tenney Frank, Westermann, Pigériol, and Paul Louis (the two latter are indeed French, but as collaborators on the *Encyclopedia of Social Sciences* they are included here) accepted those theories that concerned the delivery of grain, the barracks of the slaves on the *latifundia,* and the *coloni.* Rostovtzeff's mediation is pertinent here. As an opponent of the czars, he emigrated first to Germany and then to the United States, and influenced Weber with his idea of the condition, but not the origin, of the *coloni.* Although he rejected some of the Weberian details, he accepted others involving the *ager publicus, latifundia,* barrack slavery, and the origin of the *coloni,* and he passed them on to the American economic and social historians Frank, Haskel, Parker, and Scullard. Meanwhile the Austrian, Dopsch, deriving his evidence from an investigation of Carolingian and pre-Carolingian agrarian conditions, confirmed Weber and Rostovtzeff's thesis regarding the unbroken continuity of the *latifundia* from late Roman to early medieval times, acknowledged the two authorities, was translated in America, and was widely accepted.

On occasion there was interest in several other Weberian ideas. These were accepted: the conception of the Confucian economic ethic, by Parsons and Williams; the idea of slavery in Homeric times, by Westermann; and the idea of the old Germanic free-family farms *(Hufe),* by Geiger. On the other hand, these ideas were criticized: the definition of the *gens.* by Howard Becker, and the interpretation of the Confucian and medieval economic ethic, by Sorokin. But this latter issue is related to the incomparably more consequential discussion on religion and capitalism.

The Genesis of Capitalism

The Calvinistic-capitalistic discussion[5] in America followed these main stages: at first, appreciative reports appeared, and some of them contained supplementary examples such as those by Abel, Fullerton, and Salomon. Then came Talcott Parsons' translation with the admission that Weber, as a Kantian, had somewhat overestimated the significance of the spiritual aspect and had somewhat underestimated the changes in the internal development of Calvinism. This was followed by the first objection to the basic principle: Robertson argued that it was not permissible to explain economic changes in a one-sided way through ideological factors, and that one could trace the so-called Calvinistic attitude toward acquisition back to the Middle Ages and the Renaissance. To this, Parsons replied that his opponent, without warrant, had turned Weber into a "monistic idealist" who reduces everything to spiritual factors; furthermore, Parsons said that Robertson argued on the basis of ecclesiastic regulations, whereas Weber did not have these in mind at all but rather was thinking of the motivation of the believers. The refutation of Robertson by Howard Becker and Tawney followed the same lines. Tawney, it is true, was an Englishman, but since he lectured on similar problems in the United States and published his book here, he must be mentioned at least as an indirect link in the chain of influence.

Four new attacks followed: Hall objected that predestination was by no means the most distinctive feature of Calvinism and that this belief was disappearing as capitalism increased, that the accumulation of money had been the only means for the settler in the New World to attain social prestige, and that the typical American large-scale capitalist was by no means always of Reformed origin. Yinger's argument, partially based on Hall's, was that capitalism already flourished in Geneva before Calvin began, and, because Calvin's church could not hold back the new era, Calvin was forced to make ethical concessions; that emigrants did not come to the New World primarily for religious freedom but for economic opportunities; and that, even if religious movements are autochthonous, their ethics still develop as a product of their environment. Hyma, who, like so many persons in Michigan, was of Dutch origin, stressed chronological inaccuracies, referring mainly to Dutch contexts. Fischoff accepted the latter and went even further; he applied his epistemological objections concerning the ideal type and causal pluralism, which we outlined earlier, to the concrete case; and he assumed, as the quintessence of opposition to the idea of a causal relationship between Calvinism and capitalism, a congruence as the result of the same basic cultural elements. Further emphasizing the same point, Sorokin maintained that even in Confucianism and in the Middle Ages similar orientations had existed; that Protestantism was assumed to be more modern that it actually was; that its historical significance had been exaggerated; than Calvinism was not economically prosperous everywhere; and that, on the contrary, Japan was a country of advanced capitalism without Calvinism. Unavoidably, all such criticism concerning the genesis of capitalism affects the opinion regarding Weber's conception of other societal structures, at least to a certain degree.

Forms of Society

Weber's conceptions of particular forms of social organization[6] came to be known relatively late. Essentially this occurred in two ways: first, through Wach's book on the sociology of religion, in which the author borrowed not only the analyses of Judaism, Hinduism, Confucianism, and Taoism, but also the basic conceptions of caste, priesthood, and the role of the prophet; and second, by means of translations from the posthumous work, *Economy and Society*, initially as selections by Gerth and Mills, and then by Henderson and Parsons.

But there were some objections. Although Parsons, as Becker, Wach, and Gerth and Mills, essentially accepts a tripartite typology of leadership, he argues that the "irrational" is not simply a deviation from the norm, "irrationality" is not simply the antithesis of rationality, the legal competence of the bureaucrat is not identical with the technical, and the importance of bureaucracy is overestimated in comparison, for example, with that of the market and other economic factors. On the other hand, Parsons praises the rejection of the belief that there is a "natural self-interest" and that the occidental economic order is natural. With the rejection of such ideas, the South German liberal stands in contrast to the majority of American laissez-faire optimists, even more sharply than did Veblen. A generation earlier, Veblen had described how the Protestant ethic was disappearing in the "leisure class" in the land of the Yankees. This circumstance was taken by the translators as well as by Becker as further evidence of the correctness of Weber's thesis concerning the inevitability of secularization in occidental culture. All of these particular adoptions and rejections are certainly not of an accidental nature.

American Eclecticism Regarding Weber

The causes of the differential opinion regarding various aspects of Weber's work are these: it is understandable that Weber was not discussed intensively in terms of his politics. To be sure, people were sympathetic to this man who opposed Kaiser Wilhelm and who visited and praised the United States, but people were unfamiliar with the details of domestic politics in pre-war and revolutionary Germany, and Weber's political pessimism was foreign to them. With a surplus of land and for a long time without neighbors, Americans had come to believe that the American form of democracy represented the solution to many political problems.

This optimism also colored opinions about Weber's philosophy. Its total epistemology in its broadest sense encountered the most ready acceptance for easily obvious reasons: American sociology had grown out of practical situations; as shown at the outset, it also treated general questions. With increasing complication of the problems, the need for an epistemological foundation was felt; but such a foundation was rejected when it was anchored in the metaphysical, since the corresponding needs, insofar as they existed, were satisfied by the churches. Weber's particular interpretation of neo-Kantian doctrine did not appear so very unfamiliar to the intellectuals beyond the ocean. It underscored the character of sociology as a separate science, and it stressed the importance of religious and economic factors whose great significance one could see daily before his eyes. It did not reject statistics, so essential to Americans, but only pointed out its limitations; and, despite certain points of contact, it moved away from Marxism, which was felt to be alien.

With reference to causal pluralism, on the other hand, this interpretation seemed to be related to pragmatism, which, being a home-grown, American product, was also familiar, even to opponents. Then, if Jensen and Jordan raised objections against value neutrality, Jordan against formalism in ethics, and Sorokin against the ideal type, the basic metaphysical points at issue were of a non-American character. This was especially true of Sorokin, whose Eastern Christianity with its strong Platonic flavor could not accept neo-Kantian anti-metaphysics or the designation of concepts as methodological constructs. But, as will be explained later, counter-strikes of this kind and from such a side remained rare.

Typically American, on the other hand, is the amazement concerning three other aspects of Weberian philosophy. First, the position on psychology: in the Weber circle Emil Lask coined a phrase characterizing the fact that, at that time, philosophy chairs were rather frequently occupied by scholars who were primarily psychologists. Referring to the title of a work by Kant, Lask said that this was an attempt to introduce negative entities into world knowledge—a stark contrast to the American conviction of the value of a quantifying psychology. Because of this, Parsons, who, in so many other ways accepted Weber, protested the elimination of psychology. Second, there was the tragic ethic in antithesis to the largely unshaken American belief that most men were gentlemen. Finally, there was the issue of religion. For Weber's ethics, religiousness was fundamental. But in spite of this or, more correctly (from the standpoint of South German neo-Kantianism), because of this, it was not orthodox. It stood in sharp contrast to common custom in the United States, because here one either was religiously indifferent or found a religious home in one of the numerous denominations, even if one were not a "fundamentalist" but an "evolutionist," i.e., a Darwinist.

All of this made the acceptance of Weber considerably more difficult than in the fields of the special disciplines. Nevertheless, the acceptance was limited here, too. As an ethnologist, Weber is to be placed among scholars of anti-evolutionist historical orientation. But within this orientation he was moderate, and he died before heavy conflicts raged about the extremist, Father Schmidt. It is for this reason that, in Latin America, Schmidt is generally accepted, while in Anglo-America he is rejected. Moreover, in North America there is a considerable understanding of contemporary Orientals but less understanding of their past, because Sanskrit chairs and professors of Semitics are rare and because the alienation from orthodox Christianity is much more likely to occur because of Darwinian influences than through biblical criticism and the comparative history of religion. On the other hand there was continuity in classical philology, as well as an interest in ancient history, which was derived from English university theology and the needs of the churches, but there was only slight interest in Roman legal history. Weber's work could be incorporated here. However, Rostovtzeff worked and wrote in America and for that reason has found greater recognition. The situation was similar with respect to the Celts, Slavs, and Germans. Here Weber claimed less originality for himself, and he described himself as walking in the footsteps of his master, Meitzen, and overshadowed by Meitzen's fame.

That the Calvinist-capitalist formula raised incomparably more dust is understandable. People saw themselves caught in circumstances of which they no longer were aware or wanted to be aware. Robertson was the spokesman for those who felt particularly that, in his innermost being, Max Weber, despite all his objectivity, perceived capitalism as an oppressive fate of the Occident; this was the same capitalism which, to the average Yankee, as Parsons pointed out, was a matter of course, was identical to democracy and opposed to bureaucracy. This was not so with Sorokin; in his work, along with the previously-mentioned methodological objection which was anchored in the metaphysical realm, it was the protest against the world-historical role attributed to Calvinism that was decisive, not the American antipathy to bureaucracy. The South German democrat had warned of the danger that he perceived in bureaucratization. This made him—if we now turn to the American opinion of Weber's conception of particular forms of association—a sympathetic figure in the country to which many had fled in order to escape regimentation in their home countries. In the United States, however, people believed that they had escaped the threat; thus it was easy, even for Parsons, to see the South German liberal as a pessimist. For the rest, Parsons, even as Howard Becker, documented his particularly close affinity with Weberian thought, especially in comparison with a number of the other personalities here in question.

Weber's Intermediaries

The kind of personalities who are here on stage as protagonists is striking: a part of the discussion takes place in *Social Research*. Many articles in this journal are written and edited by members of the New School for Social Research; a great many of these are refugees who are at home in German scientific thought. This is true of Gerth and Wach. Sorokin and Rostovtzeff are Russian refugees; Becker and Parsons, both native Americans, studied in Germany as did Small and Ellwood, the American sociologists interested in history and social welfare politics, as mentioned in the beginning. Parsons studied in Heidelberg and Becker in Cologne, where, along with others, there was a Max Weber tradition. Among the intermediaries of the group are Paul Louis and André Pigériol of French origin and Tawney and Shils of English origin. (The few other discussions published by Englishmen on value relationship, causality, and nomothetic and idiographic disciplines[7] did not produce any lasting influence in America.) In any case, all of those mentioned here and a few of those mentioned earlier were at least not exclusively in the developmental continuity of American sociology depicted previously. Accordingly, they were perceived as something new. For example, Parsons' election as president of the American Sociological Association was interpreted as recognition of a "theoretician." Indirectly this facilitated the diffusion of some of Weber's basic positions and particular concepts. It was otherwise with Sorokin. The linkage of his metaphysico-historical system with statistics as well as the interest that socially conservative circles took in his holistic metaphysics originally facilitated his opportunities for publication and his teaching success. But his emphasis on metaphysics grew. In addition, like a number of other Greek Orthodox in exile, he no longer regarded Catholicism primarily as an opponent but, in increasing measure, as an ally—and this in an originally Protestant country in which many persons were apparently suddenly convinced that the American-liberal non-interference of the state in internal affairs had helped not only big business but also Catholicism into the saddle. Meanwhile, those Americans looking for systematic thought and methodology had increasing opportunity to become acquainted, through translation, with the approaches of Simmel, Sombart, Tönnies, Troeltsch, and von Wiese,[8] and to turn their interest toward these and away from Sorokin. All of this decreased Sorokin's influence and thereby the weight of the objections to neo-Kantianism, particularly because these objections were closely connected with the anti-nominalist group ontology. Finally the special function of German refugees in the process of assimilating Weber's work is part of the wider problem of a sociology of anti-Hitler refugees. Such a problem, however important it may be, lies outside the scope of this article.

Notes

1. For the development of American sociology and ethnology, cf.: Harry Elmer Barnes and Howard Becker, *Social Thought from Lore to Science*, Vols. I and II (Boston: D.C. Heath and Co., 1938), especially (I) pp. 719, 748-750, and (11) pp. 956-965; Harry Elmer Barnes, Howard Becker, and Frances Bennett Becker (eds.), *Contemporary Social Theory* (New York: D. Appleton-Century Co., 1947), pp. 54-58,134-135, 202-203, 372-373, 453-490, 648-665, 851-853, 861-866; Harry Elmer Barnes (ed.), *An Introduction to the History of Sociology* (Chicago: University of Chicago Press, 1 948), pp. 138, 191, 774-883. For the conflict between evolutionists and antievolutionists, cf. Leslie A. White, "L. H. Morgan," in Barnes, *ibid.*, pp. 138-154; Leslie A. White, "History, Evolution and Functionalism," *Southwest Journal of Anthropology*, I (1945), pp. 221-248; Leslie A. White, "Morgan's Attitude toward Religion and Science," *American Anthropologist*, XLVII (1944), pp. 218-230; Leslie A. White, "Diffusion vs. Evolution," *American Anthropologist*, XLVII (1945), pp. 339-356; Robert H. Lowie, "Evolution in Cultural Anthropology," *American Anthropologist*, XLVIII (1946), pp. 223-233; and Paul Honigsheim, "The Problem of Diffusion and Parallel Evolution," *Michigan Academy of Science Papers*, XXVII (1942), pp. 515-524.
2. Max Weber, *Gesammelte politische Schriften* (Munich: Drei Masken Verlag, 1921). For more on this, see H. H. Gerth and C. Wright Mills (trans. and eds.), *From Max Weber: Essays in Sociology* (New York: Oxford University Press, 1946), pp. 8-29, 32-50; Paul Honigsheim, Review of *German Youth: Bond or Free*, by Howard Becker, *American Journal of Sociology*, 53 (July, 1947), pp. 159-160. Also see: Max Weber, *Jugendbriefe*, ed. Marianne Weber (Tübingen: J. C. B. Mohr, 1936), especially pp. 64, 75, 187-193, 204, 294, 300, 334, 417-419, 456. The most important American works on this are: H. W. Brann, "Max Weber and the United States," *The Southwest Social Science Quarterly*, XXV (1 944), pp. 18-30; Werner Falk, "Democracy and Capitalism in Weber's Sociology," *The Sociological Review*, XXVII (1935), pp. 373-390; Albert Salomon, "Weber's Political Ideas," *Social Research*, II (1935), pp. 368-383. For the matter as a whole, see Marianne Weber, *Max Weber*

(Tübingen: J. C. B. Mohr, 1926); Paul Honigsheim, "Max Weber as a Rural Sociologist," *Rural Sociology,* XI (September, 1946) pp. 207-218; and Paul Honigsheim, "Max Weber as Applied Anthropologist," *Applied Anthropology,* VII (Fall, 1948), pp. 27-35.

3.   Max Weber, *Gesammelte Aufsätze zur Wissenschaftslehre* (Tübingen: J.C. B. Mohr, 1922); and Max Weber, *Gesammelte politische Schriften, op. cit.* Both are treated in Gerth and Mills, *op. cit.,* pp. 129-158 (see also Introduction, pp. 45-50); and Max Weber, *On the Methodology of the Social Sciences,* trans. and ed. E. A. Shils and H. H. Finch (Glencoe: The Free Press, 1949) (See Foreword, pp. v, ix, x). The most important American works on this are: Theodore Abel, *Systematic Sociology in Germany* (New York: Columbia University Press, 1929), pp. 116-159; Barnes, *op. cit.,* pp. 60-61; Barnes and Becker, *op. cit.,* Vol. 1, p. 110, Vol. II, pp. 894-898; Barnes, Becker, and Becker, *op. cit.,* p. 30 n.10, pp. 509, 515, 518-519, 521, Howard Becker, "Cultural Case Study and Ideal Type Methodology," *Social Forces,* XII (1933-34), pp. 399-404; A. K. Davis, "Veblen and the Decline of Private Enterprise," *Social Forces,* XXII (1944), pp. 282-286; Charles Diehl, "The Life and Works of Max Weber," *The Quarterly Journal of Economics,* XXXVIII (1924), pp. 87-107; Heinrich Jordan, "Some Philosophical Implications of Max Weber's Methodology," *International Journal of Ethics,* XLVIII (1937-38), pp. 22 1-230; E. M. Manasse, "Moral Principles and Alternatives in Max Weber," *Journal of Philosophy,* XXXI (1911), pp. 31, 35, 42-43, 60, 66; Talcott Parsons, "Capitalism in Recent German Literature," *The Journal of Political Economy,* XXXVII (1929), pp. 48-50, Talcott Parsons, "Max Weber's Sociological Analysis of Capitalism and Modern Institutions," in Barnes, *op. cit.,* pp. 287, 293-295; Talcott Parsons, "Introduction," in Max Weber, *The Theory of Social and Economic Organization,* trans. A. M. Henderson and Talcott Parsons (New York: Oxford University Press, 1947), pp. 6, 10, 13, 54; Albert Salomon, "Max Weber's Methodology," *Social Research,* I (1934), pp. 154-156, 165; Ephraim Fischoff, "The Protestant Ethic and the Spirit of Capitalism," *Social Research,* XI (1944), pp. 72, 75; Pitirim A. Sorokin, *Contemporary Sociological Theories* (New York: Harper & Brothers, 1928), pp. 530, 587, 659, n. 89, 691, 720; Pitirim A. Sorokin, *Society, Culture and Personality* (New York: Harper & Brothers, 1947), p. 500 n.17. For the matter as a whole, see Paul Honigsheim, "Max Weber: His Religious and Ethical Background and Development," *Church History,* XIX (1950), pp. 3-23.

4.   Max Weber, *Die römische Agrargeschichte in ihrer Bedeutung für das Staats- und Privatrecht* (Amsterdam: P. Schippers, 1891); Max Weber, *Gesammelte Aufsätze zur Sozial- und Wirtschaftsgeschichte* (Tübingen: J. C. B. Mohr, 1924) (translated by F. H. Knight as *General Economic History* [New York: Collier Publishing Company, 1927]). Weber's direct influence on America is shown in N. S. B. Gras, *A History of Agriculture* (New York: H. F. Crofts & Co., 1940), pp. 61, 257; N. S. B. Gras, *An Introduction to Economic History* (New York: Harper & Brothers, 1922);

N. S. B. Gras, "Agriculture in Antiquity and the Middle Ages," *Encyclopedia of Social Sciences*, I (New York: The Macmillan Company, 1944), pp. 574-577; W. L. Westermann, "Slavery, Ancient," *Encyclopedia of Social Sciences*, XIV (New York: The Macmillan Company, 1944), pp. 75-77; Paul Louis, "Agrarian Movements," *Encyclopedia of Social Sciences*, I (New York: The Macmillan Company, 1944), p. 494; André Pigériol, "Latifundia," *Encyclopedia of Social Sciences*, XI (New York: The Macmillan Company, 1944), pp. 186-188; Tenney Frank, *Roman Imperialism* (New York: The Macmillan Company, 1921), p. 241. On the relationship of Weber, Rostovtzeff, and Dopsch, cf.: Max Weber, *Die römische Agrargeschichte* . . . , *op. cit.*, pp. 119-121, 149, 185, 220, 252, 286; Max Weber, *Gesammelte Aufsätze zur Sozial- und Wirschaftsgeschichte, op. cit.*, p. 286; Mikhail I. Rostovtzeff, *A History of the Ancient World*, Vol. II (New York: Oxford University Press, 1926), pp. 98, 231, 296-297, 351-356; Mikhail I. Rostovtzeff, "Studien zur Geschichte der römischen Kolonats," *Archiv für Papyrusforschungen*, No. 3 (1914), pp. 116, 133, 259 n. 1, 313 n. 1, 377, 403; Mikhail I. Rostovtzeff, "Geschichte der Staatspacht," *Philologus*, Suppl. 9 (1901); Mikhail I. Rostovtzeff, "*Die Ursprung der Kolonats* (Leipzig: Dieterich, 1901); Alfons Dopsch, *The Economic and Social Foundations of European Civilization* (London: K. Paul, Trench, Trubner and Co., 1937), pp. 137, 337. The adoption of Rostovtzeff and Weber's ideas in America is shown in: Tenney Frank, *An Economic History of Rome* (Baltimore: The Johns Hopkins Press, 1927), Introduction; Henry J. Haskell, *New Deal in Old Rome* (New York: Alfred A. Knopf, 1939), pp. 202-204; H. H. Scullard, *A History of the Roman World* (New York: Barnes and Noble, 1935), pp. 316-318; H. M. D. Parker, *A History of the Roman World from 138-337* (London: Methuen and Company, 1929), p. 288. An allusion to the Weberian theory of economic history, which does not refer to Rome, may be found in: Westermann, *op. cit.*, p. 75; G. R. Geiger, *The Theory of the Land Question* (New York: The Macmillan Company, 1936), p. 112; Howard Becker, "In Defense of Morgan's Grecian Gens," *Southwest Journal of Anthropology*, VI (1950), pp. 317-318 (A more comprehensive work on this subject by Becker will follow [author's note]); Talcott Parsons, "Sociological Elements in Economic Thought," in Barnes, Becker, and Becker, *op. cit.*, p. 635; M. J. Williams, "Representative Sociological Contributions to Religion and Ethics," in Barnes, Becker, and Becker, *ibid.*, p. 843; Pitirim A. Sorokin, *Contemporary Sociological Theories, op. cit.*, pp. 694-695. On the matter as a whole, see Paul Honigsheim, "Max Weber as Historian of Agriculture and Rural Life," *Agricultural History*, XXIII (1949), pp. 195, 198, where there are extensive references to the literature.

5.   Max Weber, *Gesammelte Aufsätze zur Religionssoziologie*, 3 vols. (Tübingen: J. C. B. Mohr 1920-1921). Part of this work has been translated as: Max Weber, *The Protestant Ethic and the Spirit of Capitalism*, trans. Talcott Parsons (New York: Charles Scribner's Sons, 1930). For the controversy on this, see: Abel, *op. cit.*, pp. 142-143; Kemper Fuller-

ton, "Calvinism and Capitalism," *Harvard Theological Review*, XXI (1928), pp. 163-195; Albert Salomon, "Max Weber's Sociology," *Social Research*, II (1935), pp. 60-62; H. M. Robertson, *Aspects of the Rise of Economic Individualism* (Cambridge: The University Press, 1935); Talcott Parsons, "H. M. Robertson on Weber and His School," *Journal of Political Economy*, XLII (1935), pp. 688-696; Talcott Parsons, "Capitalism in Recent German Literature," *op. cit.;* Talcott Parsons, "Sociological Elements ... , in Barnes, Becker, and Becker, *op. cit.*, pp. 633-635; Howard Becker, "Sociology in the Germanic Languages," in Barnes and Becker, *op. cit.*, Vol. II, p. 894; Howard Becker, "Historical Sociology," in Barnes, Becker, and Becker, *op. cit.*, p. 520-522; Richard H. Tawney, *Religion and the Rise of Capitalism* (New York: Harcourt, Brace & Co., 1926), pp. 290 n. 12, 316-317; T. C. Hall, *The Religious Background of American Culture* (Boston: Little, Brown and Company, 1930), pp. 207-224; J. Milton Yinger, *Religion in the Struggle for Power* (Durham: Duke University Press, 1946), pp. 78-128 (cf. Honigsheim, Review of *German Youth, op. cit.);* Albert Hyma, *Christianity, Capitalism and Communism: A Historical Analysis* (Ann Arbor: By the author, 1937), pp. 126, 161; Fischoff, *op. cit.*, pp. 70-76; Sorokin, *Contemporary Sociological Theories, op. cit.*, pp. 531 n. 38, 539 n. 51, 691, 695 n. 58, 697; Pitirim A. Sorokin, *Social and Cultural Dynamics* (New York: Bedminister Press, 1937), (I) p. 500, (III) p. 224, (IV) p. 123 n. 25, 175, 312, 362 n.14; Sorokin, *Society, Culture ... , op. cit.*, pp. 591 n. 4, 657, 672 n. 30.

6. Max Weber, *Wirtschaft und Gesellschaft* (Tübingen: J. C. B. Mohr, 1922), selected portions of which have been translated in Gerth and Mills, *op. cit.* (cf. pp. 51-55, 61-70), and Max Weber, *The Theory of Social and Economic Organization, op. cit.* (cf. pp. 14-17, 26-31, 35, 40, 54-60, 75-76, 80). Cf.: Howard Becker, "Cultural Case Study ...," *op. cit.;* Davis, *op. cit.*, p. 284 n. 3; Parsons, "Weber's Sociological Analysis . . . ," *op. cit.*, p. 300; Parsons, "Capitalism in Recent ... ," *op. cit.*, pp. 38, 51; Talcott Parsons, *The Structure of Social Action* (Glencoe: The Free Press, 1949), Ch. XVII; Joachim Wach, *Sociology of Religion* (Chicago: The University of Chicago Press, 1944), pp. 49, 212, 260, 337, 347, 366.

7. Cf., for example, F. H. von Hayek, "Scientism and the Study of Society, Part II," *Economica*, X (1943), pp. 54-55; F. H. von Hayek, "Scientism and the Study of Society, Part III, *Economica*, XI (1944), p.35; Karl Popper, "The Poverty of Historicism," *Economica*, XII (1945), pp. 83-84.

8. *The Sociology of Georg Simmel*, trans. and ed. Kurt Wolff (Glencoe: The Free Press, 1950); Werner Sombart, *A History of Economic Institutions of Europe*, trans. F. L. Nussbaum (New York: F. S. Crofts, 1933); Ferdinand Tönnies, *Fundamental Concepts of Sociology: Gemeinschaft und Gesellschaft*, trans. and suppl. Charles P. Loomis (New York: American Book Company, 1940); Ernst Troeltsch, *The Social Teaching of the Christian Churches*, trans. Olive Wyon (New York: The Macmillan Company, 1931); Leopold von Wiese, *Systematic Sociology*, adapted and amplified by Howard Becker (New York: John Wiley & Sons, Inc., 1932).

Name Index

Abel, Theodore, 264, 267
Ahlwardt, Theodor Wilhelm, 211
Ahrens, Heinrich, 199
Alexander the Great, 58
Alm, Richard von der (pseud. von
  Ghillany), 230
Anemüller, Detmold, 161
Ankermann, Bernhard, 36
Anschütz, Gerhard, 195
Archiv für Sozialwissenschaft, 143,
  191, 231
Aron, Raymond R., 136, 247
Ashley, William J., 78
Augustine, Saint, 144

Baader, Franz Xaver von, 68
Bachofen, Johann Jakob, 39, 41, 55,
  159, 169
Baines, Henri, 46, 52
Bakunin, Mikhail, 211
Balzac, Honore de, 202
Barnes, Harry Elmer, 264
Barth, Karl, 237
Basserman, Heinrich, 224, 234
Bastian, Adolf, 36, 179, 180, 181, 182
Bauer, Bruno, 229
Bauer, Edgar, 229
Bauer, Ferdinand Christian, 229, 235
Baumbach, Rudolf, 202
Baumgarten, Hermann, 100, 216
Baumgarten, Otto, 49, 100, 102, 216,
  230, 232
Bebel, August, 37, 39, 65
Beccaria, Cesare Bonesana, Marchese
  di, 198
Becker, Howard, ix, 17, 247-249, 263-
  264, 266-269, 272
Beethoven, Ludwig von, 210, 214
Behn, Siegfried, 138
Bekker, Immanuel, 159, 160. 170
Below, Georg von, 6l-63, 75-79, 82,
  130, 161, 183

Bendix, Reinhard, xii
Bennigsen, Rudolf von, 126, 169
Bergson, Henri, 191, 254
Berlioz, Louis Hector, 210
Bernays, Maria, 139, 152, 174
Bernoulli, Karl A., 159, 169
Bernstein, Eduard, 157
Bezold, Carl, 209
Biach, Rudolf, 191
Bismarck, Otto von, 27, 100, 104,
  125, 126, 133, 142, 161, 162, 166,
  169, 173, 176, 207, 216, 217, 245
Björnson, Bjönstjerne, 200
Bloch, Ernst, 132, 147, 151, 152, 190,
  204, 206, 213, 214, 216, 217, 235,
  236
Boas, Franz, 262
Boccalini, Traiano, 163
Bodin, Jean, 163
Boeckh, August, 159
Böhm-Bawerk, Eugen von, 187
Bopp, Franz, 65
Bornhak, Konrad, 195-198
Boswell, James, 64
Bougle, C., 46-48, 52
Brahms, Johannes, 210
Brann, H. W., 263
Brentano, Lujo, 187, 239
Breysig, Kurt, 165, 173, 178
Buber, Martin, 144, 147
Bubnoff, Nikolai von, 146, 206, 236
Bucher, Carl, 73
Buhler, Georg, 46, 52
Bülow, Bernhard, Prince von, 126
Bülow, Hans von, 211
Bultmann, Rudolf, 237
Burckhardt, Jakob, 166, 179, 194,
  208, 220

Caesar, Julius, 74, 75, 77-78
Calas, Jean, 133
Campanella, Tommaso, 163

Subject Index